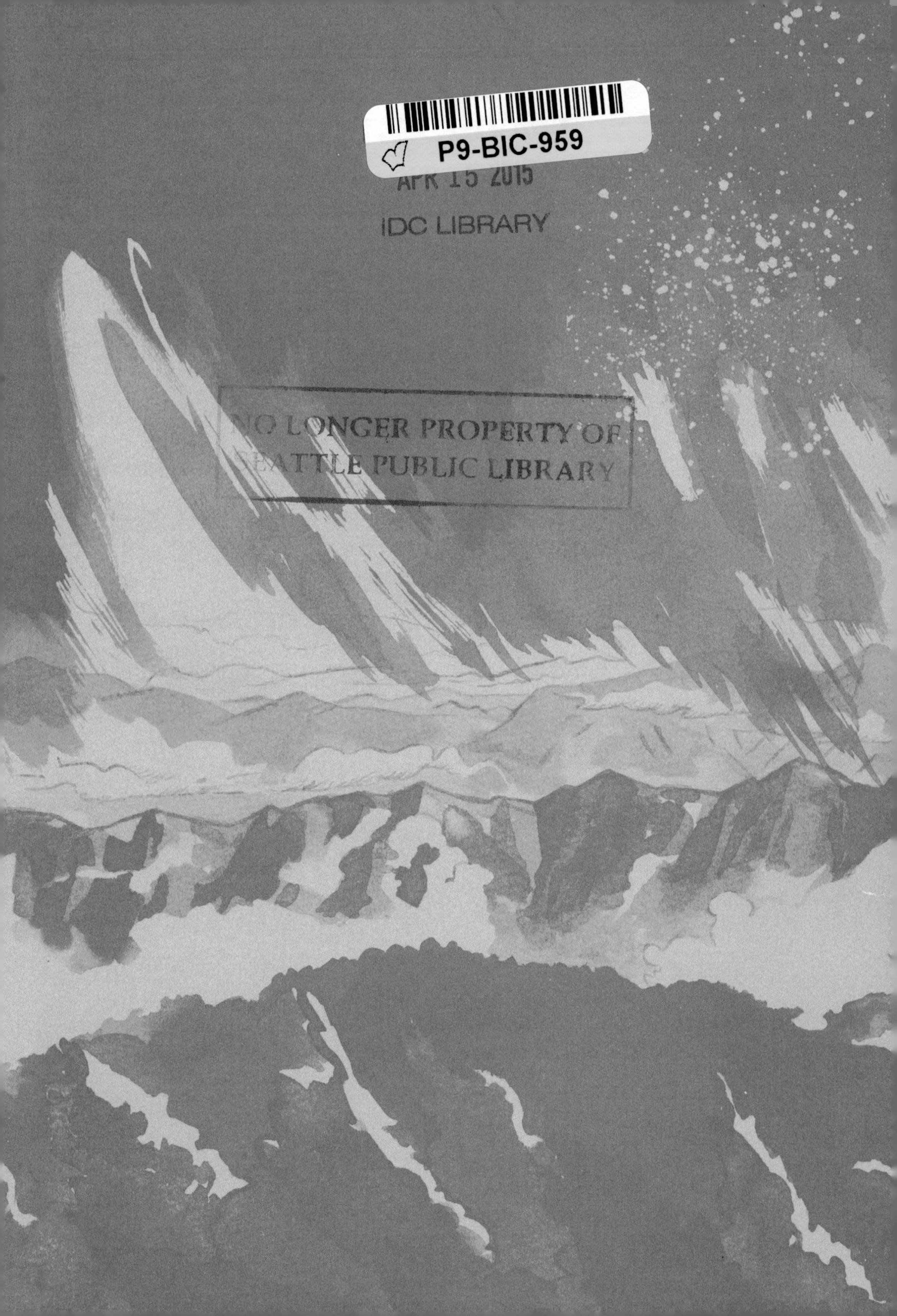

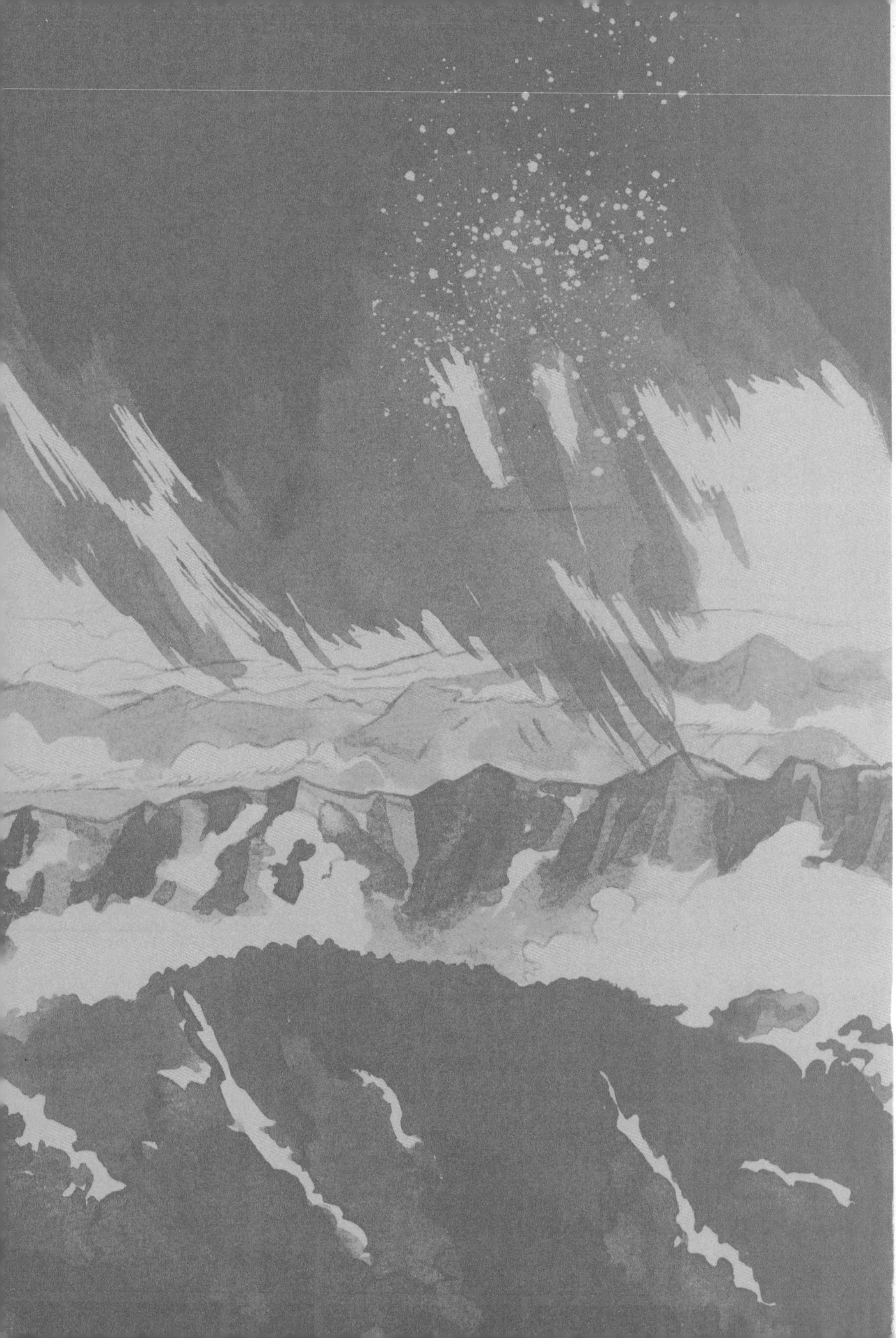

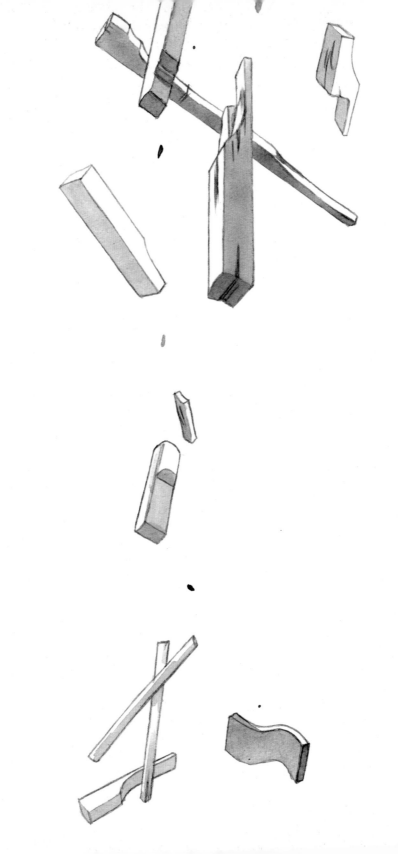

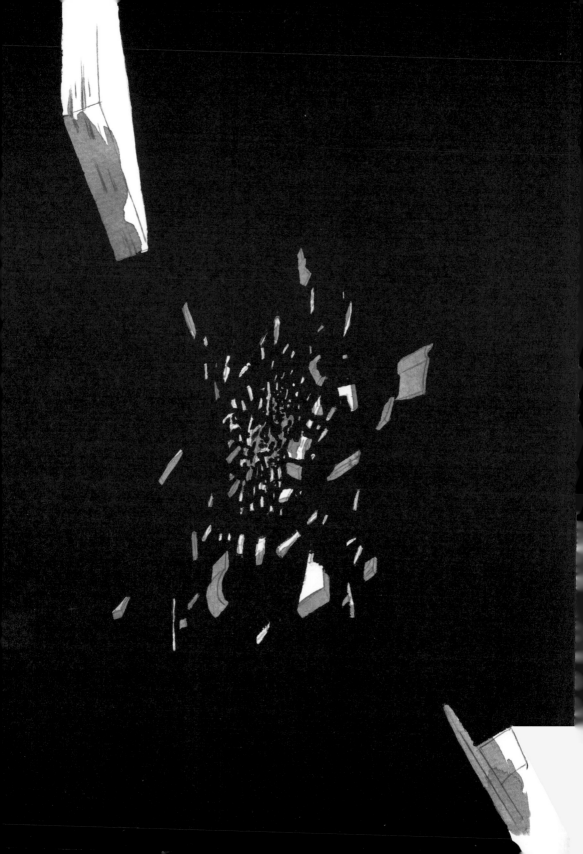

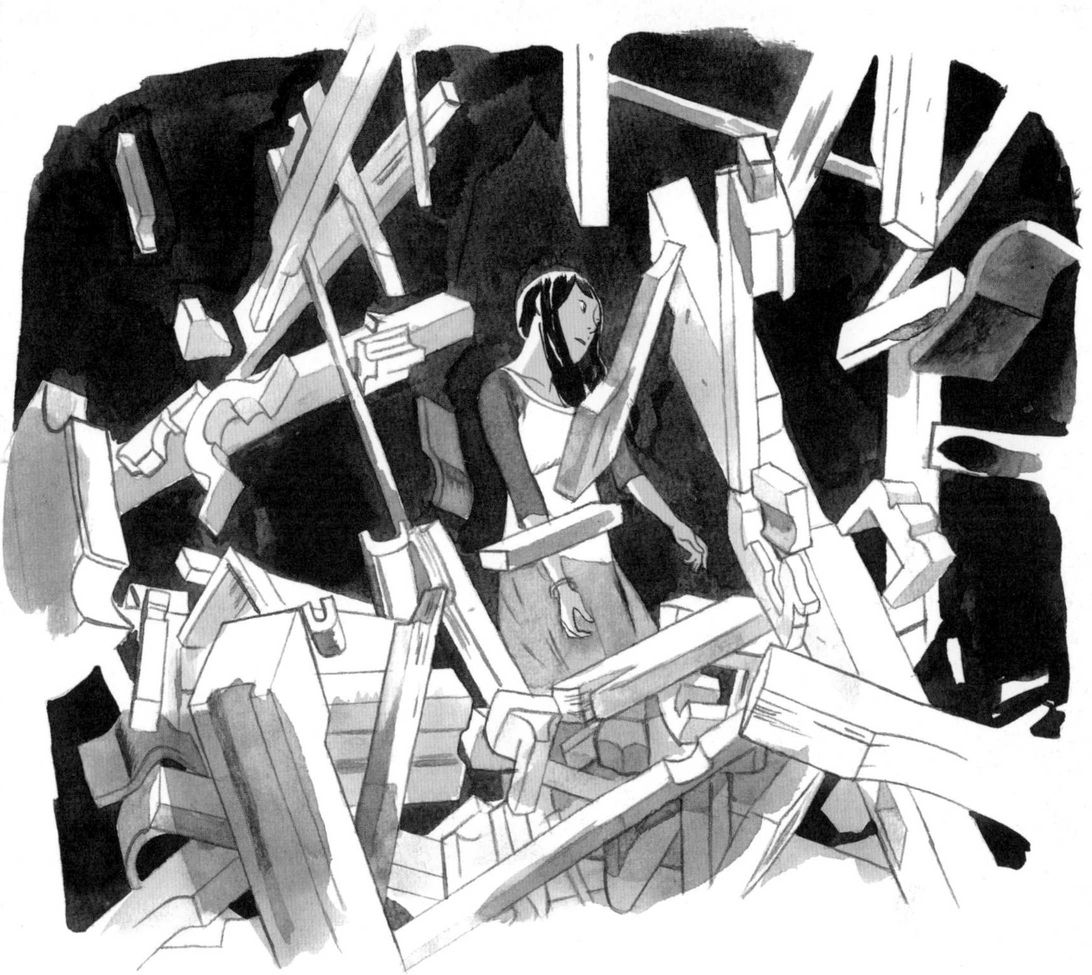

JUST SO HAPPENS

FUMIO OBATA

Abrams ComicArts • New York

Editor: Carol M. Burrell
Designer: Pamela Notarantonio
Managing Editor: Jen Graham
Production Manager: Kathy Lovisolo

Library of Congress
Control Number:
2014948131

Hardcover ISBN:
978-1-4197-1595-2
Paperback ISBN:
978-1-4197-1596-9

First published
in the United
Kingdom
in 2014 by
Jonathan Cape/
Random House
Group Ltd.

Printed and bound in China
10 9 8 7 6 5 4 3 2 1

Abrams ComicArts books are available
at special discounts when purchased in
quantity for premiums and promotions
as well as fundraising or educational
use. Special editions can also be created
to specification. For details, contact
specialsales@abramsbooks.com or the
address below.

ABRAMS
THE ART OF BOOKS SINCE 1549
115 West 18th Street
New York, NY 10011
www.abramsbooks.com

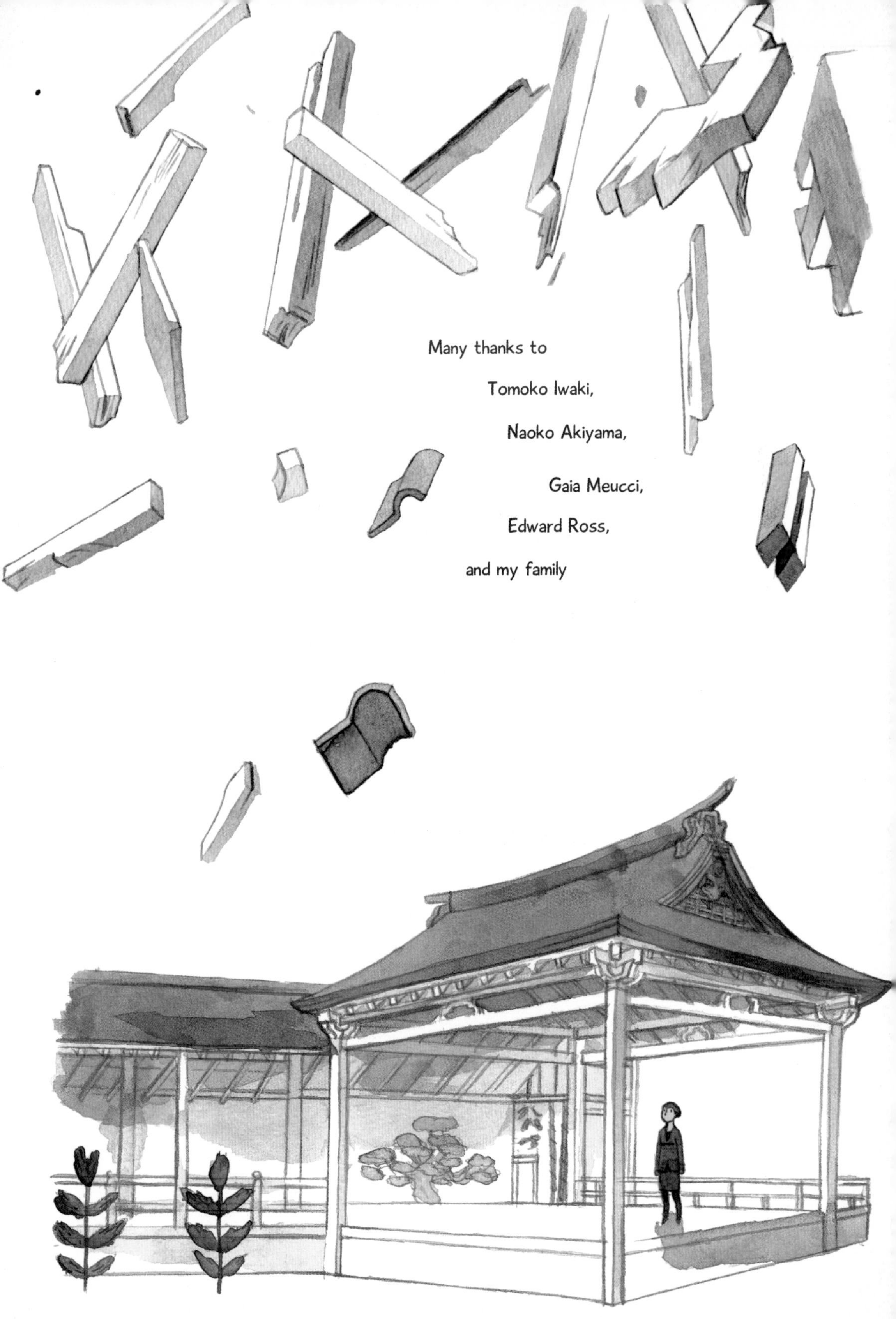

Many thanks to
Tomoko Iwaki,
Naoko Akiyama,
Gaia Meucci,
Edward Ross,
and my family

I

OK!
derma

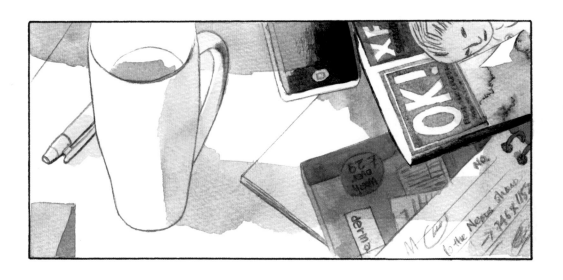

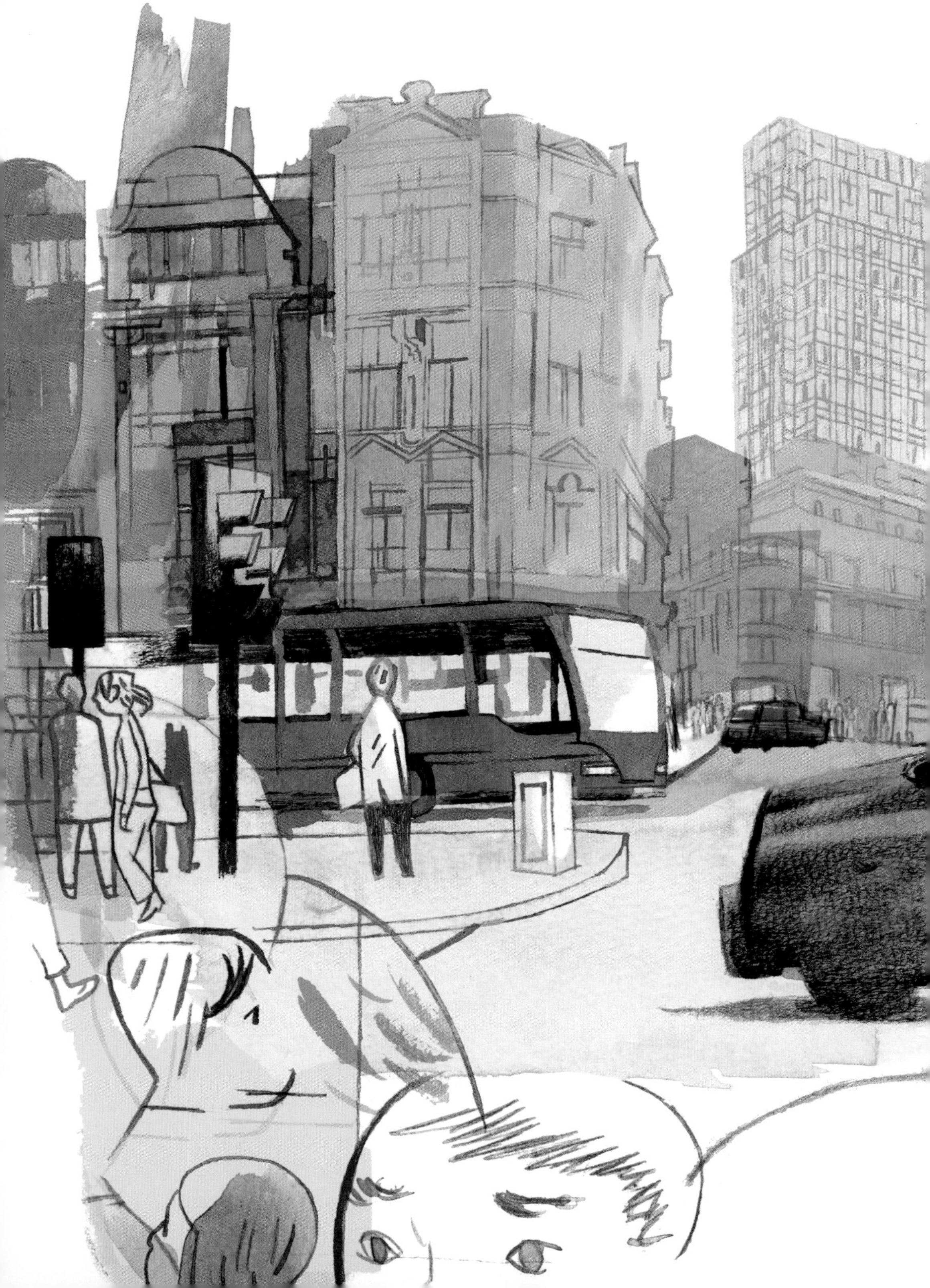

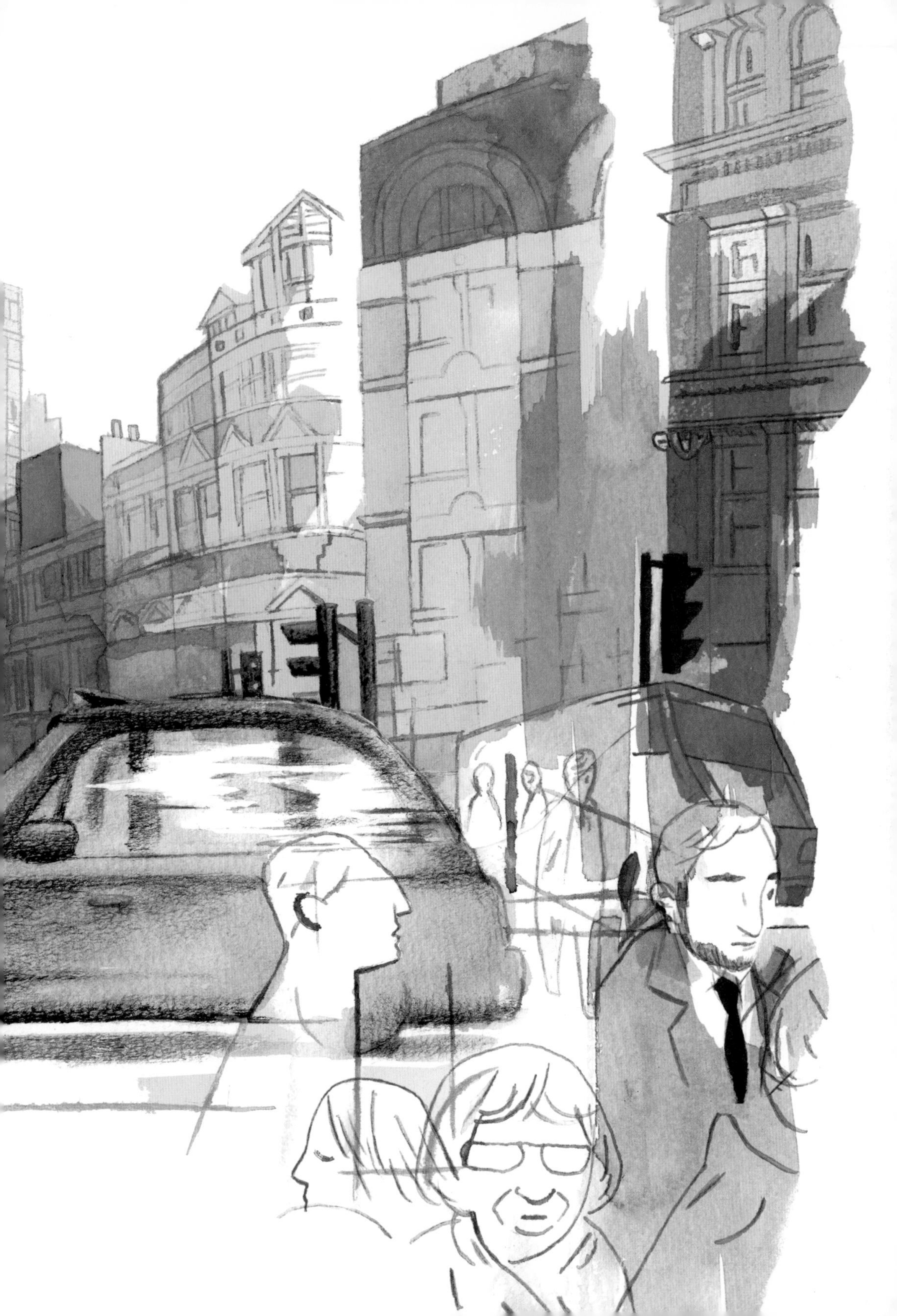

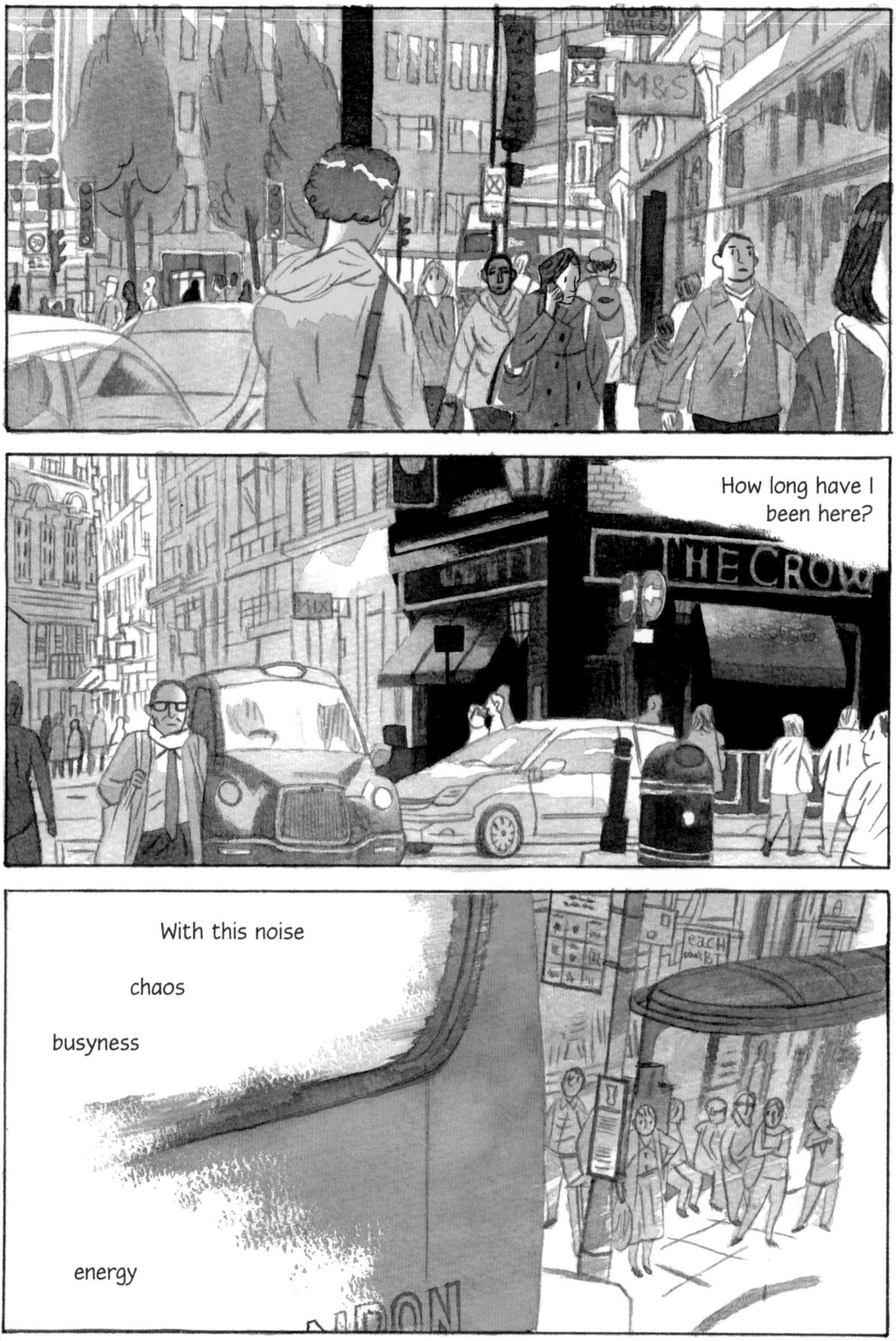
How long have I been here?
With this noise
chaos
busyness
energy

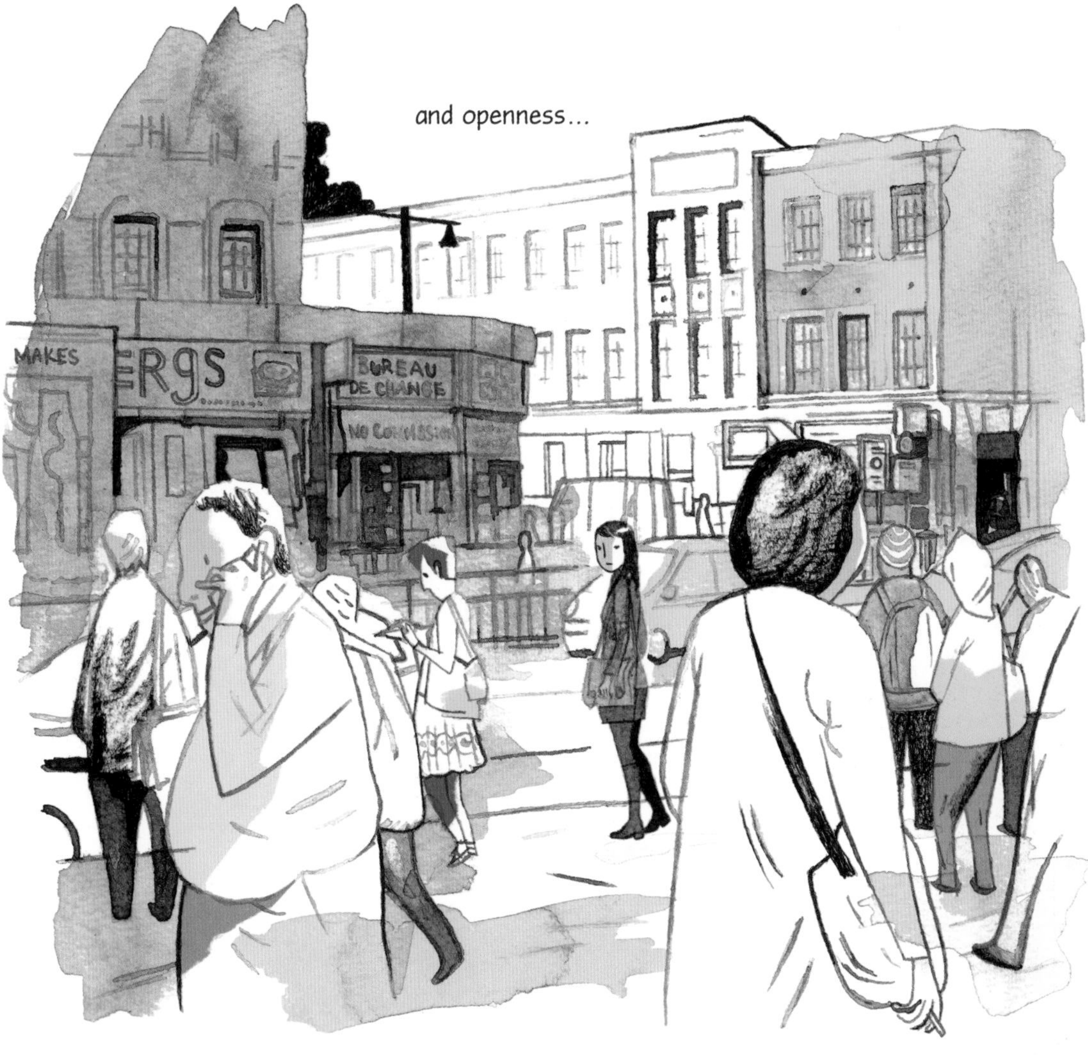
and openness...
MAKES
ERGS
BUREAU DE CHANGE
NO COMMISSION

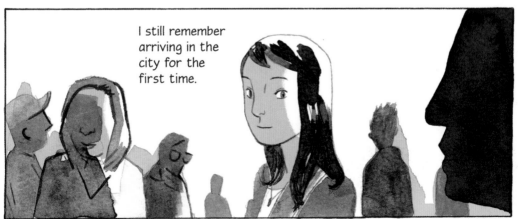

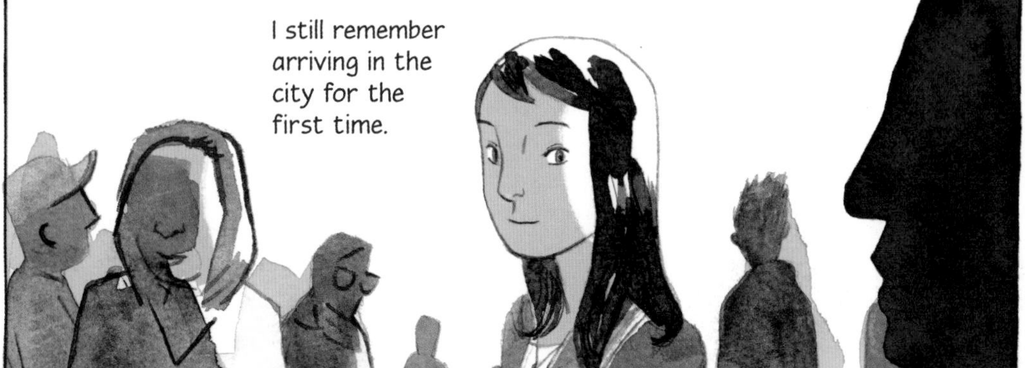
I still remember arriving in the city for the first time.

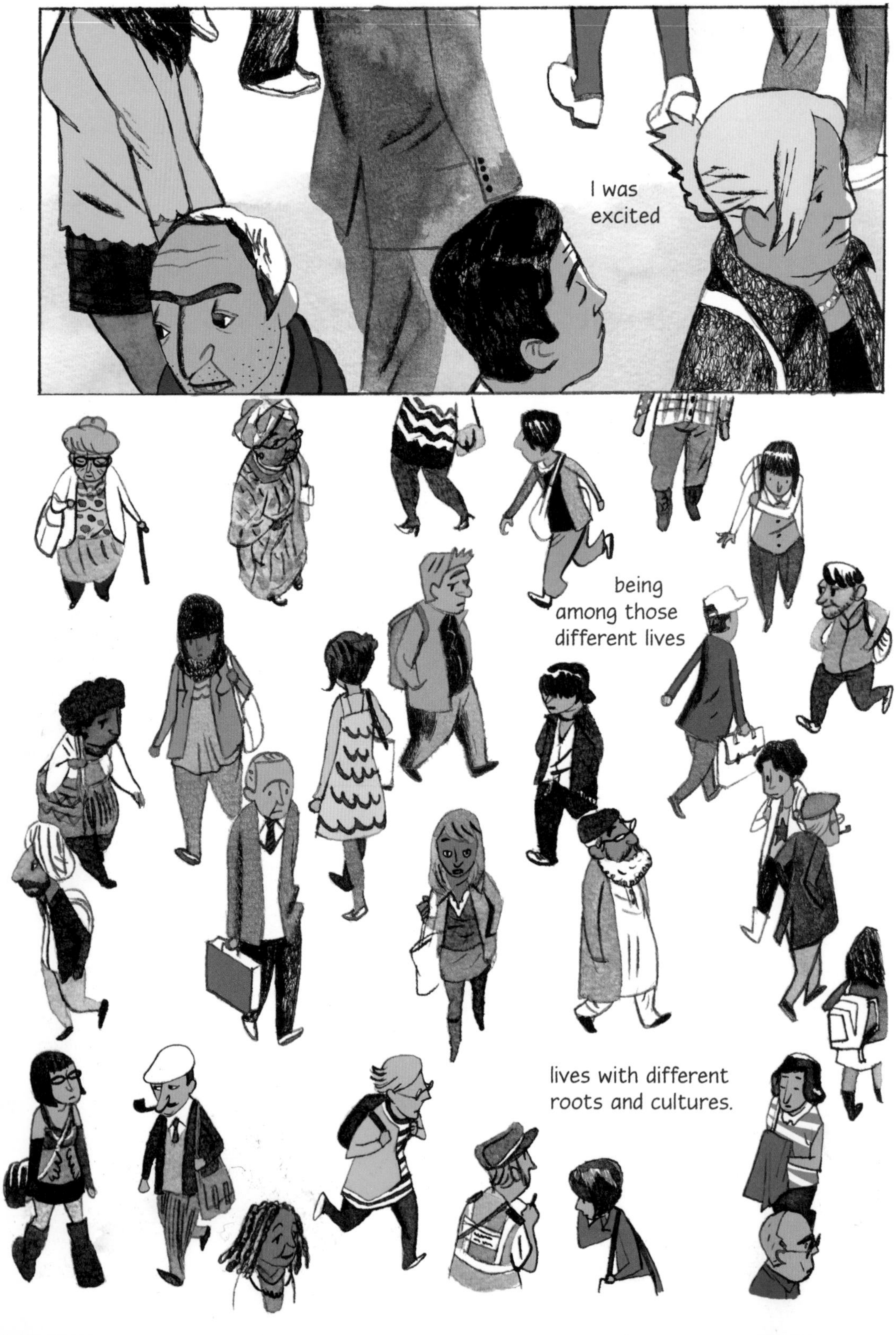
I was excited
being among those different lives
lives with different roots and cultures.

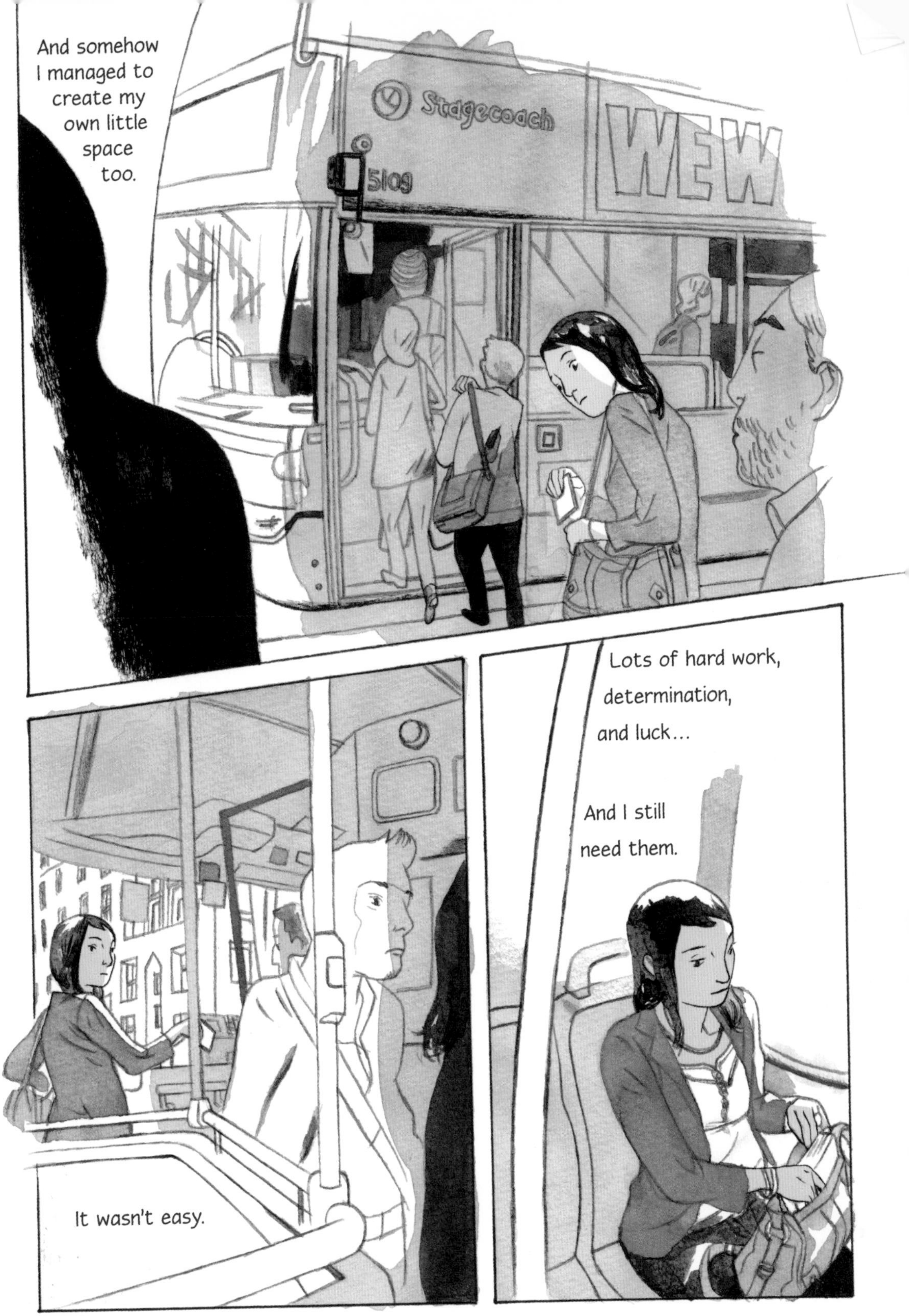
And somehow I managed to create my own little space too.
Stagecoach
5109
WEW
It wasn't easy.
Lots of hard work, determination, and luck...
And I still need them.

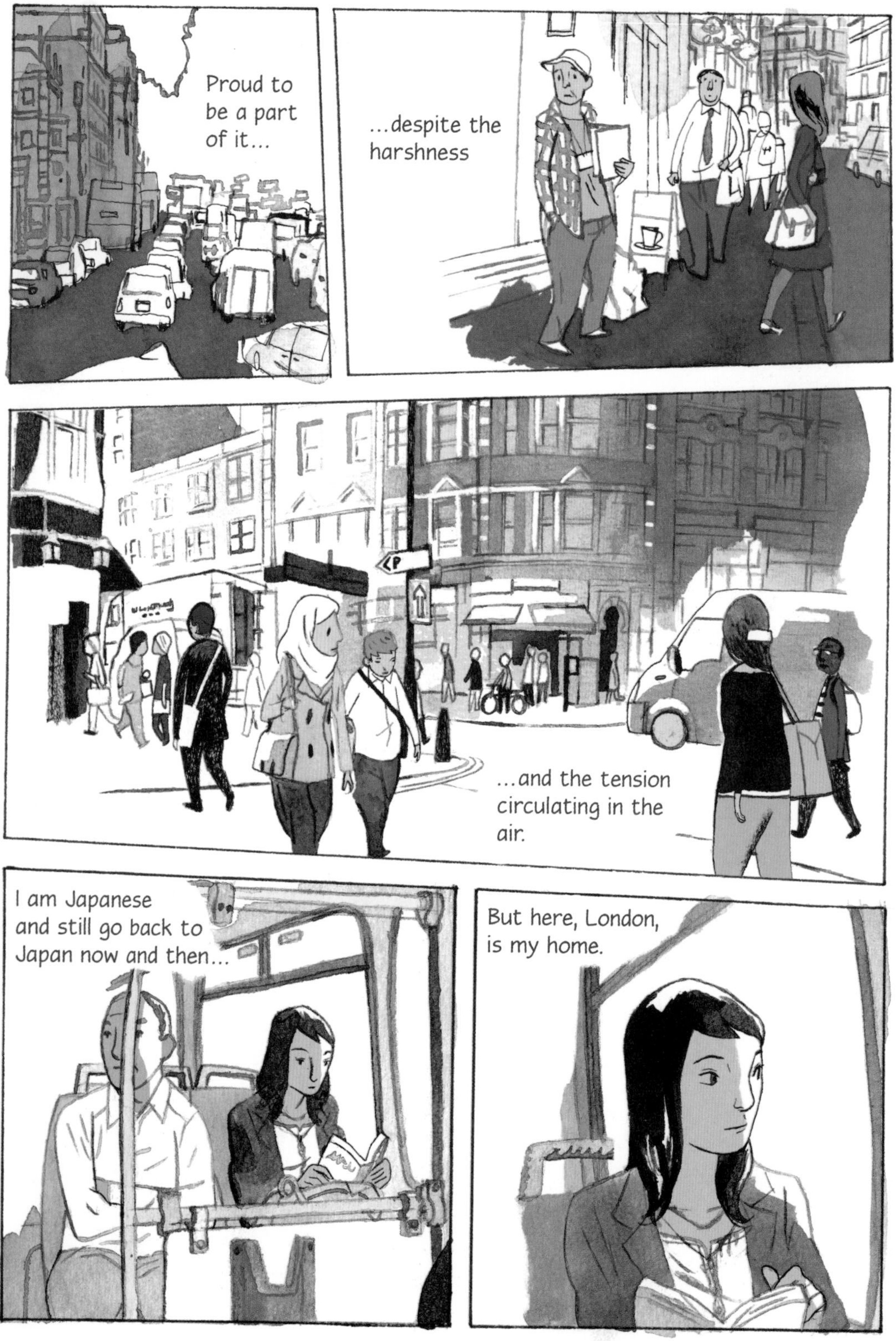
Proud to be a part of it...
...despite the harshness
...and the tension circulating in the air.
I am Japanese and still go back to Japan now and then...
But here, London, is my home.

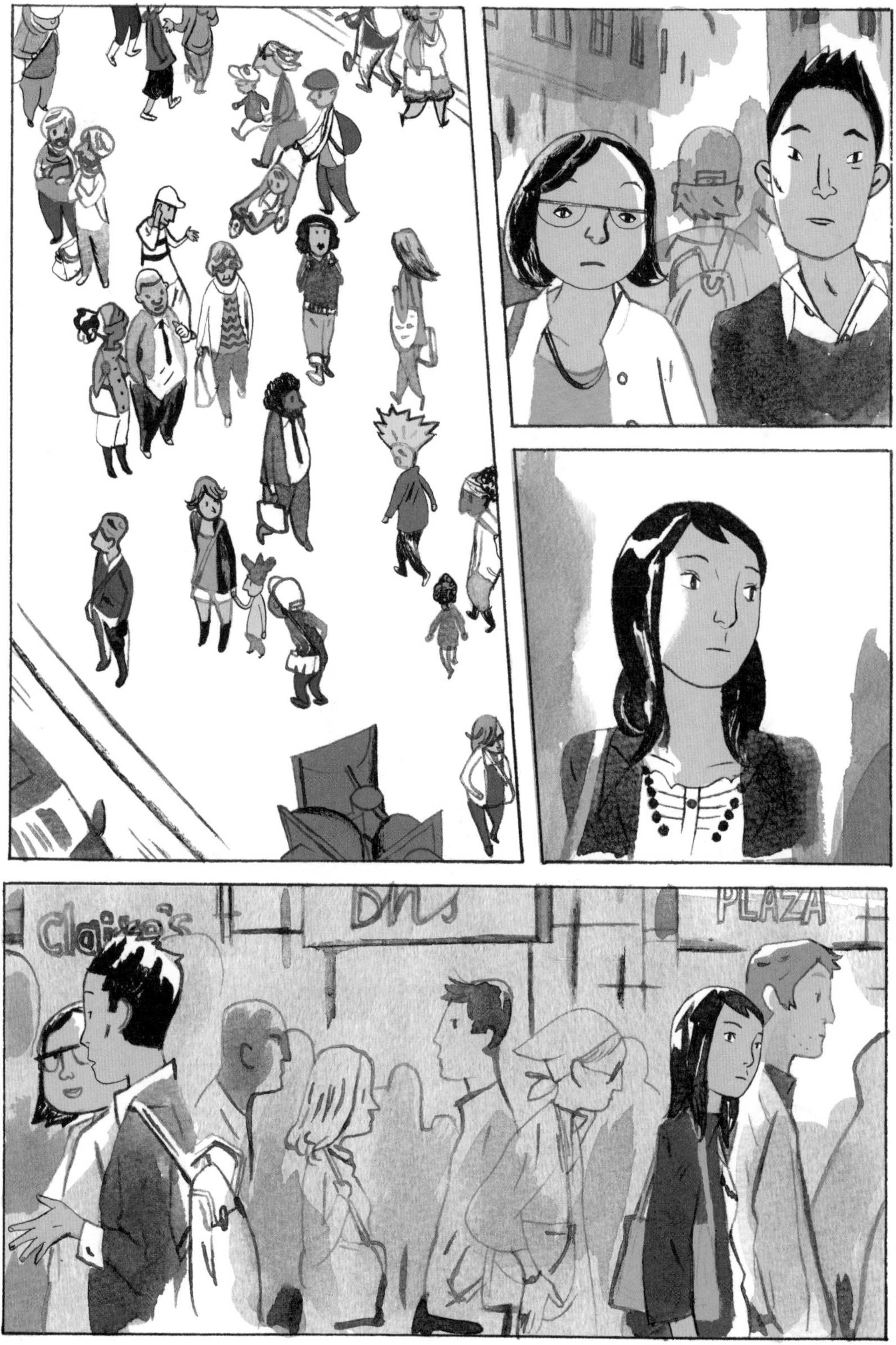
Claire's
PLAZA

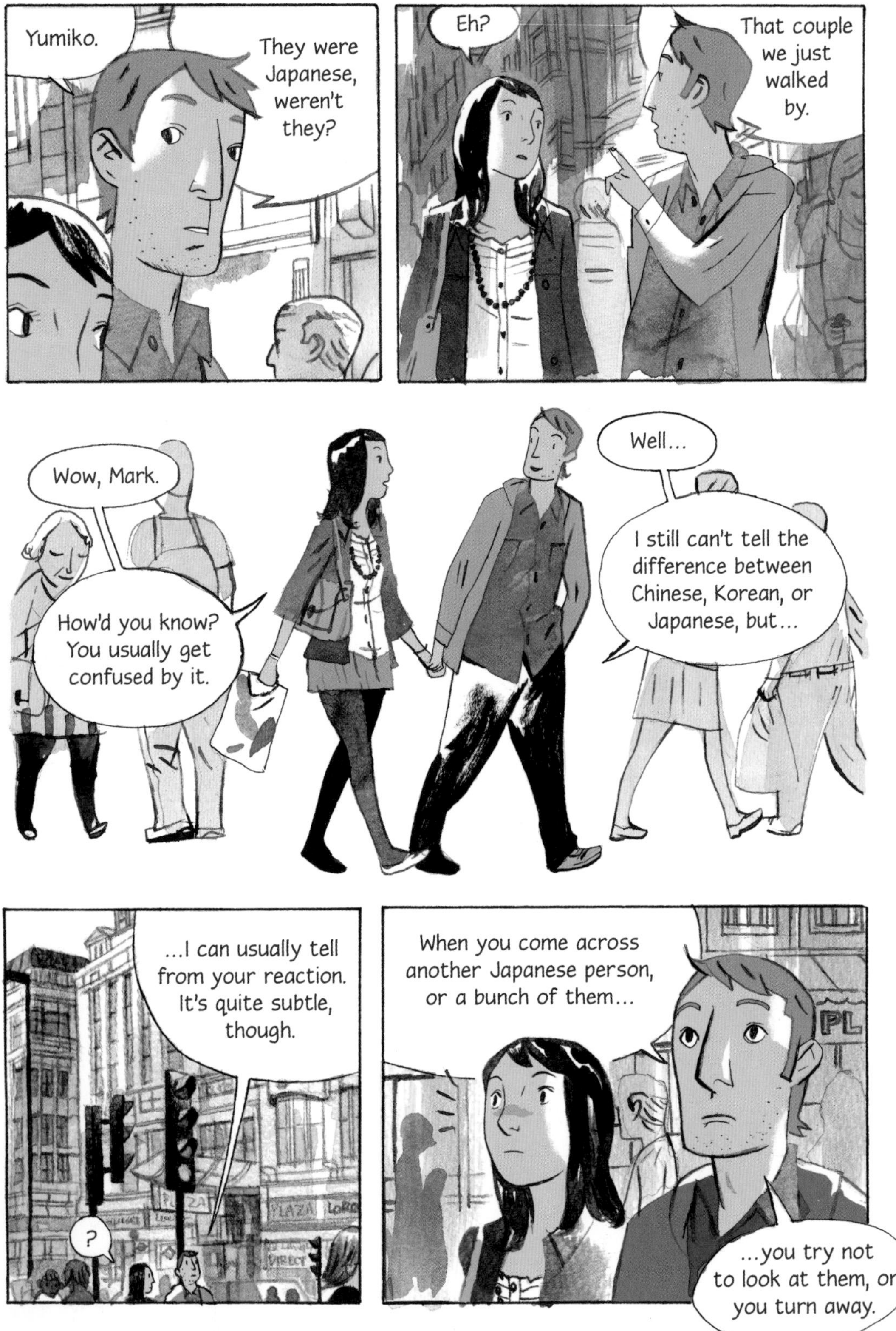
Yumiko.
They were Japanese, weren't they?
Eh?
That couple we just walked by.
Wow, Mark.
How'd you know? You usually get confused by it.
Well...
I still can't tell the difference between Chinese, Korean, or Japanese, but...
...I can usually tell from your reaction. It's quite subtle, though.
?
When you come across another Japanese person, or a bunch of them...
...you try not to look at them, or you turn away.

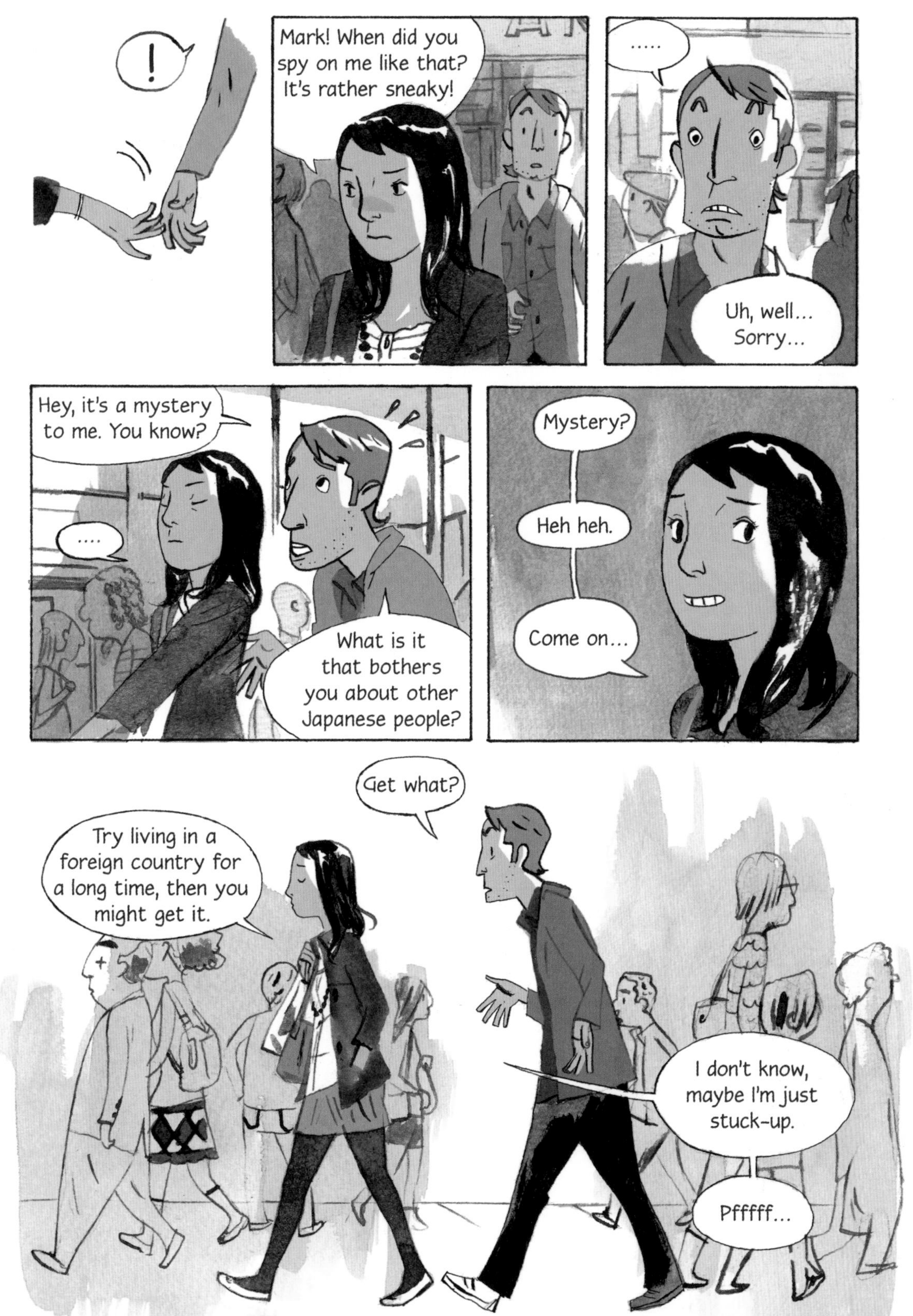
!
Mark! When did you spy on me like that? It's rather sneaky!
.....
Uh, well... Sorry...
Hey, it's a mystery to me. You know?
....
What is it that bothers you about other Japanese people?
Mystery?
Heh heh.
Come on...
Get what?
Try living in a foreign country for a long time, then you might get it.
I don't know, maybe I'm just stuck-up.
Pffffff...

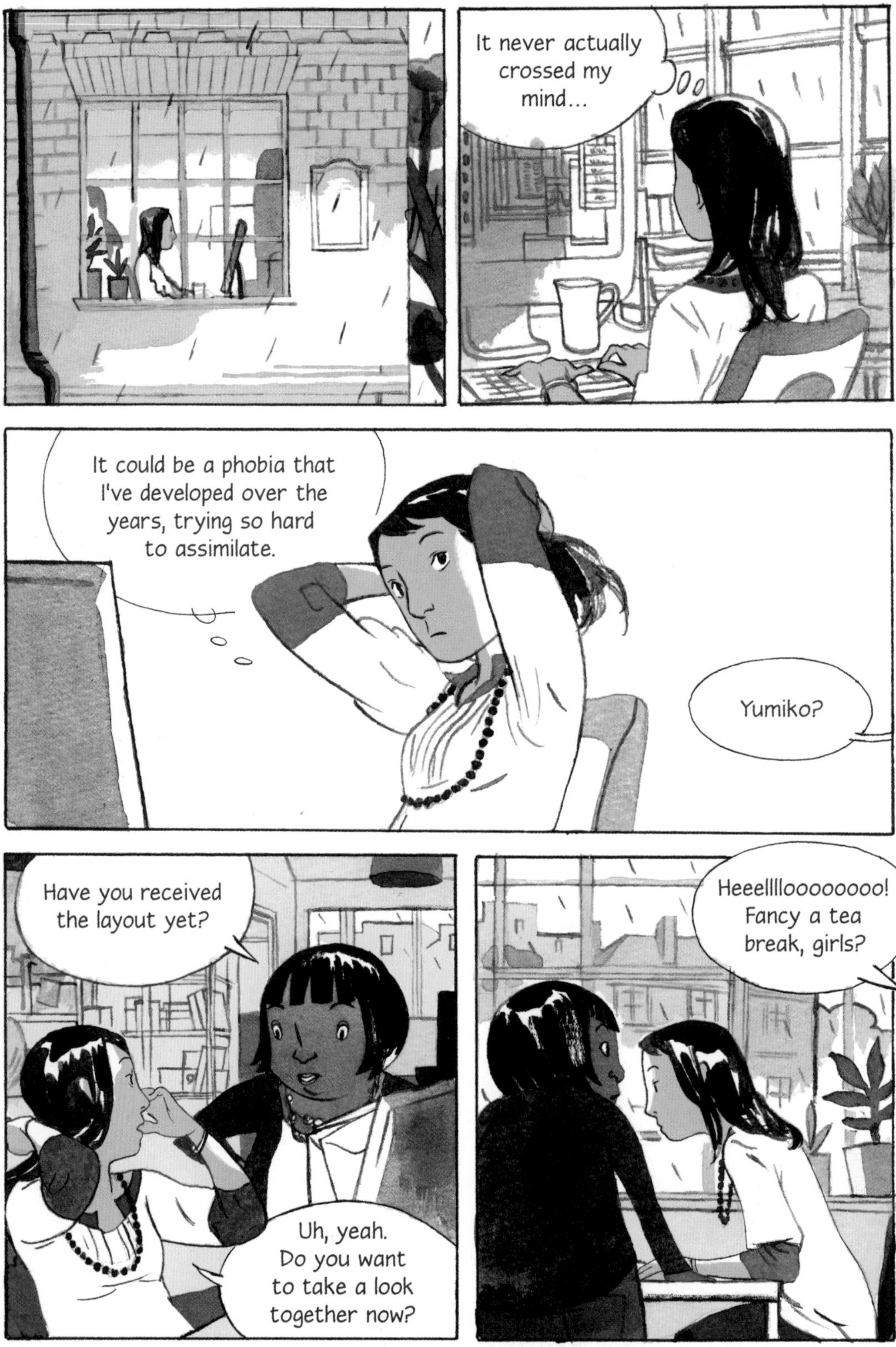
It never actually crossed my mind...
It could be a phobia that I've developed over the years, trying so hard to assimilate.
Yumiko?
Have you received the layout yet?
Uh, yeah. Do you want to take a look together now?
Heeellllooooooooo! Fancy a tea break, girls?

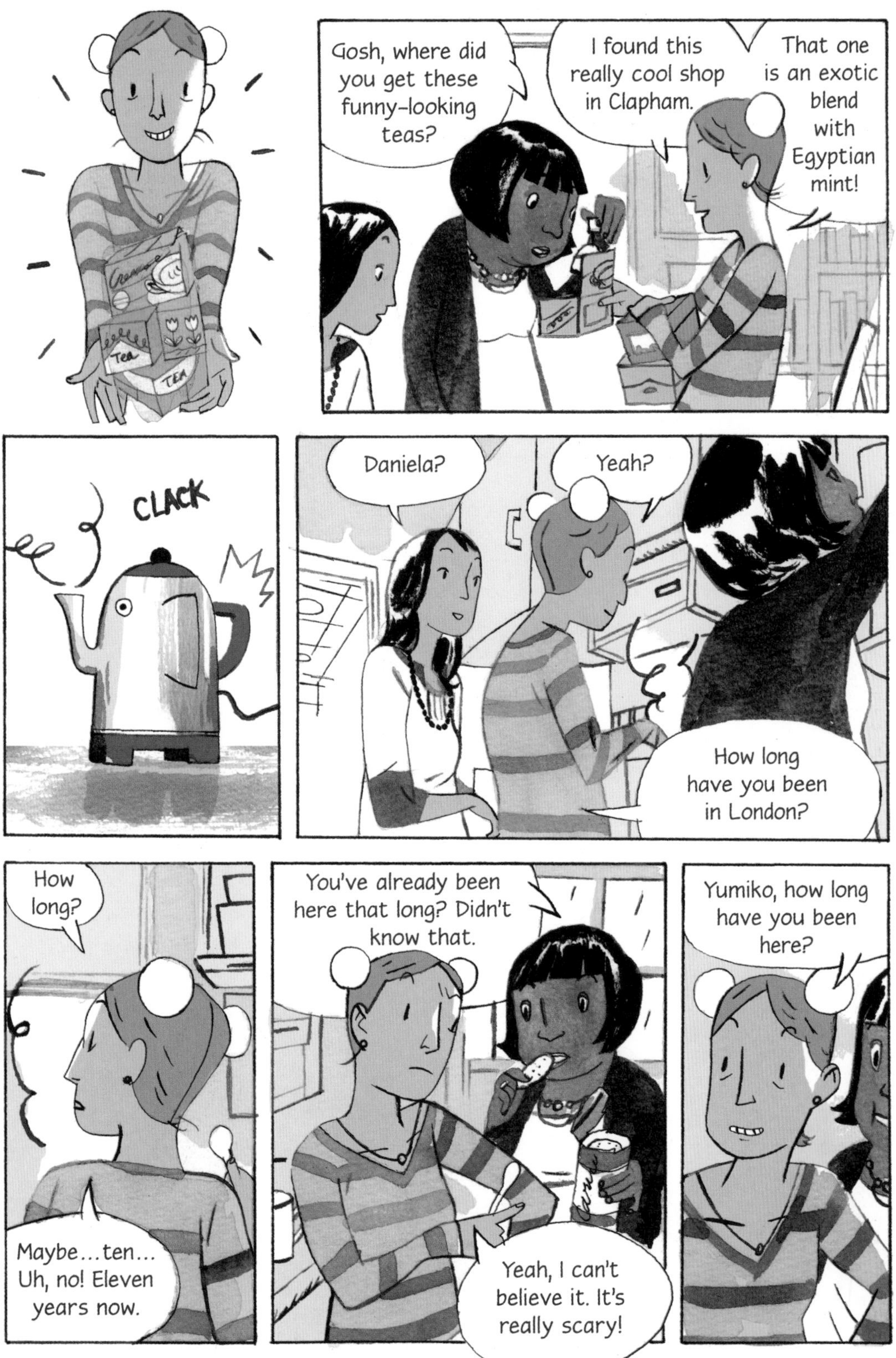
Gosh, where did you get these funny-looking teas?
I found this really cool shop in Clapham.
That one is an exotic blend with Egyptian mint!
CLACK
Daniela?
Yeah?
How long have you been in London?
How long?
Maybe...ten... Uh, no! Eleven years now.
You've already been here that long? Didn't know that.
Yeah, I can't believe it. It's really scary!
Yumiko, how long have you been here?

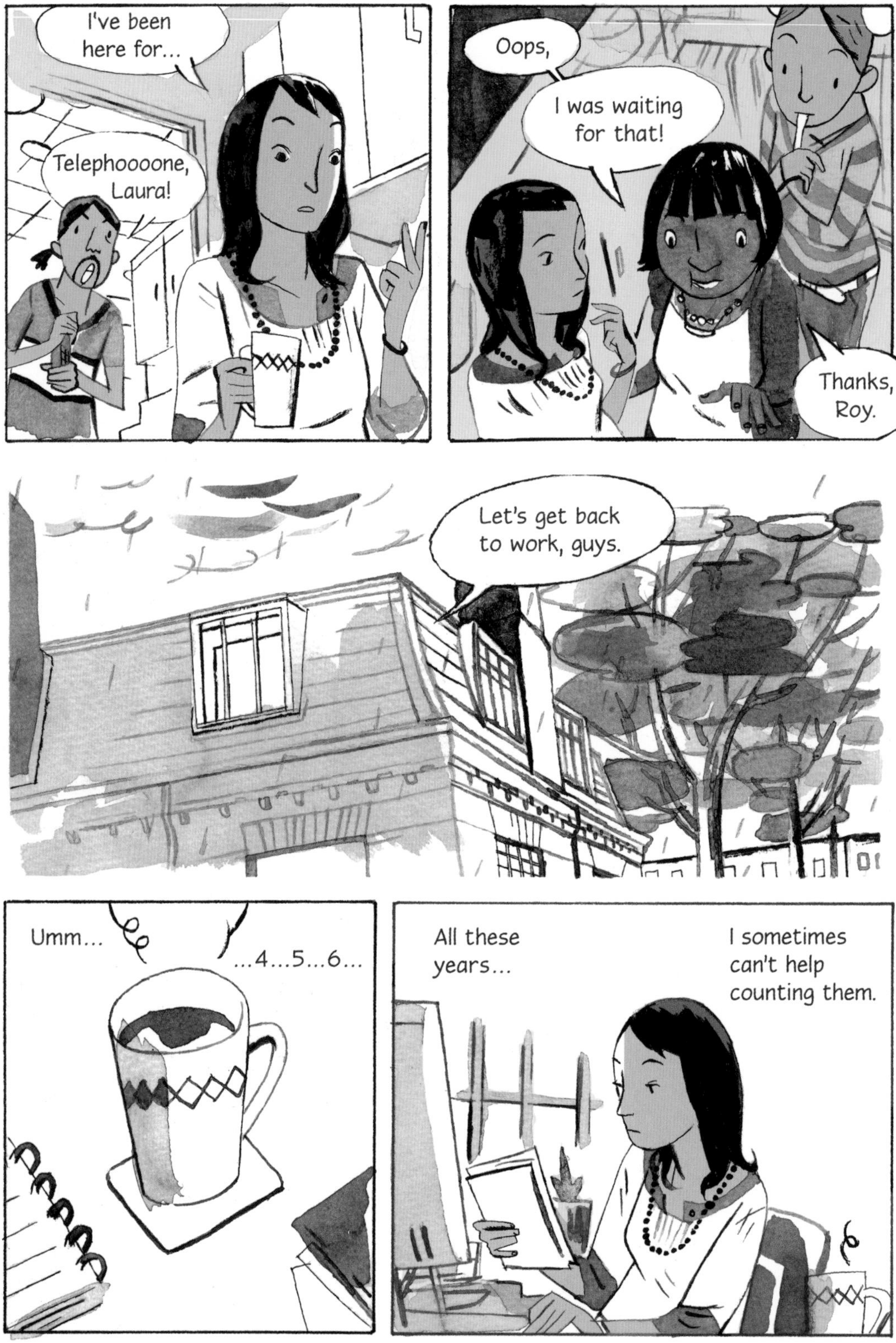
I've been here for...
Telephoooone, Laura!
Oops,
I was waiting for that!
Thanks, Roy.
Let's get back to work, guys.
Umm...
...4...5...6...
All these years...
I sometimes can't help counting them.

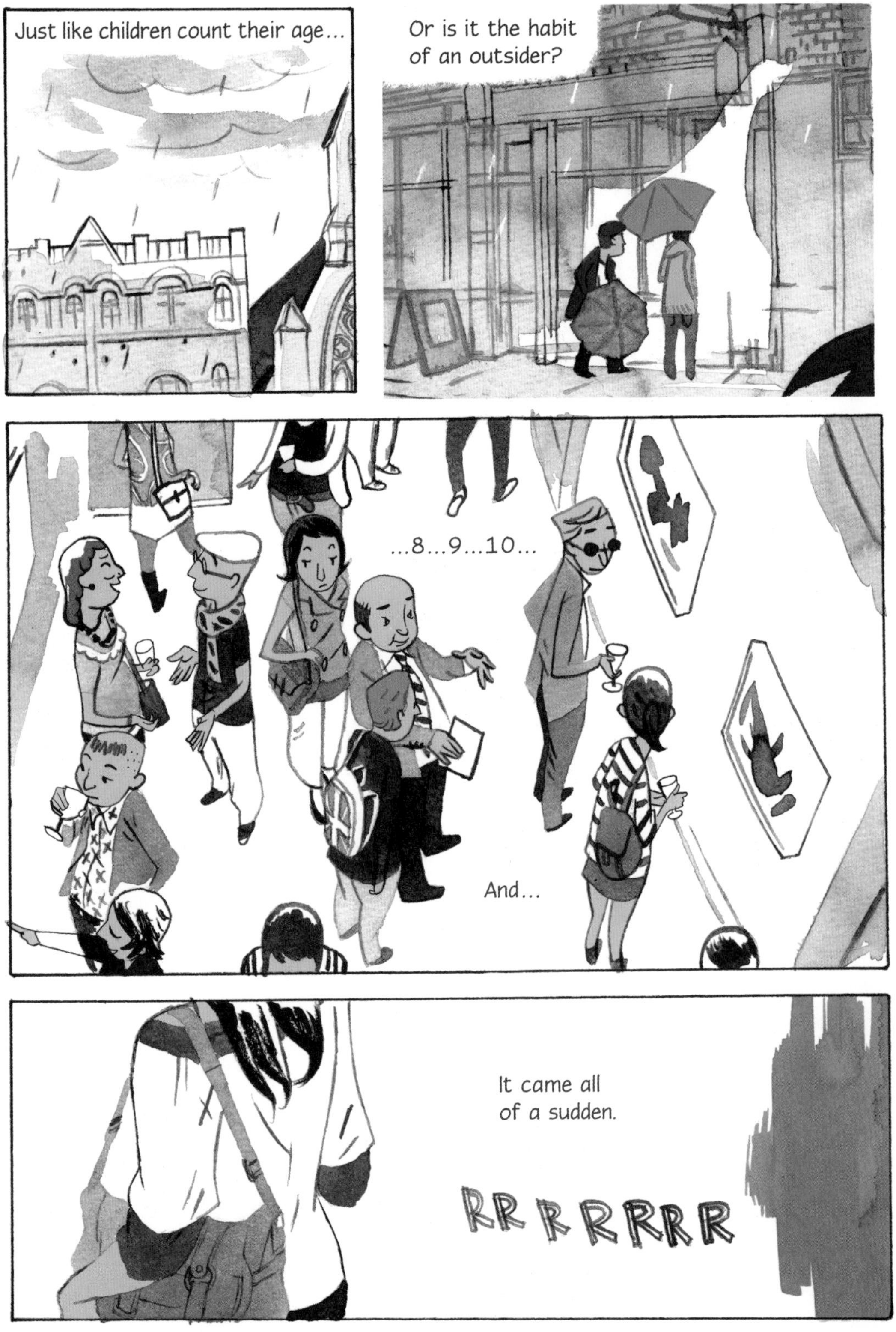
Just like children count their age…
Or is it the habit
of an outsider?
…8…9…10…
And…
It came all
of a sudden.
RRRRRRR

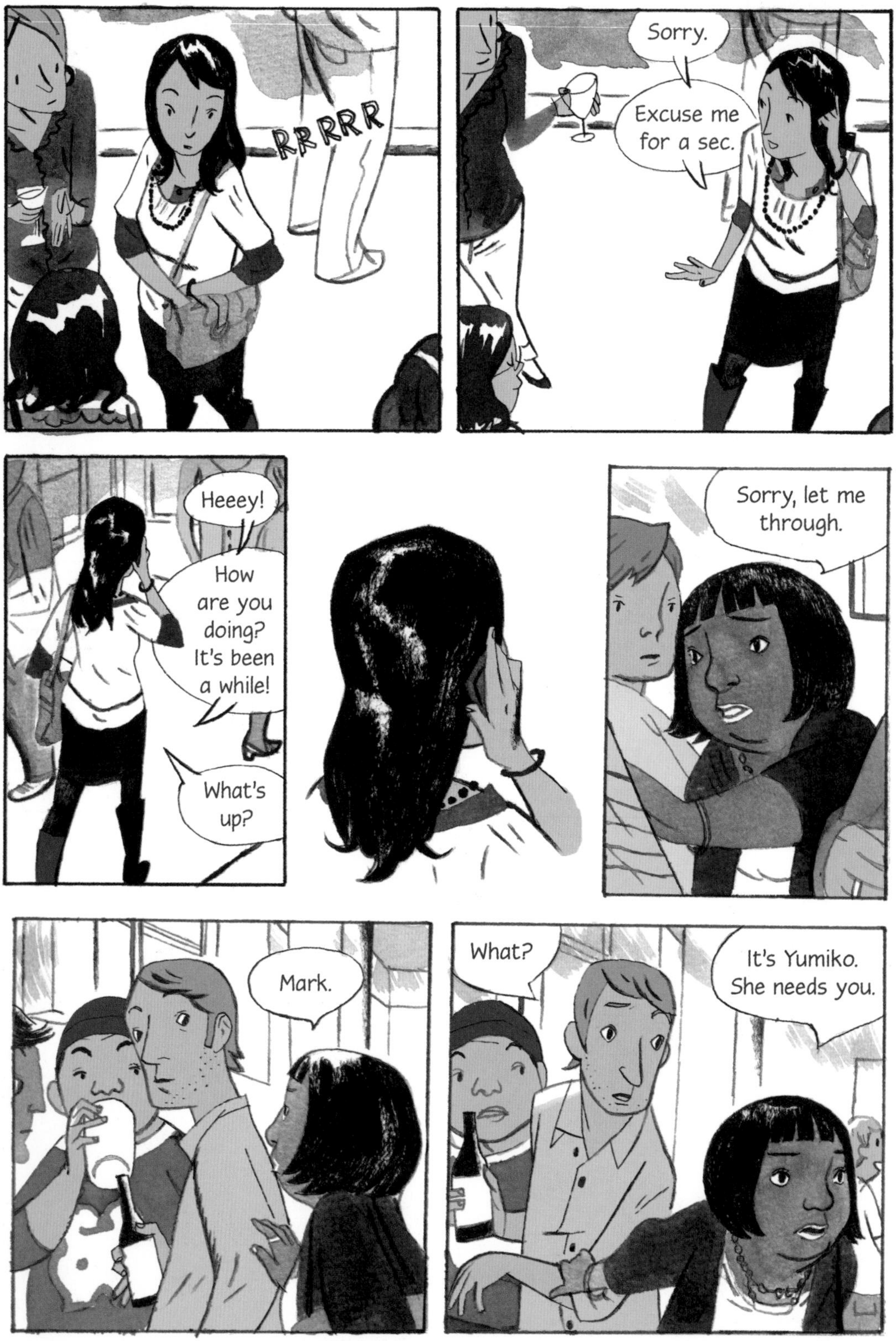
RRRRR
Sorry.
Excuse me for a sec.
Heeey!
How are you doing? It's been a while!
What's up?
Sorry, let me through.
Mark.
What?
It's Yumiko. She needs you.

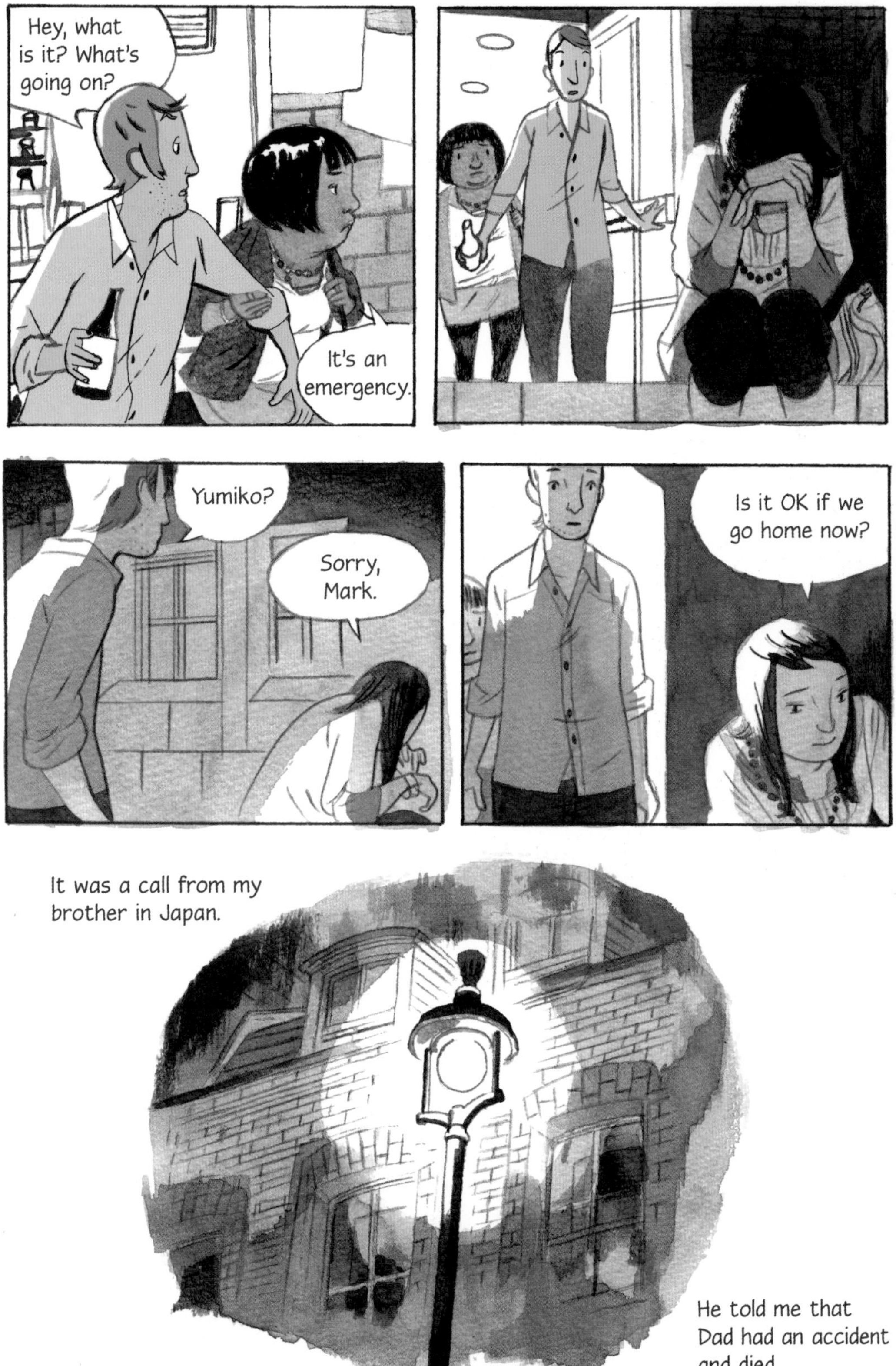
Hey, what is it? What's going on?
It's an emergency.
Yumiko?
Sorry, Mark.
Is it OK if we go home now?
It was a call from my brother in Japan.
He told me that Dad had an accident and died.

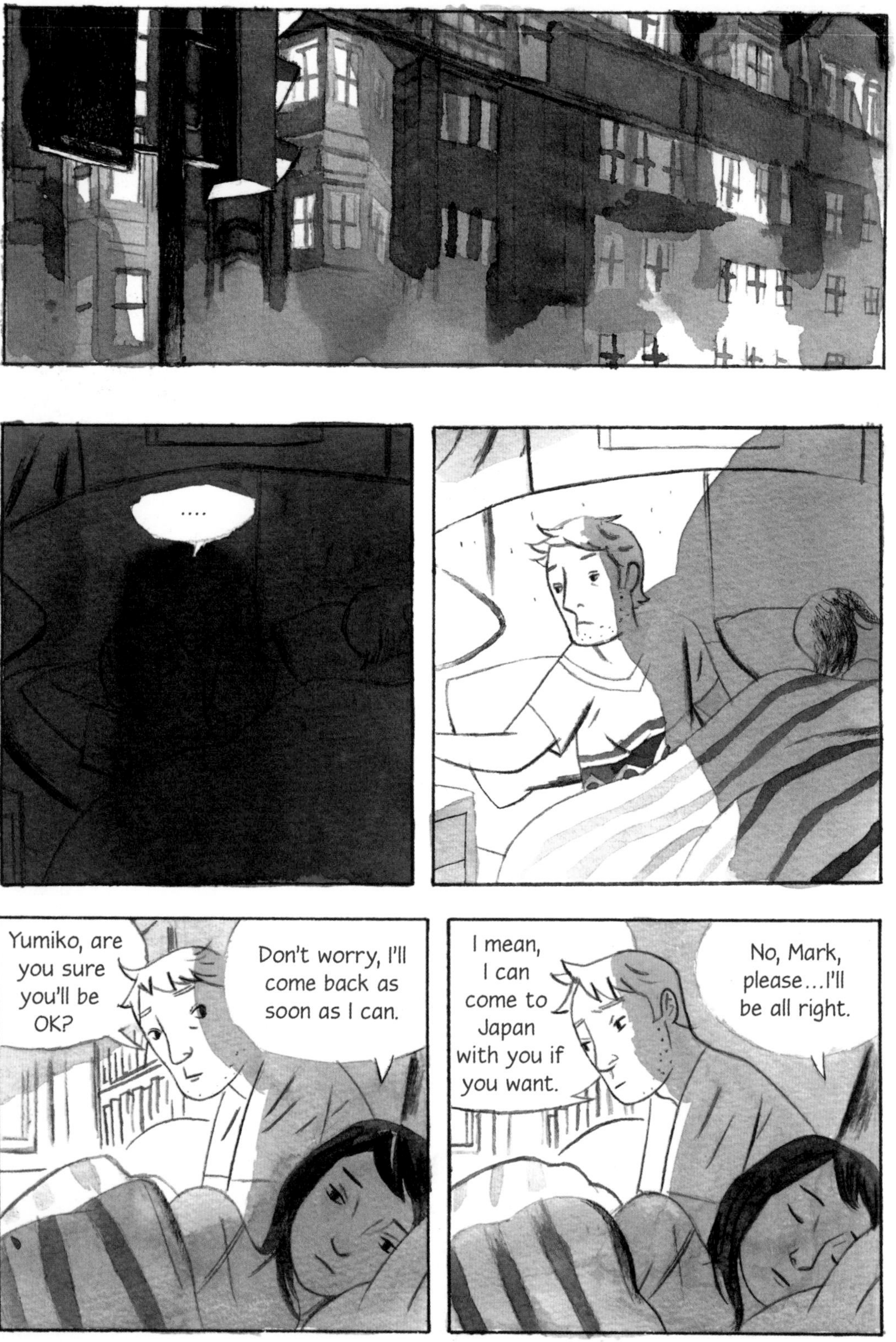
....
Yumiko, are you sure you'll be OK?
Don't worry, I'll come back as soon as I can.
I mean, I can come to Japan with you if you want.
No, Mark, please...I'll be all right.

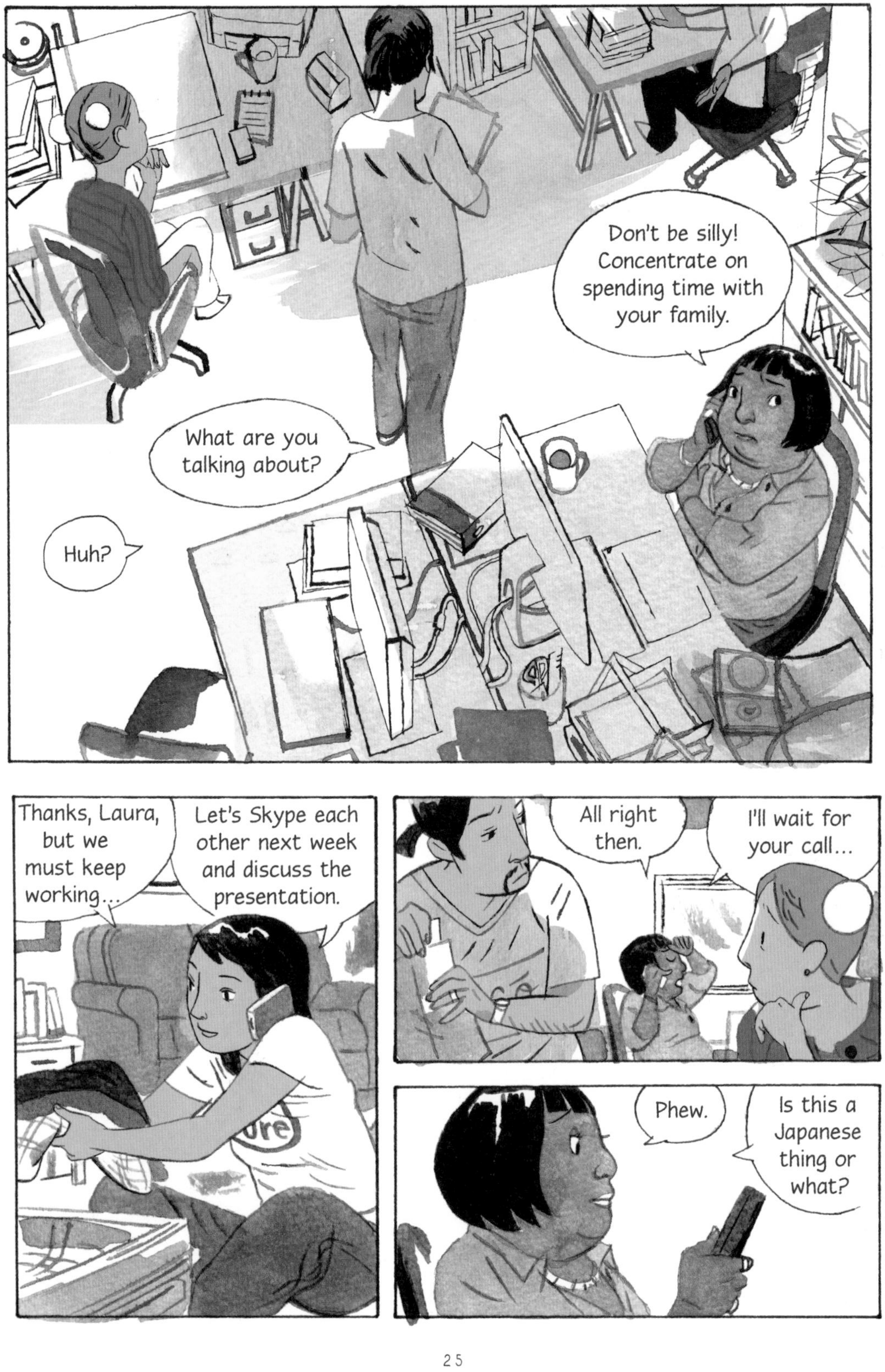
Don't be silly! Concentrate on spending time with your family.
What are you talking about?
Huh?
Thanks, Laura, but we must keep working...
Let's Skype each other next week and discuss the presentation.
All right then.
I'll wait for your call...
Phew.
Is this a Japanese thing or what?

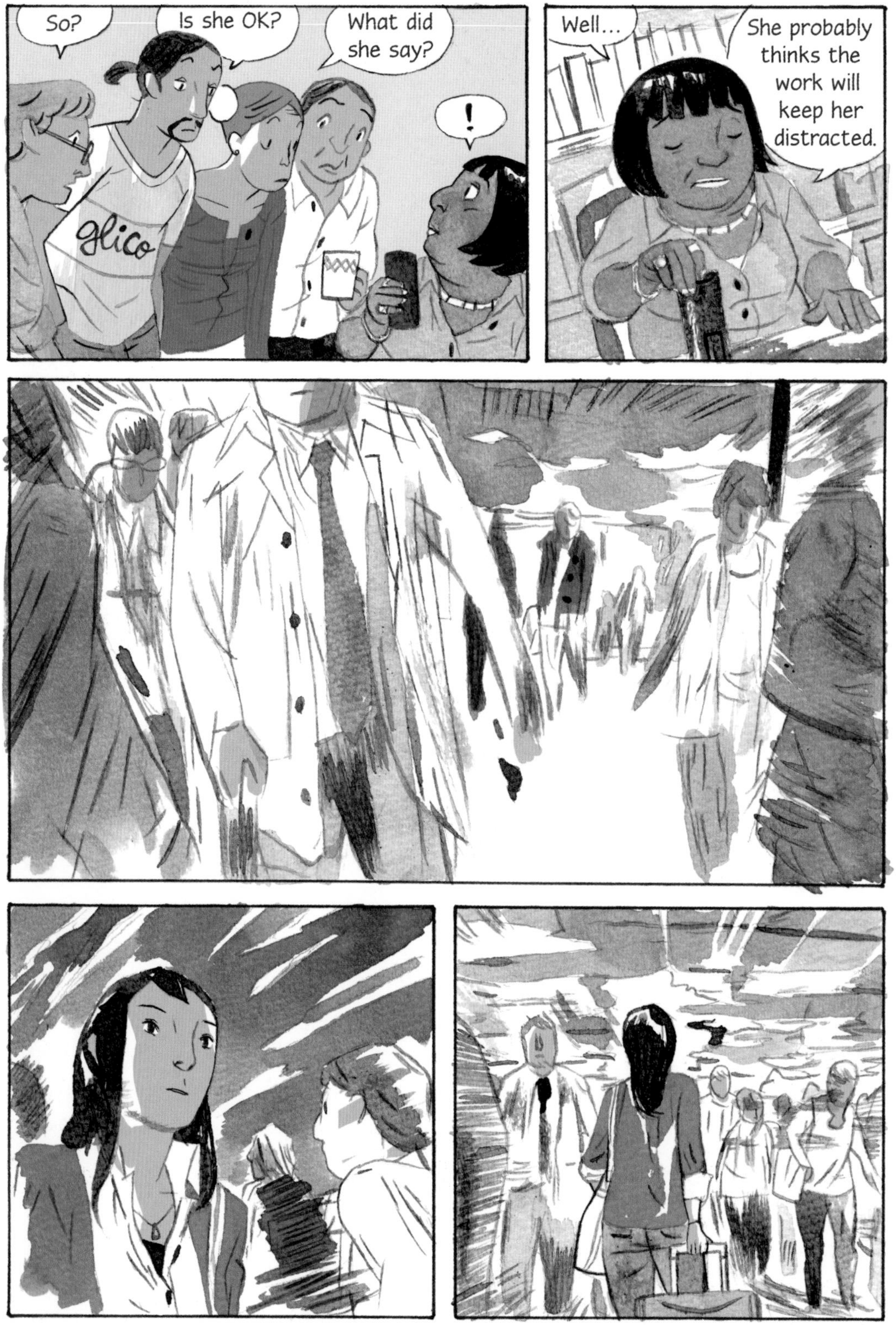
So?
Is she OK?
What did she say?
!
glico
Well...
She probably thinks the work will keep her distracted.

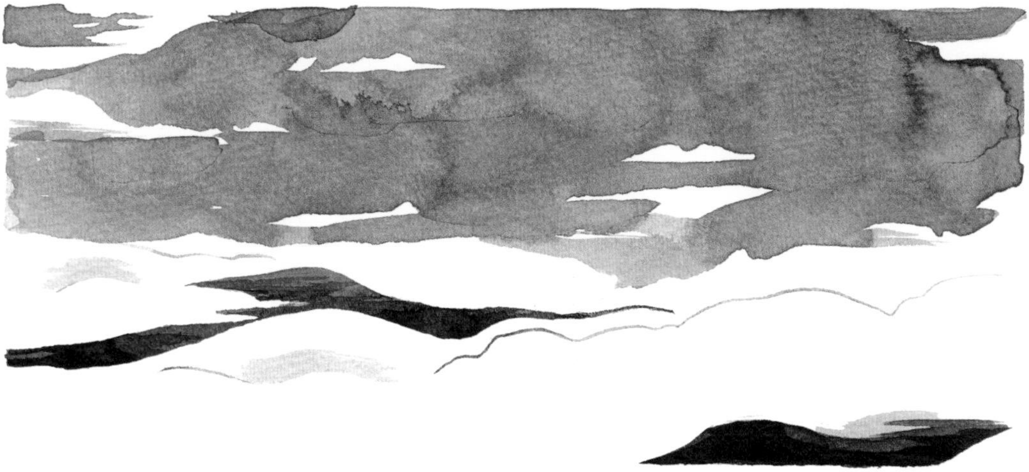

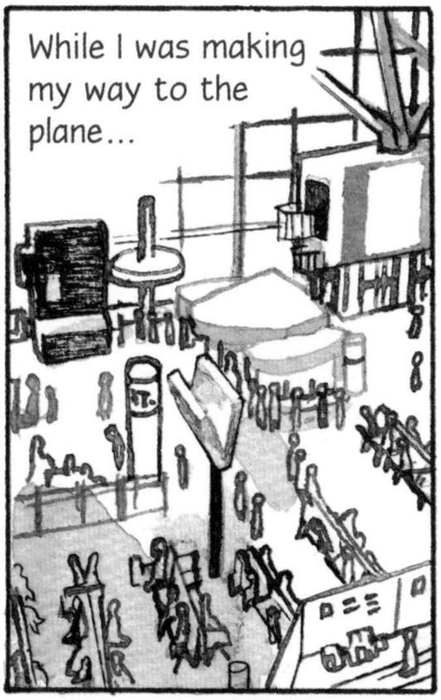
While I was making my way to the plane...

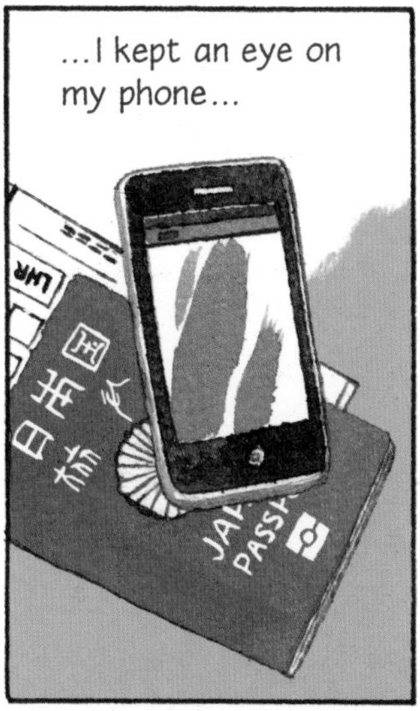
...I kept an eye on my phone...

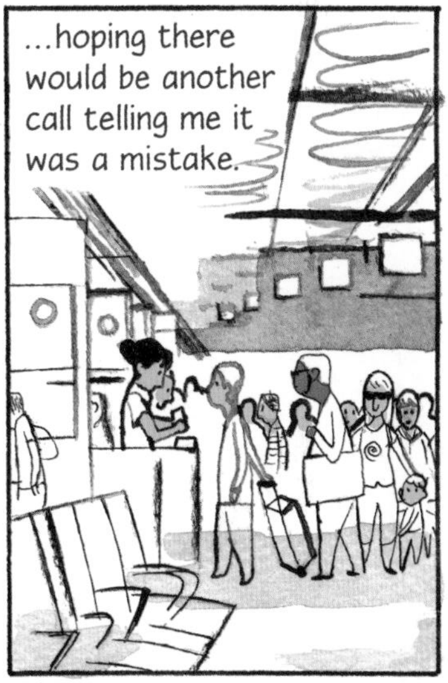
...hoping there would be another call telling me it was a mistake.

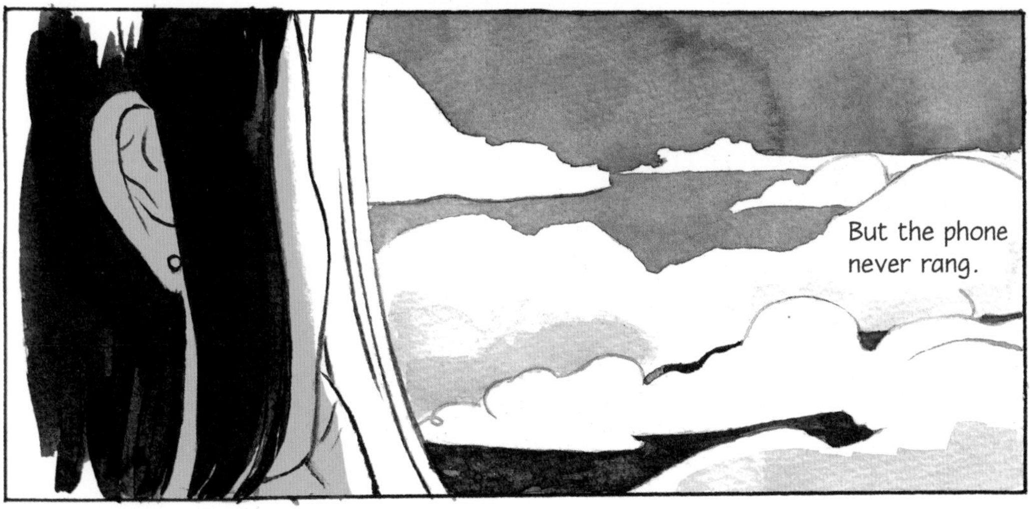
But the phone never rang.

Another trip back home...
but this time it's
different...

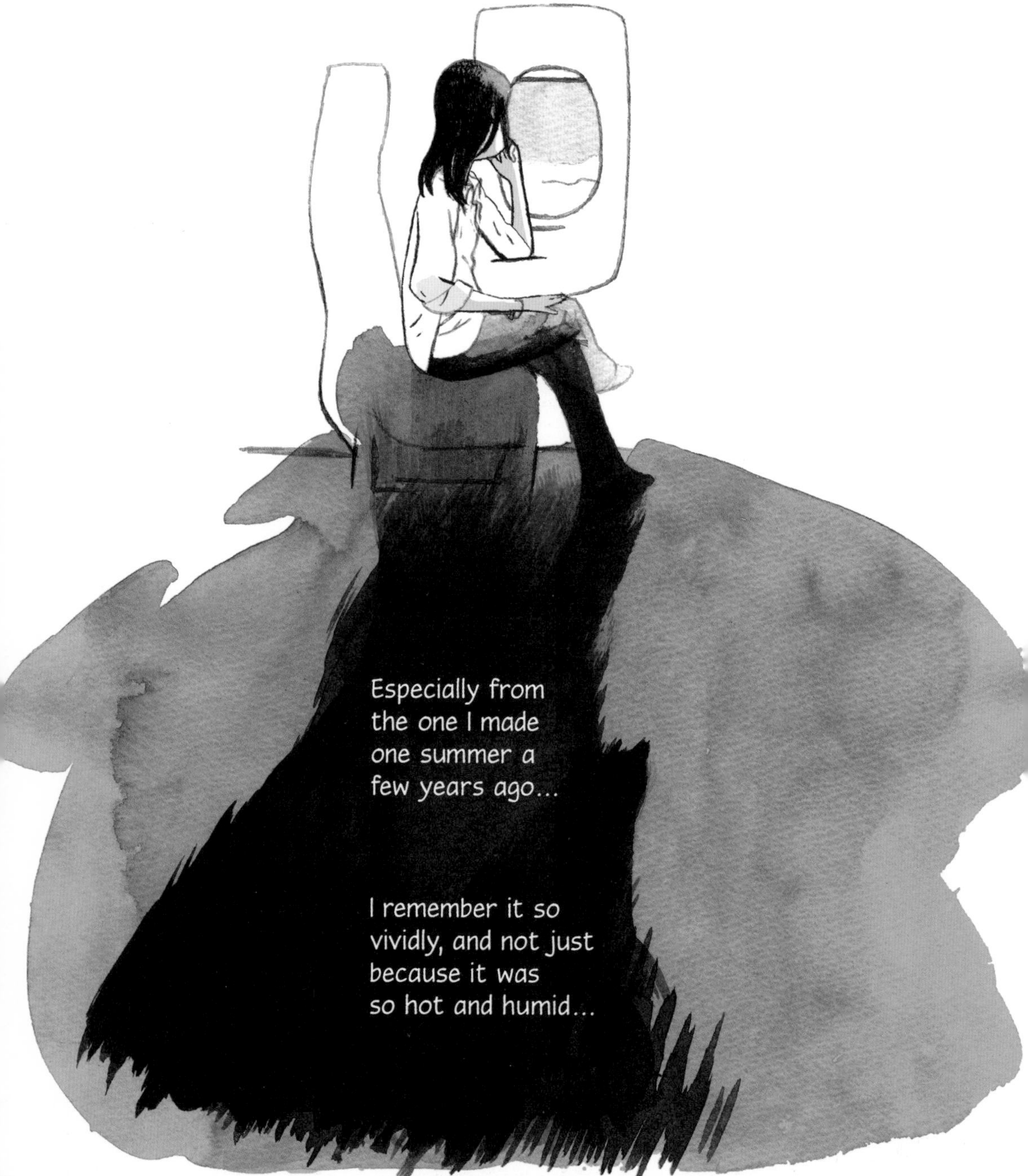
Especially from the one I made one summer a few years ago...
I remember it so vividly, and not just because it was so hot and humid...

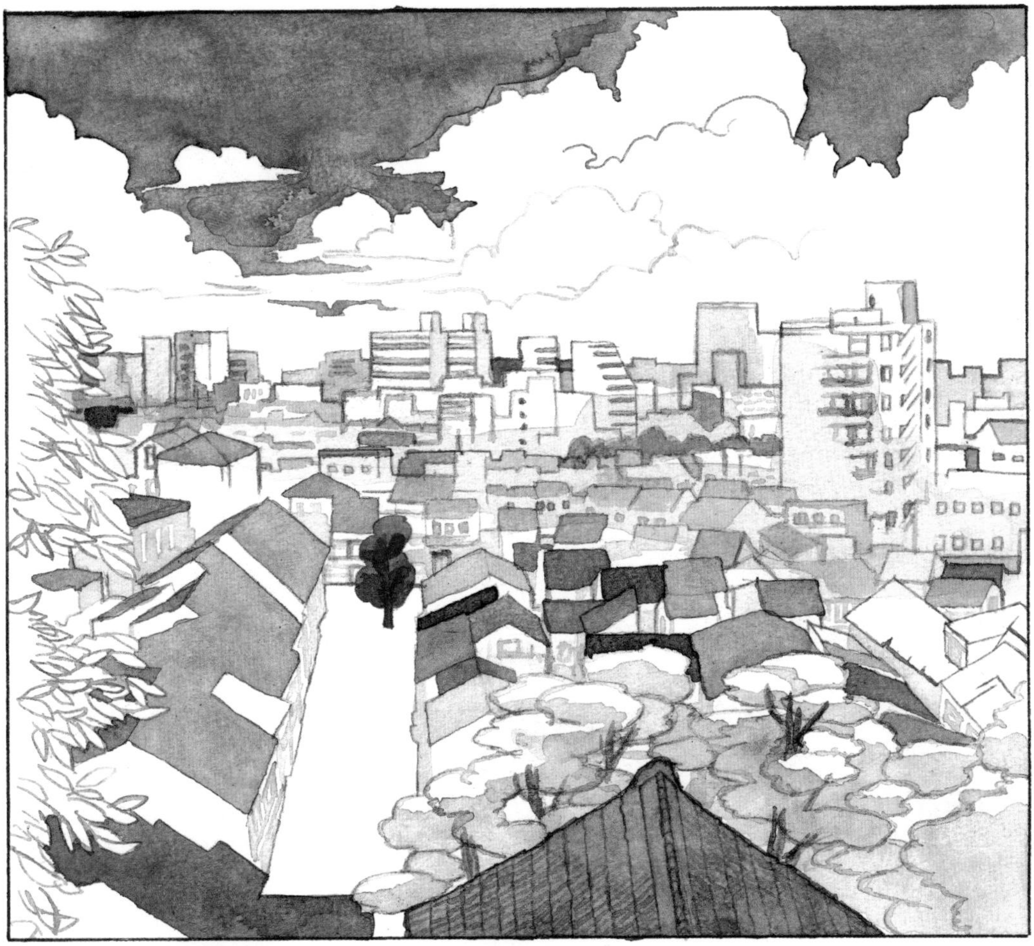

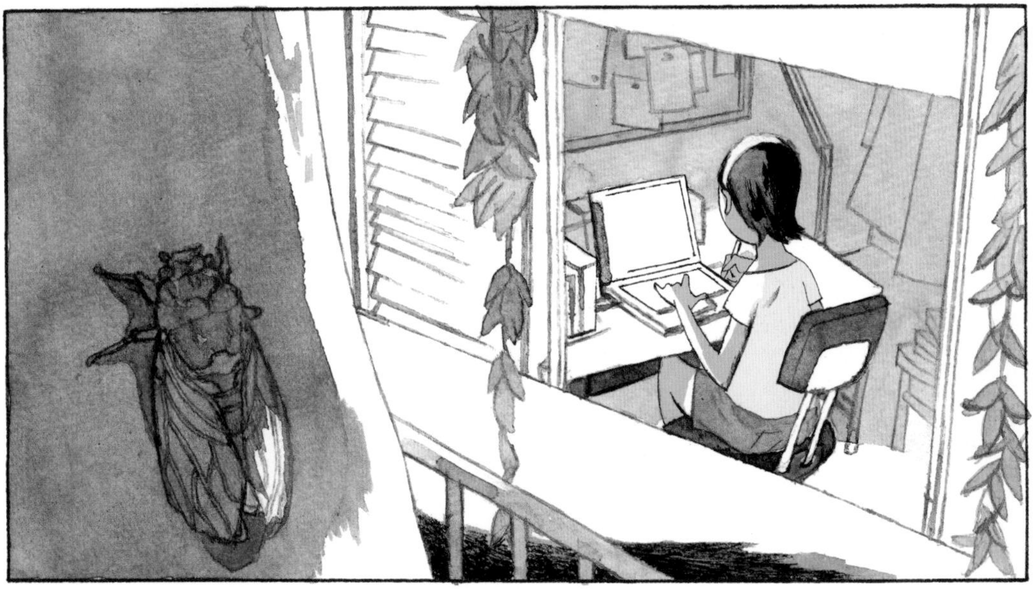

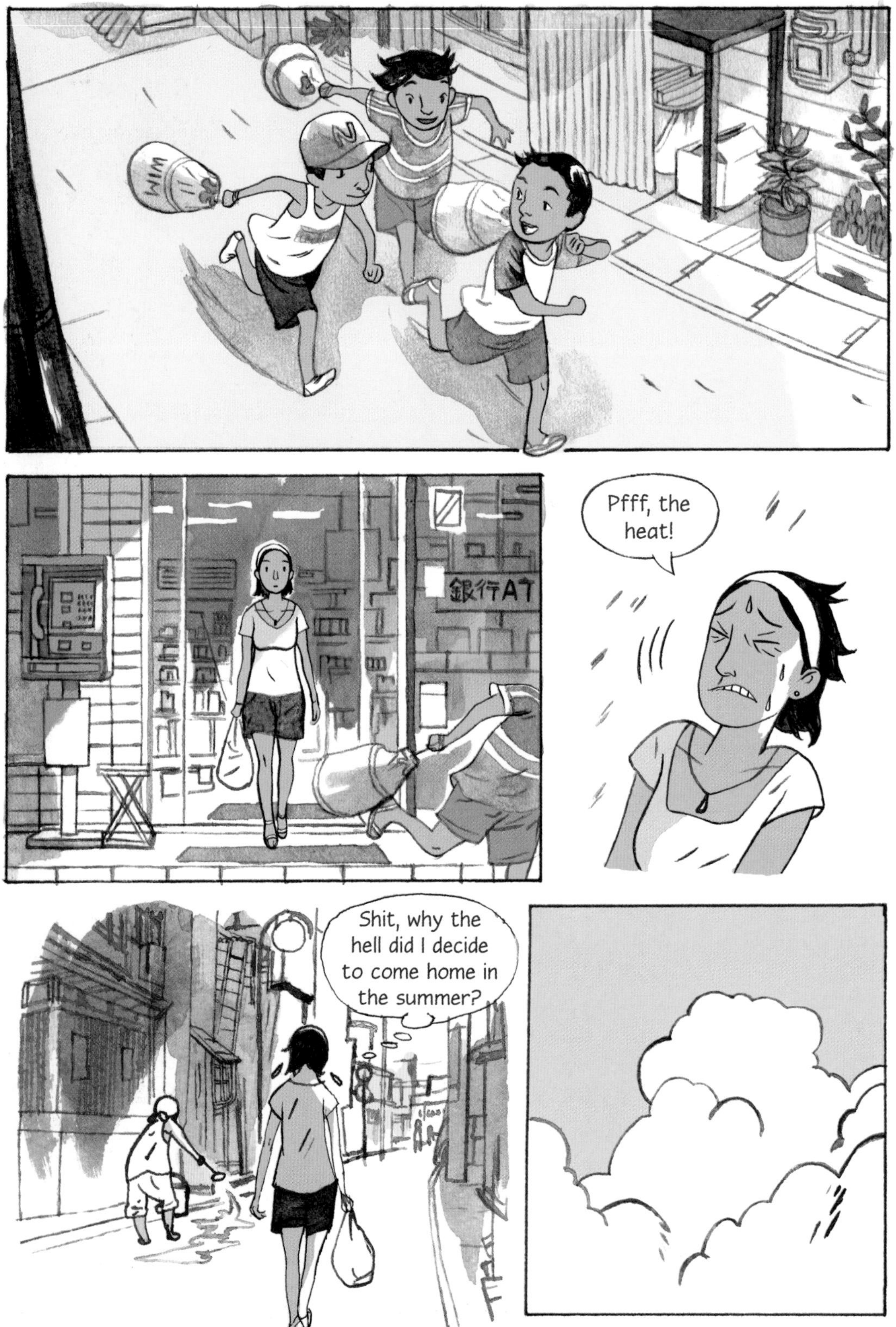
銀行AT
Pfff, the heat!
Shit, why the hell did I decide to come home in the summer?

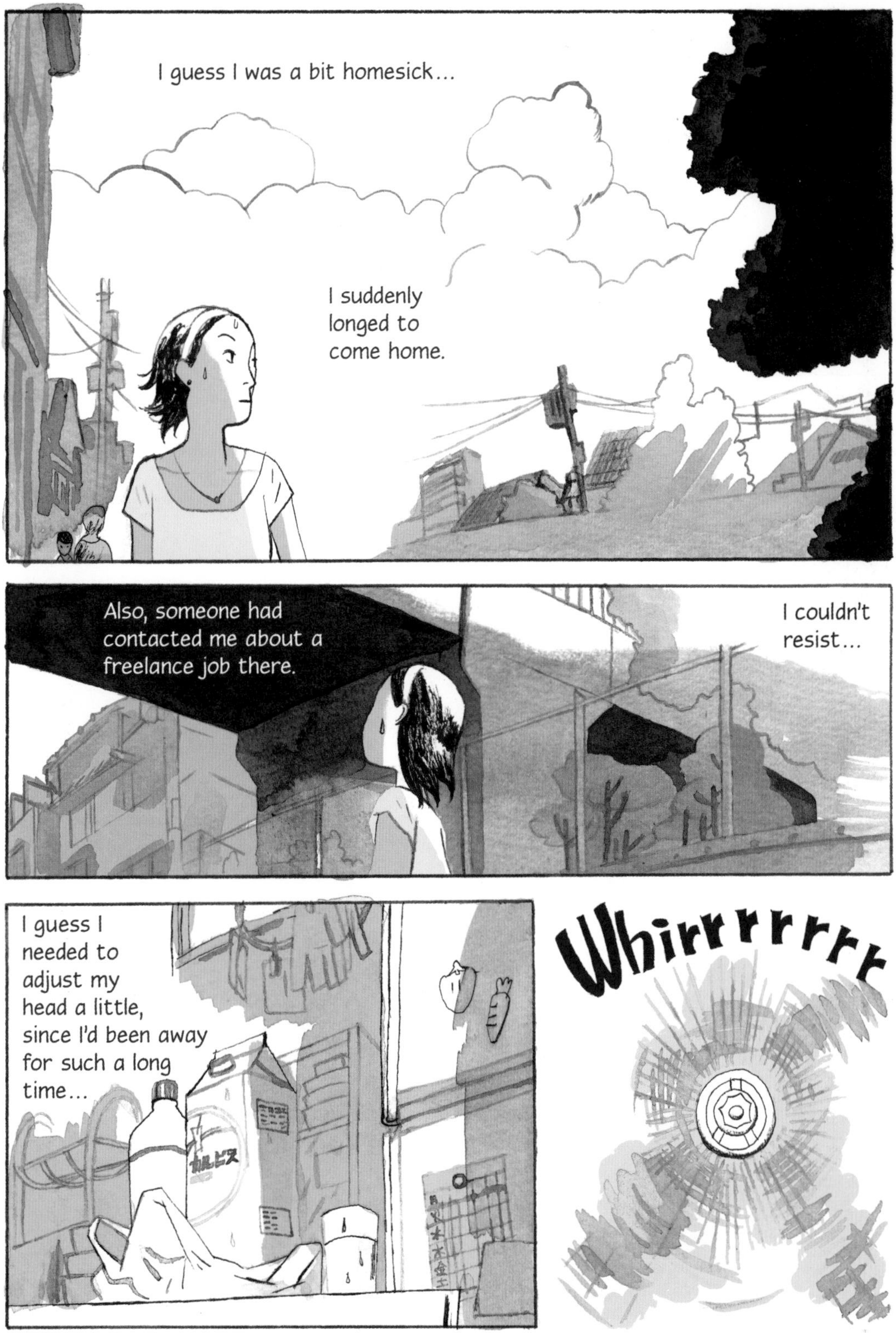
I guess I was a bit homesick…
I suddenly longed to come home.
Also, someone had contacted me about a freelance job there.
I couldn't resist…
I guess I needed to adjust my head a little, since I'd been away for such a long time…
カルピス
Whirrrrrrt

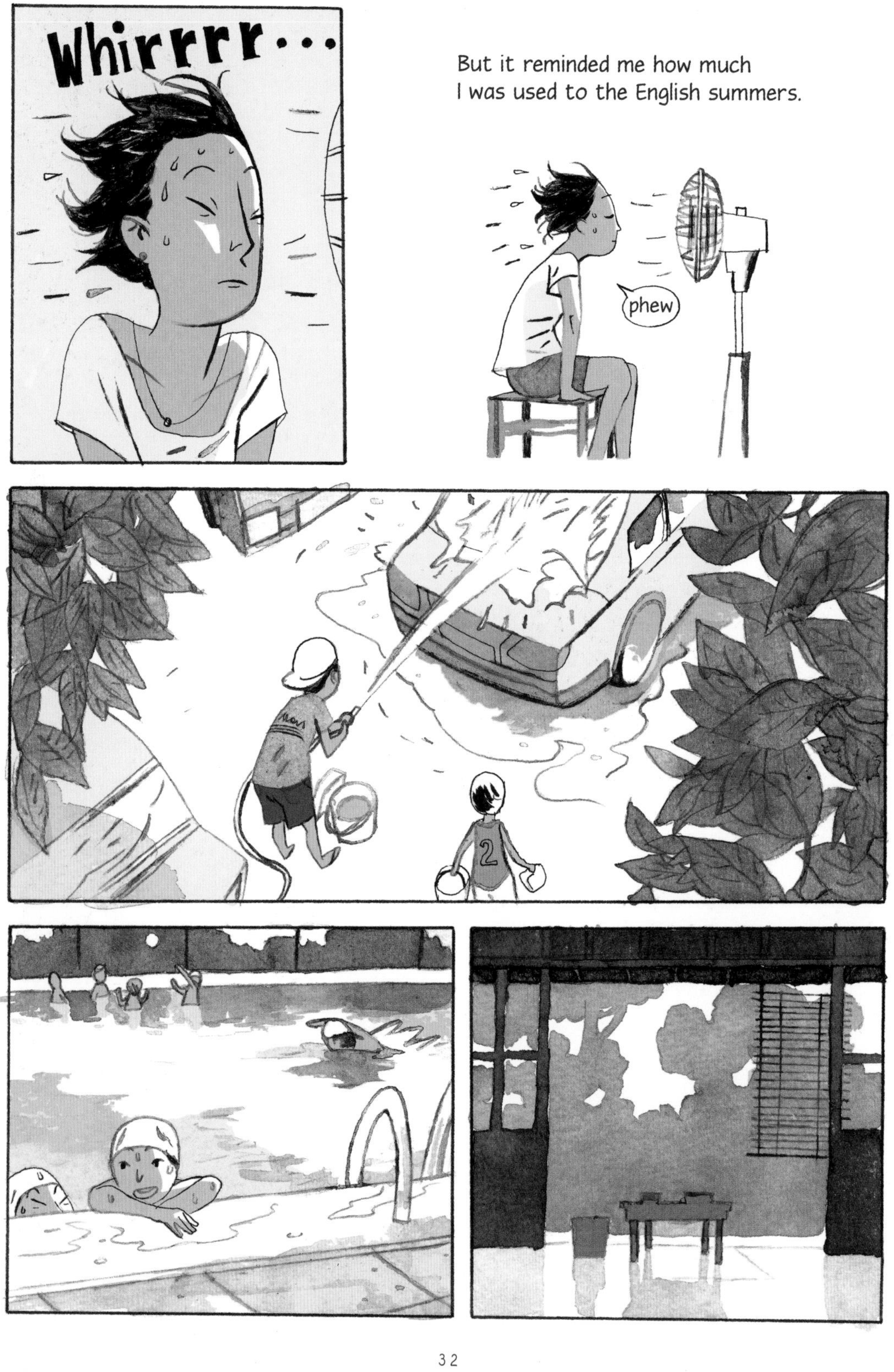
Whirrrr...
But it reminded me how much
I was used to the English summers.
phew

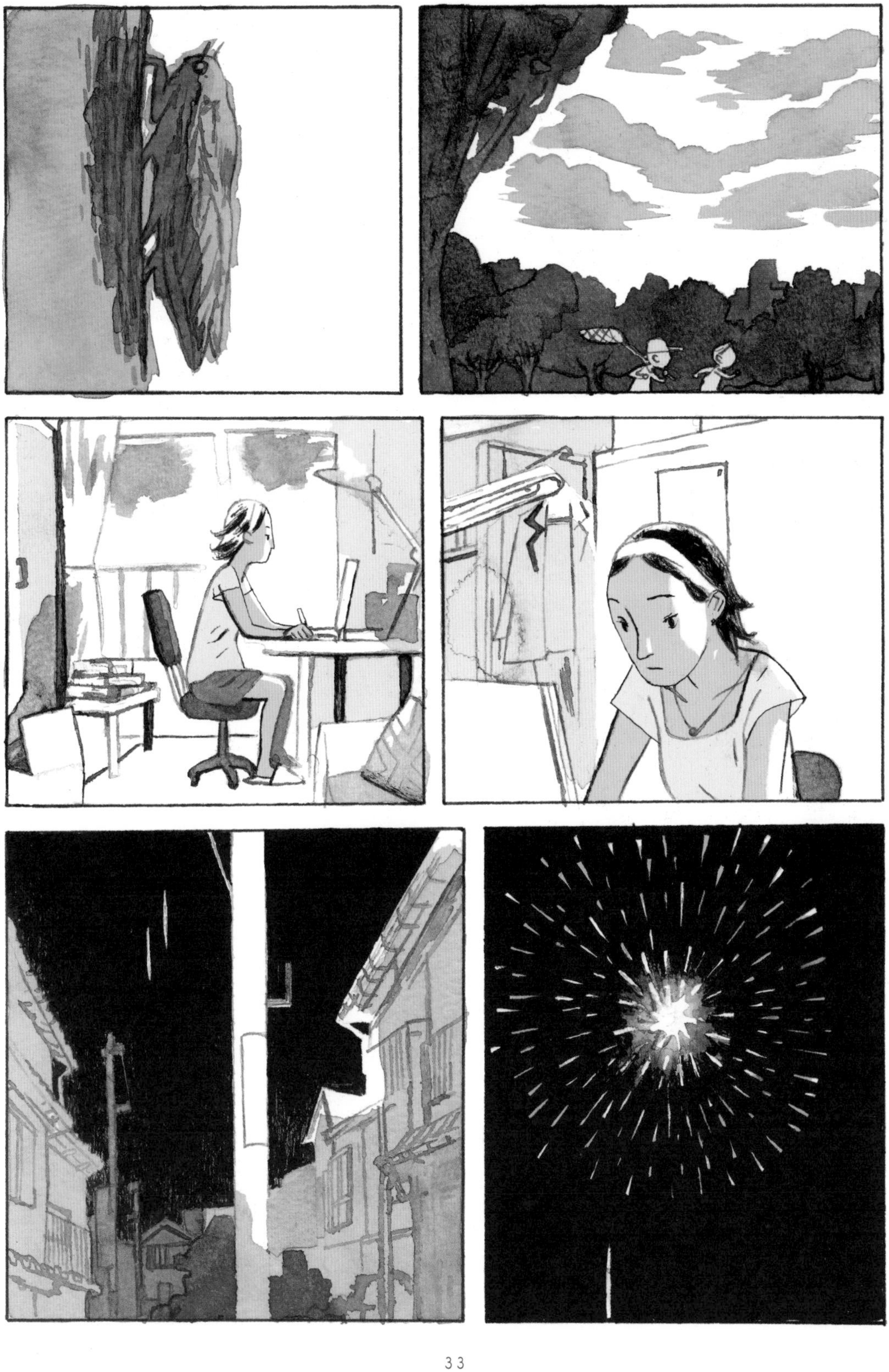

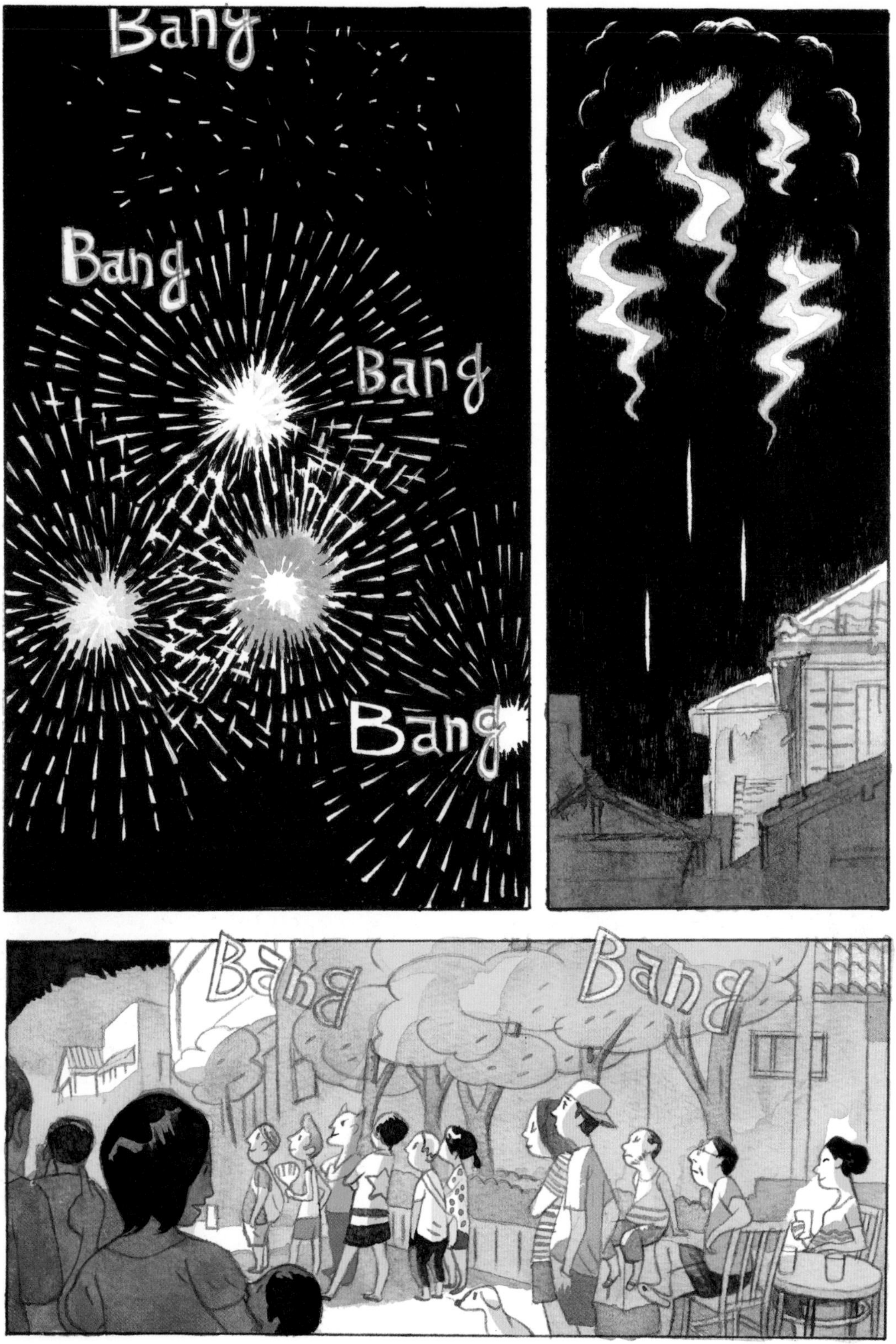
Bang
Bang
Bang
Bang
Bang
Bang

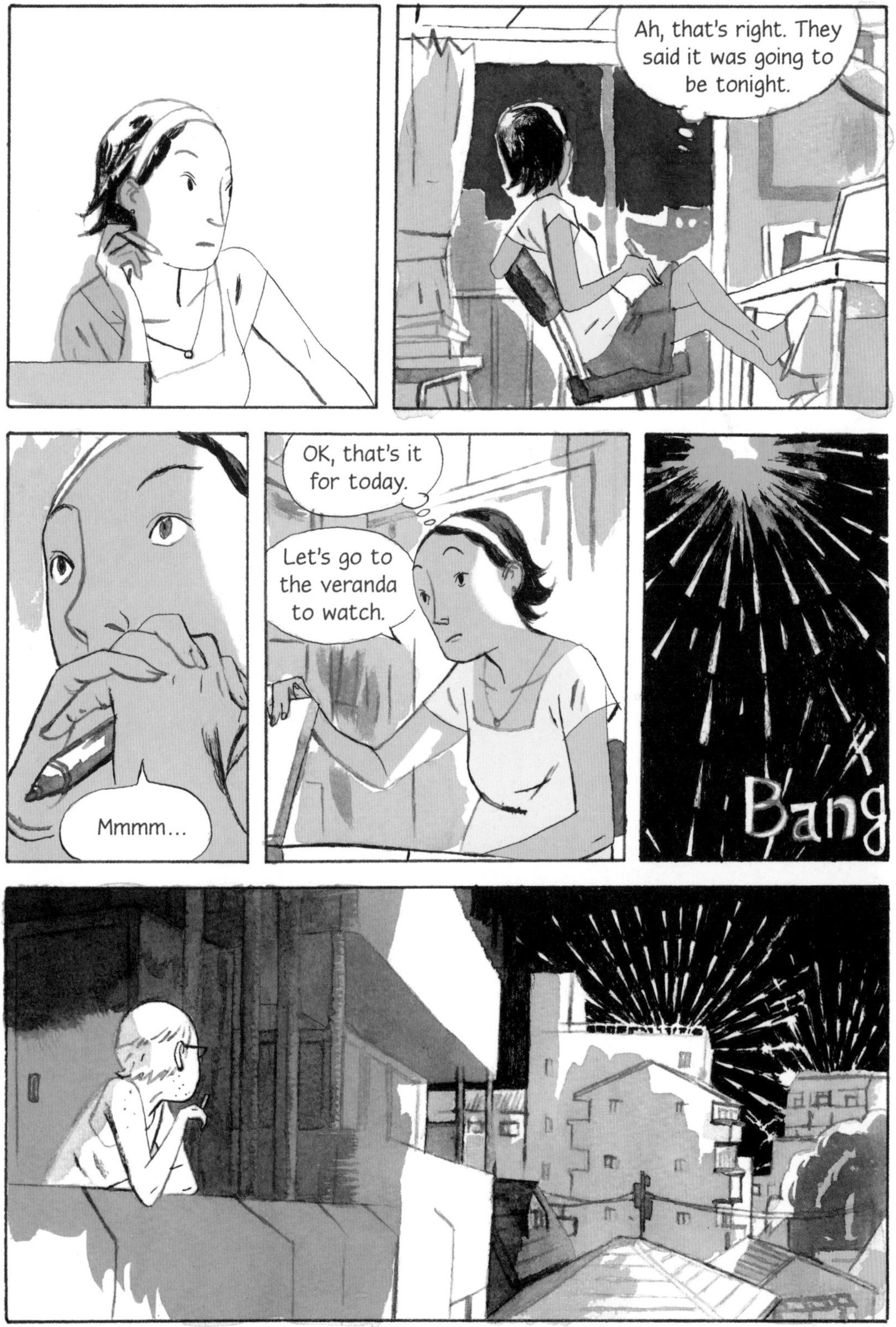
Ah, that's right. They said it was going to be tonight.
Mmmm...
OK, that's it for today.
Let's go to the veranda to watch.
Bang

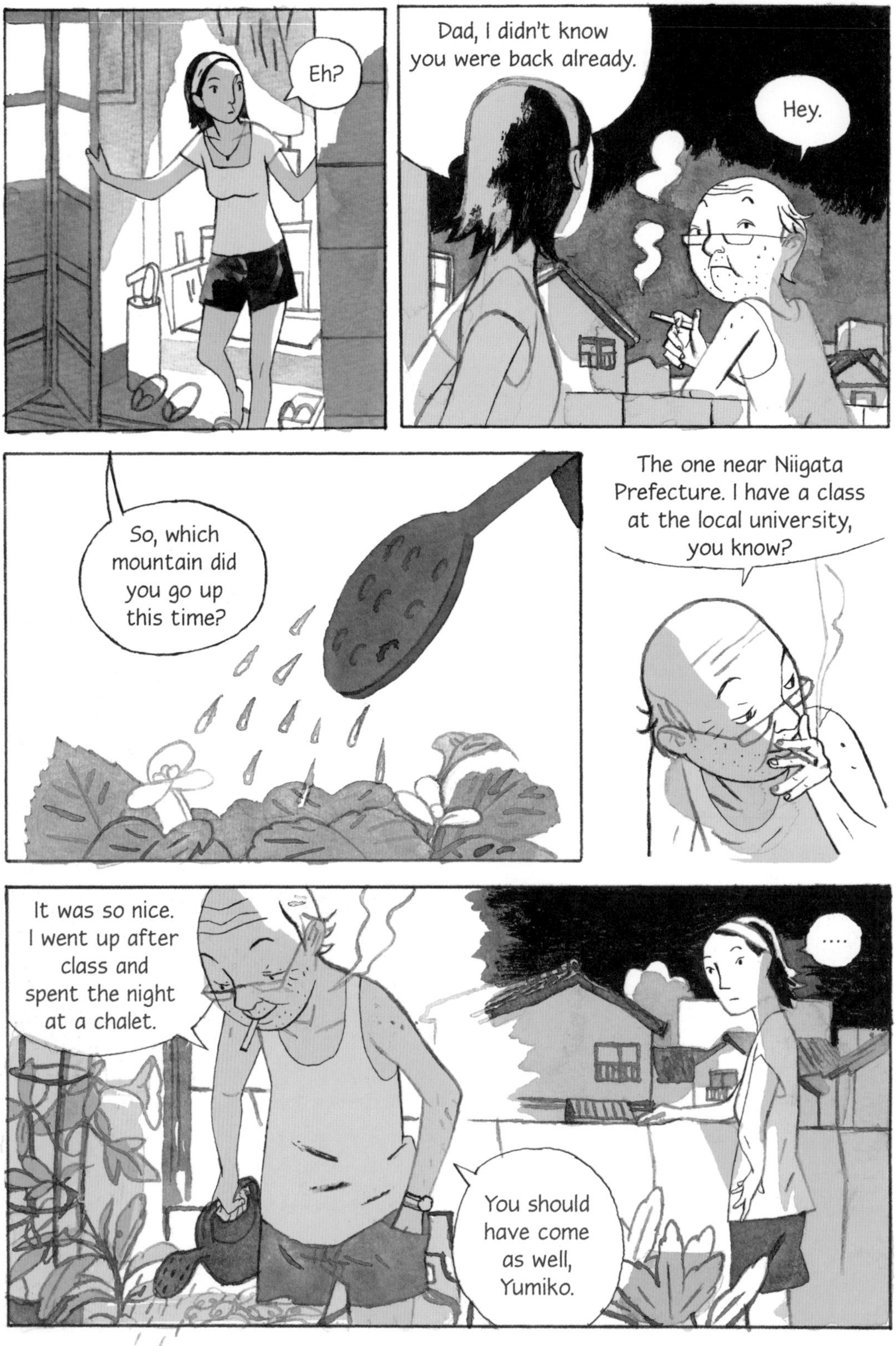

Eh?
Dad, I didn't know you were back already.
Hey.
So, which mountain did you go up this time?
The one near Niigata Prefecture. I have a class at the local university, you know?
It was so nice. I went up after class and spent the night at a chalet.
....
You should have come as well, Yumiko.

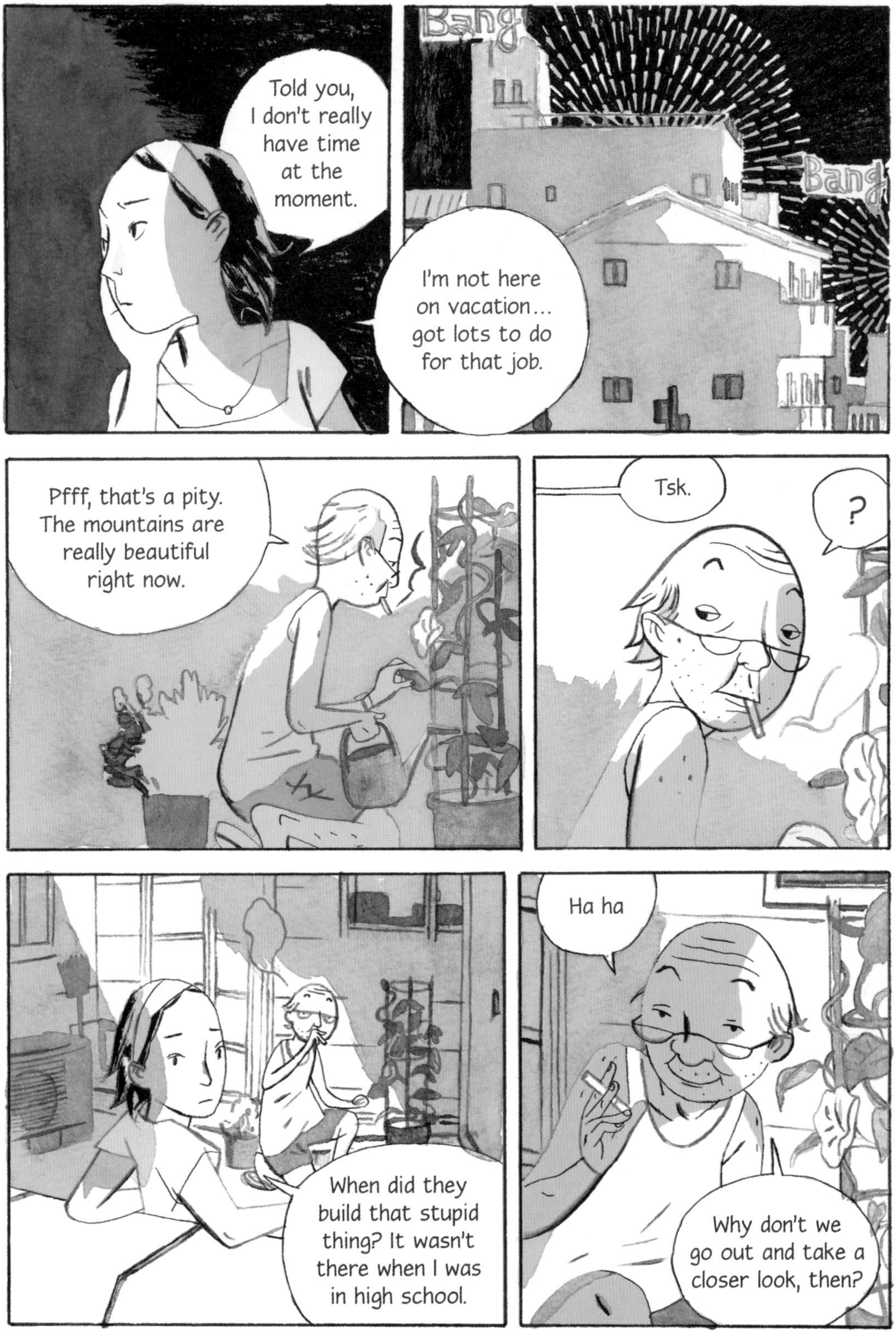
Told you, I don't really have time at the moment.
Bang
Bang
I'm not here on vacation... got lots to do for that job.
Pfff, that's a pity. The mountains are really beautiful right now.
Tsk.
?
When did they build that stupid thing? It wasn't there when I was in high school.
Ha ha
Why don't we go out and take a closer look, then?

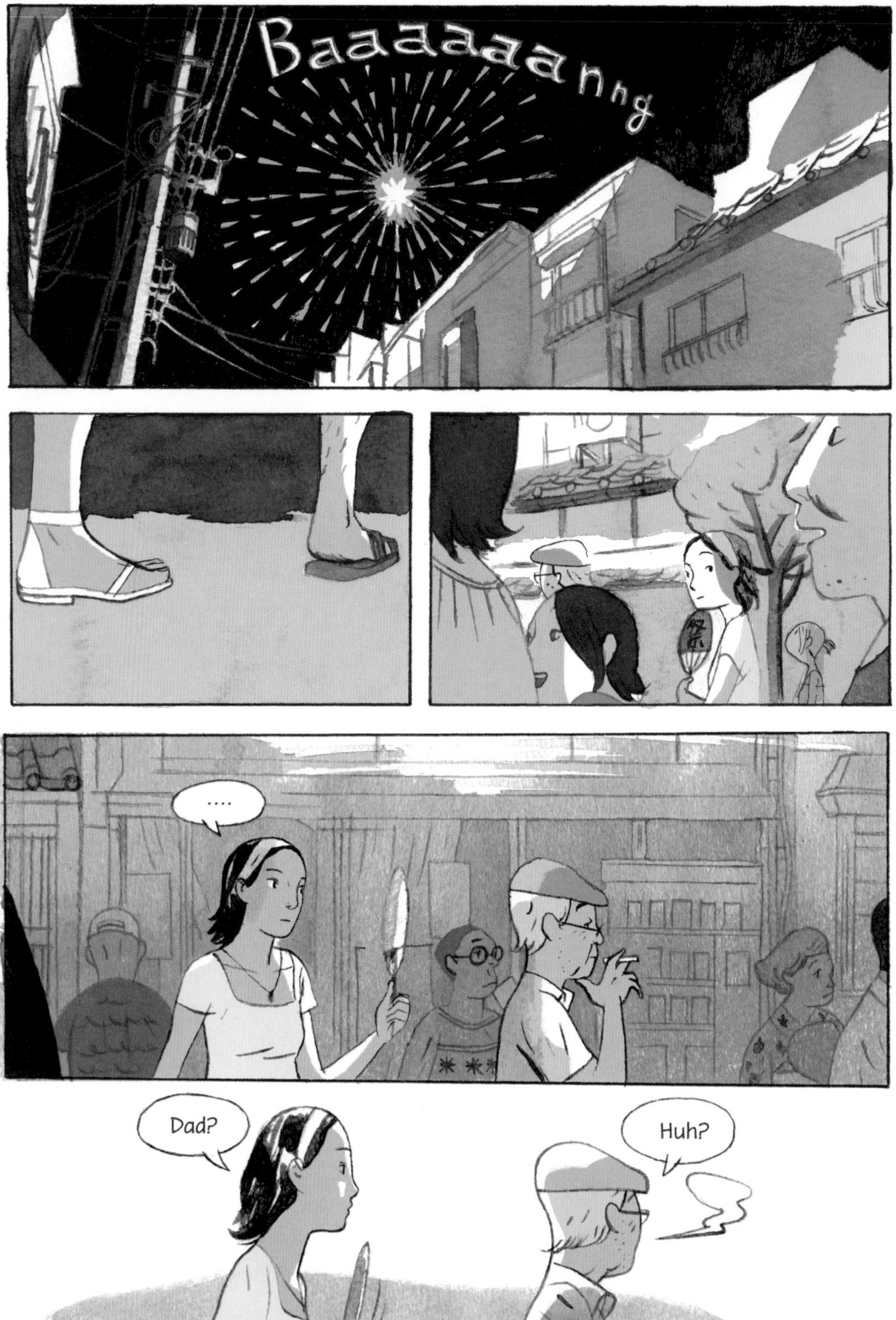
Baaaaaaanng
....
Dad?
Huh?

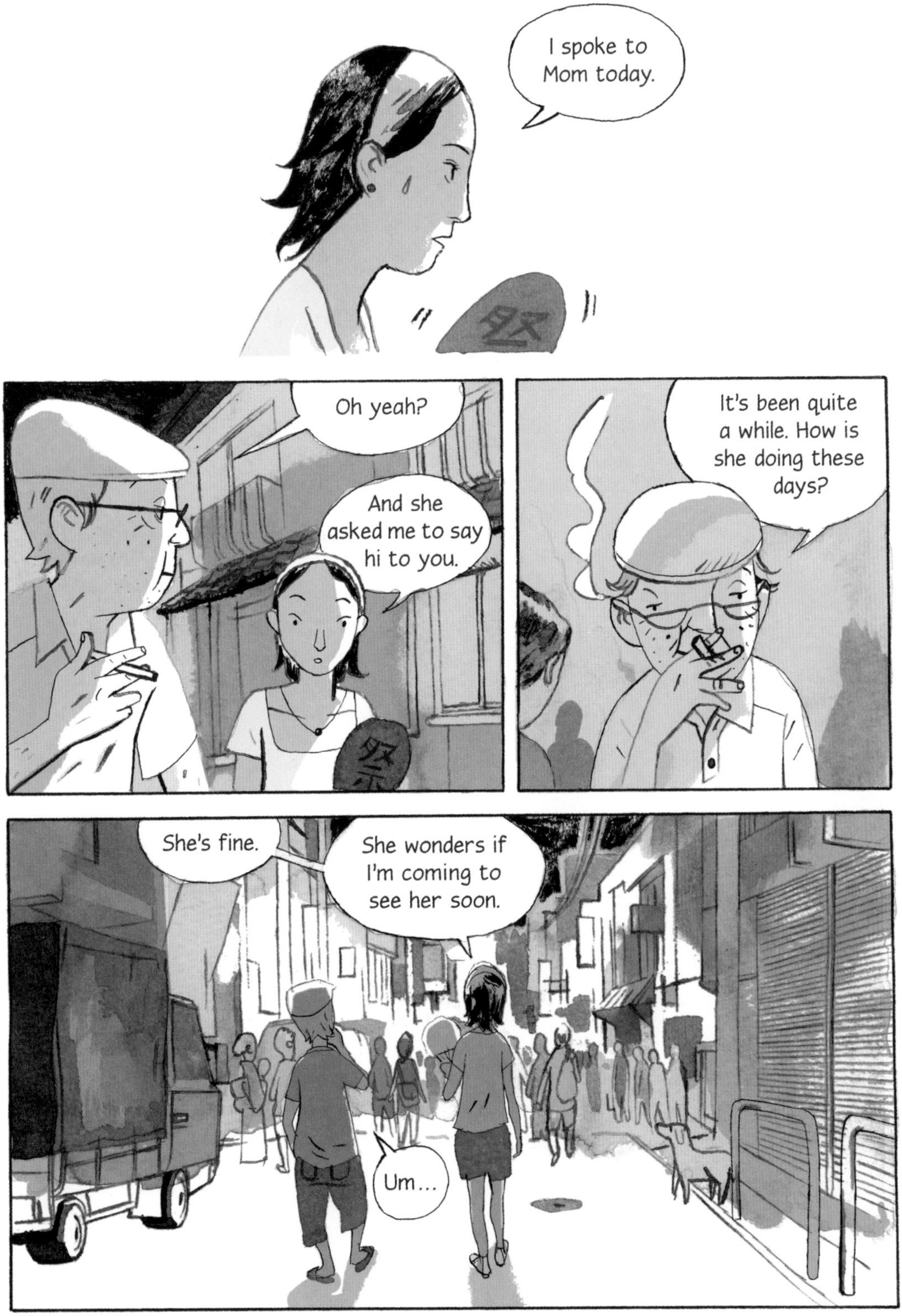
I spoke to Mom today.
Oh yeah?
And she asked me to say hi to you.
It's been quite a while. How is she doing these days?
She's fine.
She wonders if I'm coming to see her soon.
Um...

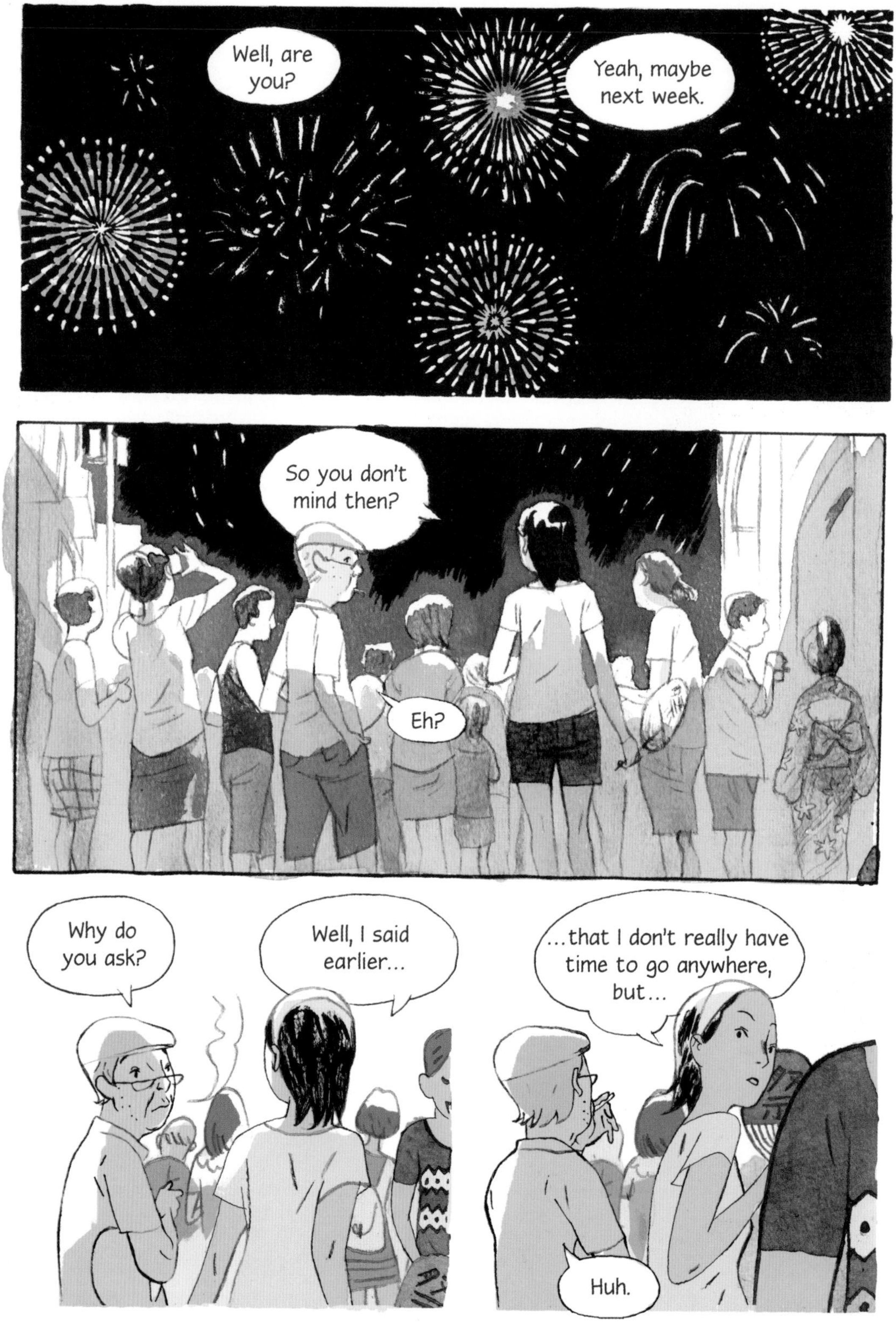
Well, are you?
Yeah, maybe next week.
So you don't mind then?
Eh?
Why do you ask?
Well, I said earlier...
...that I don't really have time to go anywhere, but...
Huh.

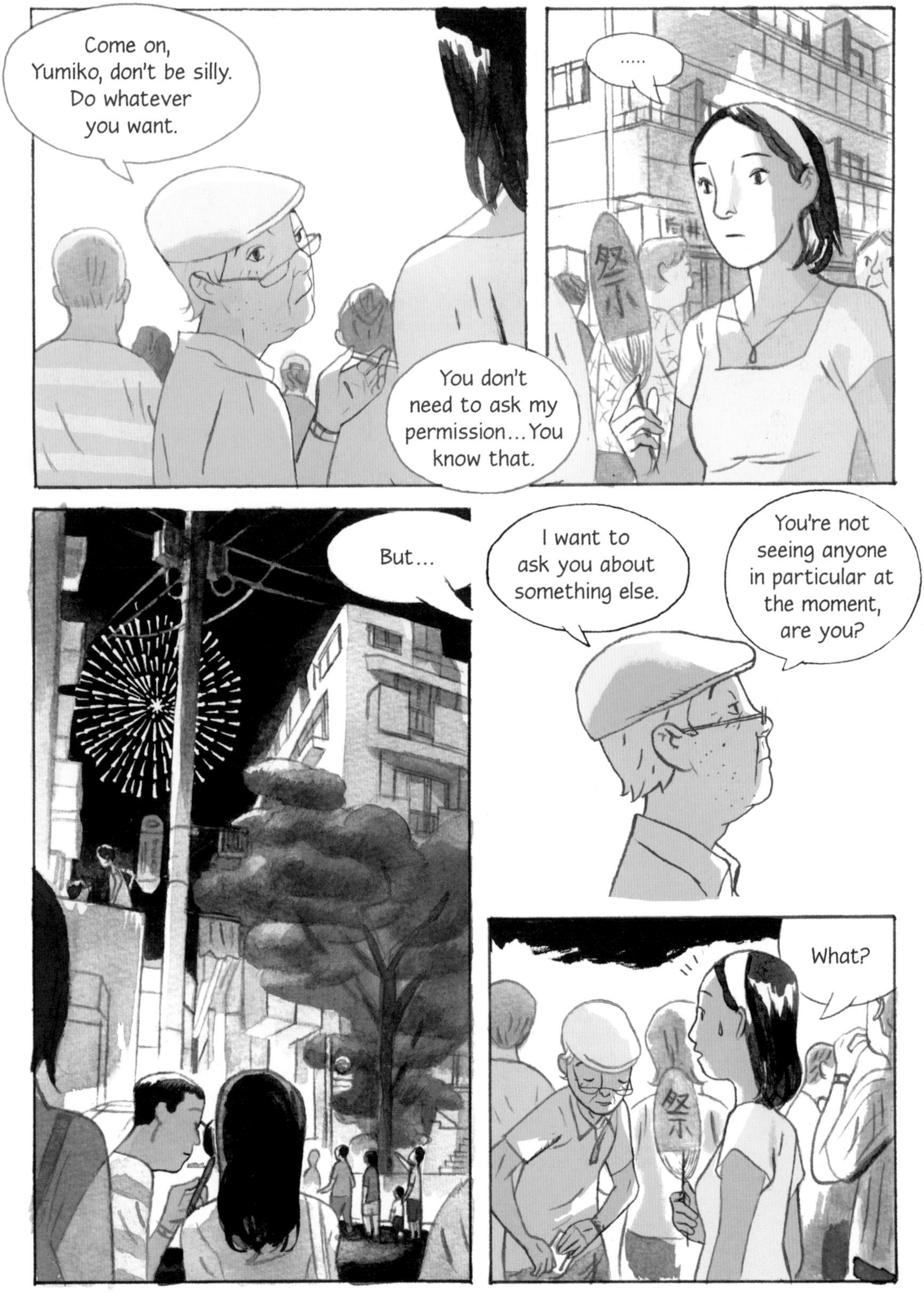

Come on, Yumiko, don't be silly. Do whatever you want.
You don't need to ask my permission... You know that.
.....
But...
I want to ask you about something else.
You're not seeing anyone in particular at the moment, are you?
What?

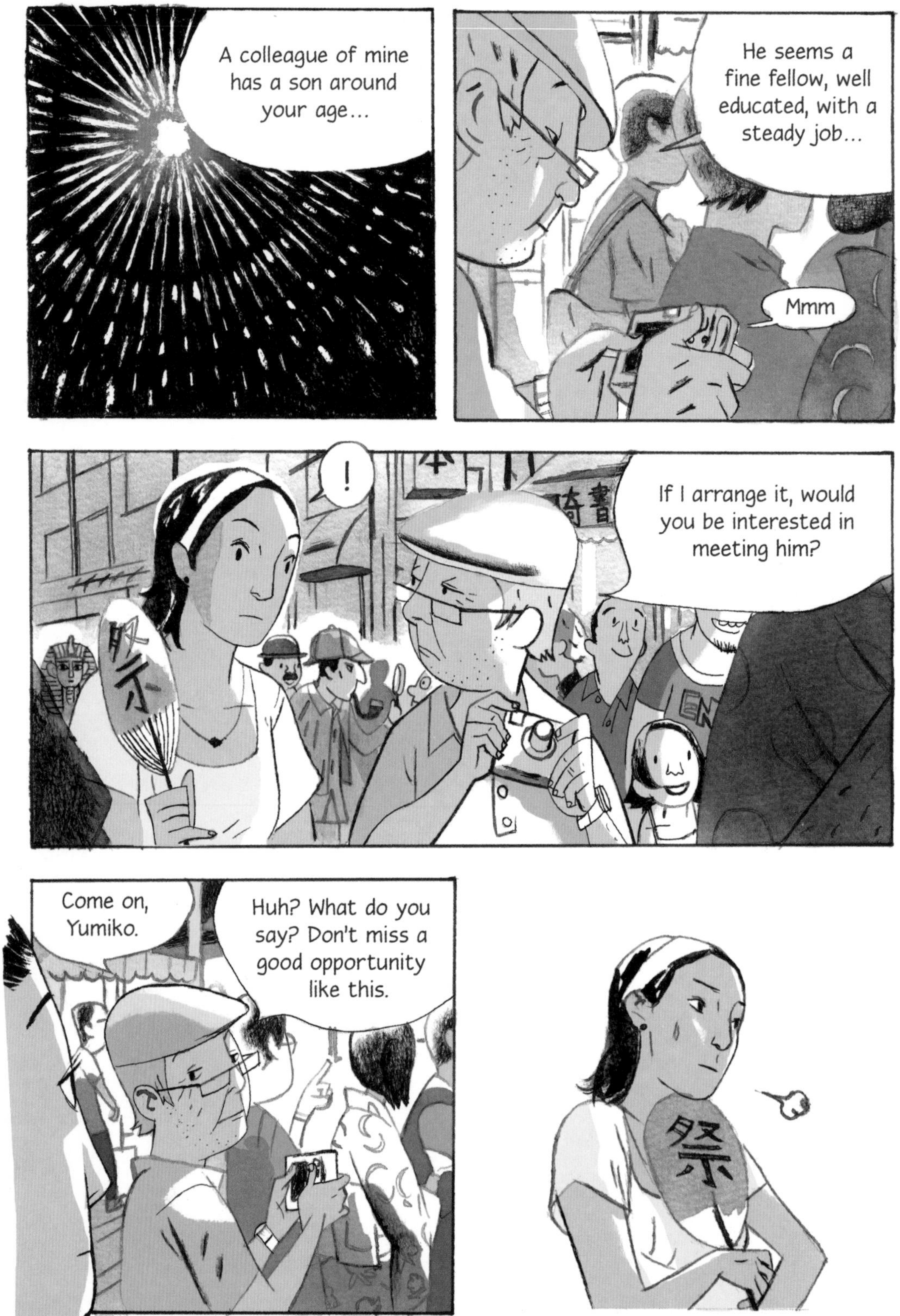
A colleague of mine has a son around your age...
He seems a fine fellow, well educated, with a steady job...
Mmm
!
If I arrange it, would you be interested in meeting him?
Come on, Yumiko.
Huh? What do you say? Don't miss a good opportunity like this.
祭

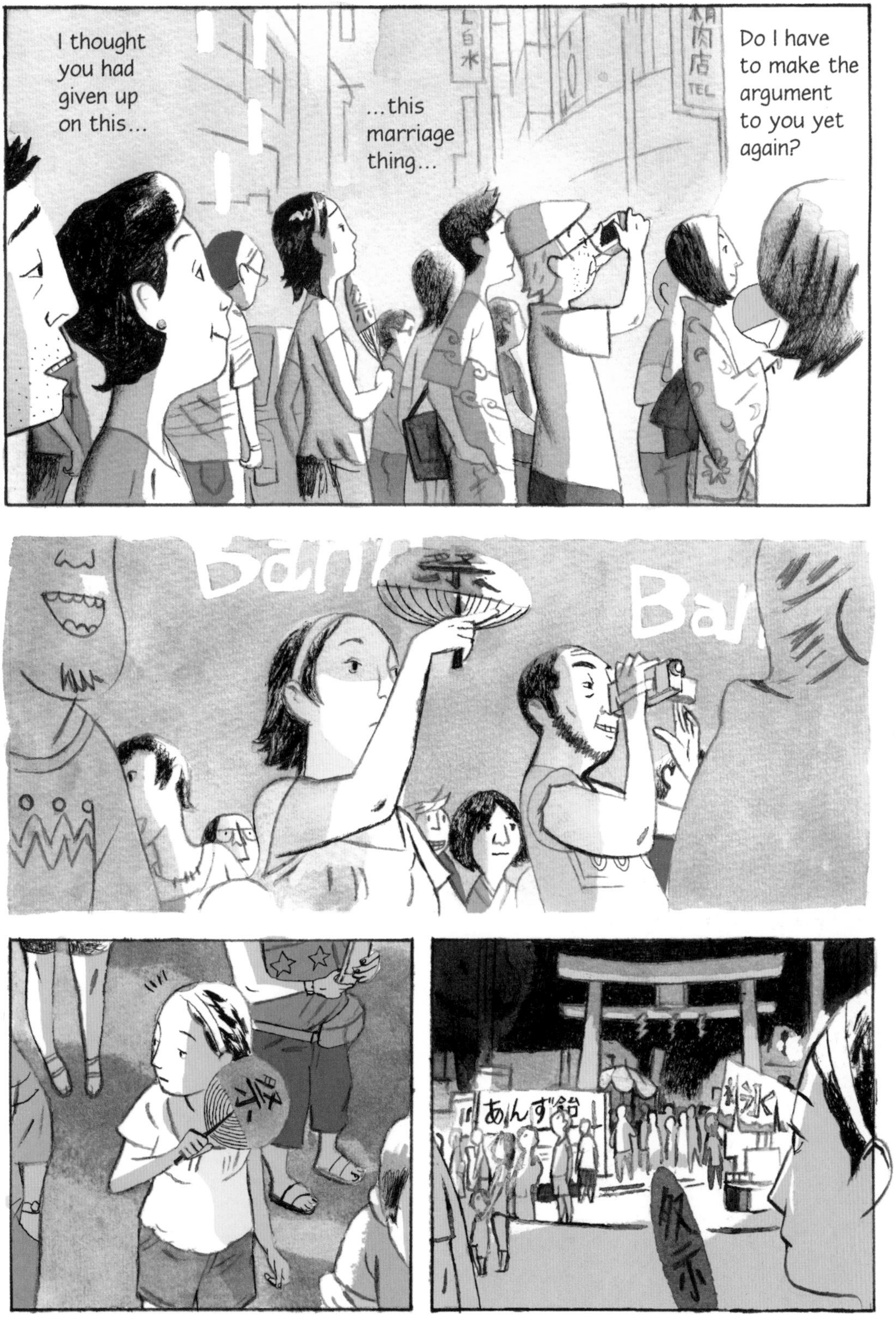
I thought you had given up on this...
...this marriage thing...
Do I have to make the argument to you yet again?

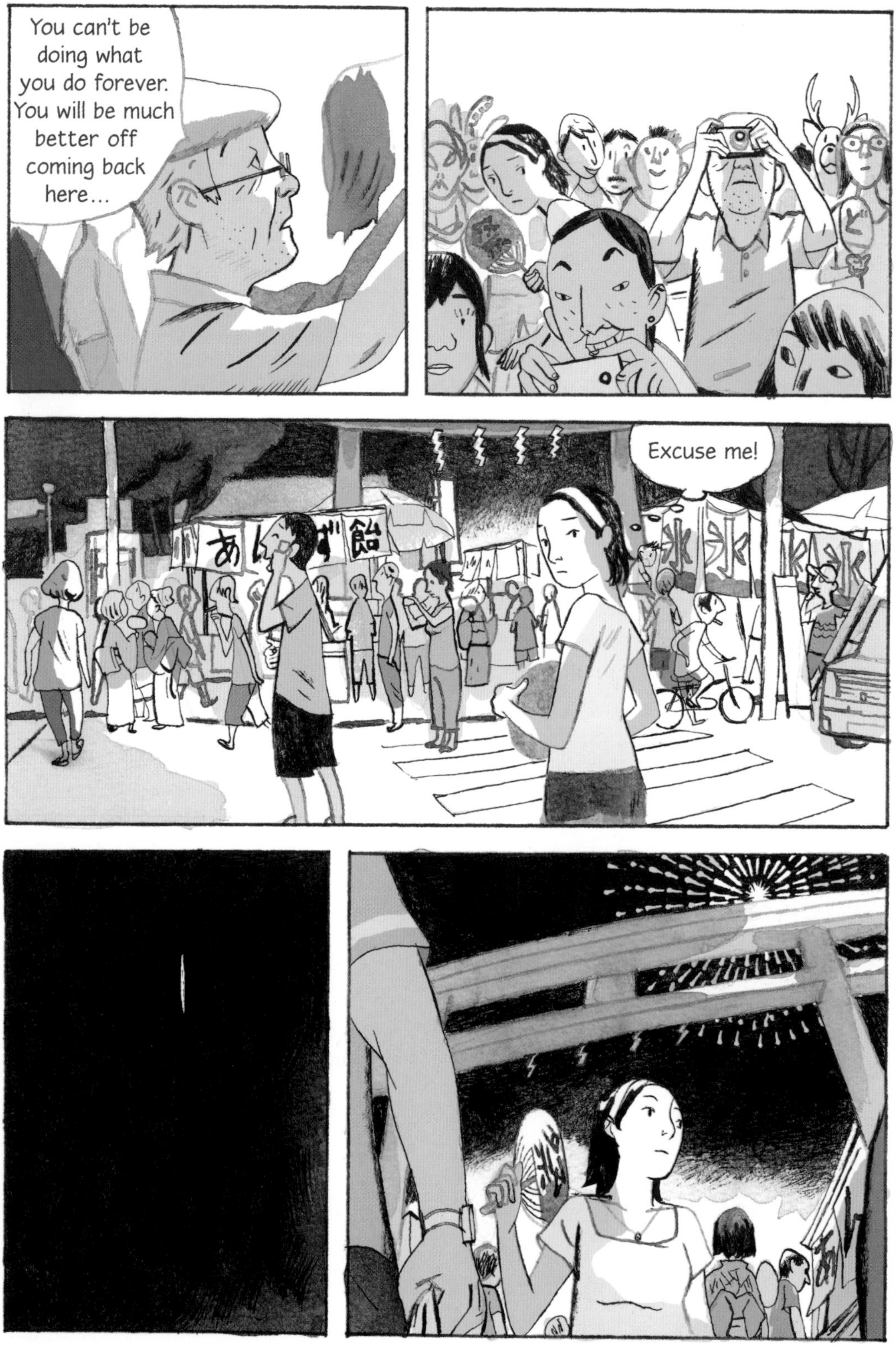
You can't be doing what you do forever. You will be much better off coming back here...
Excuse me!

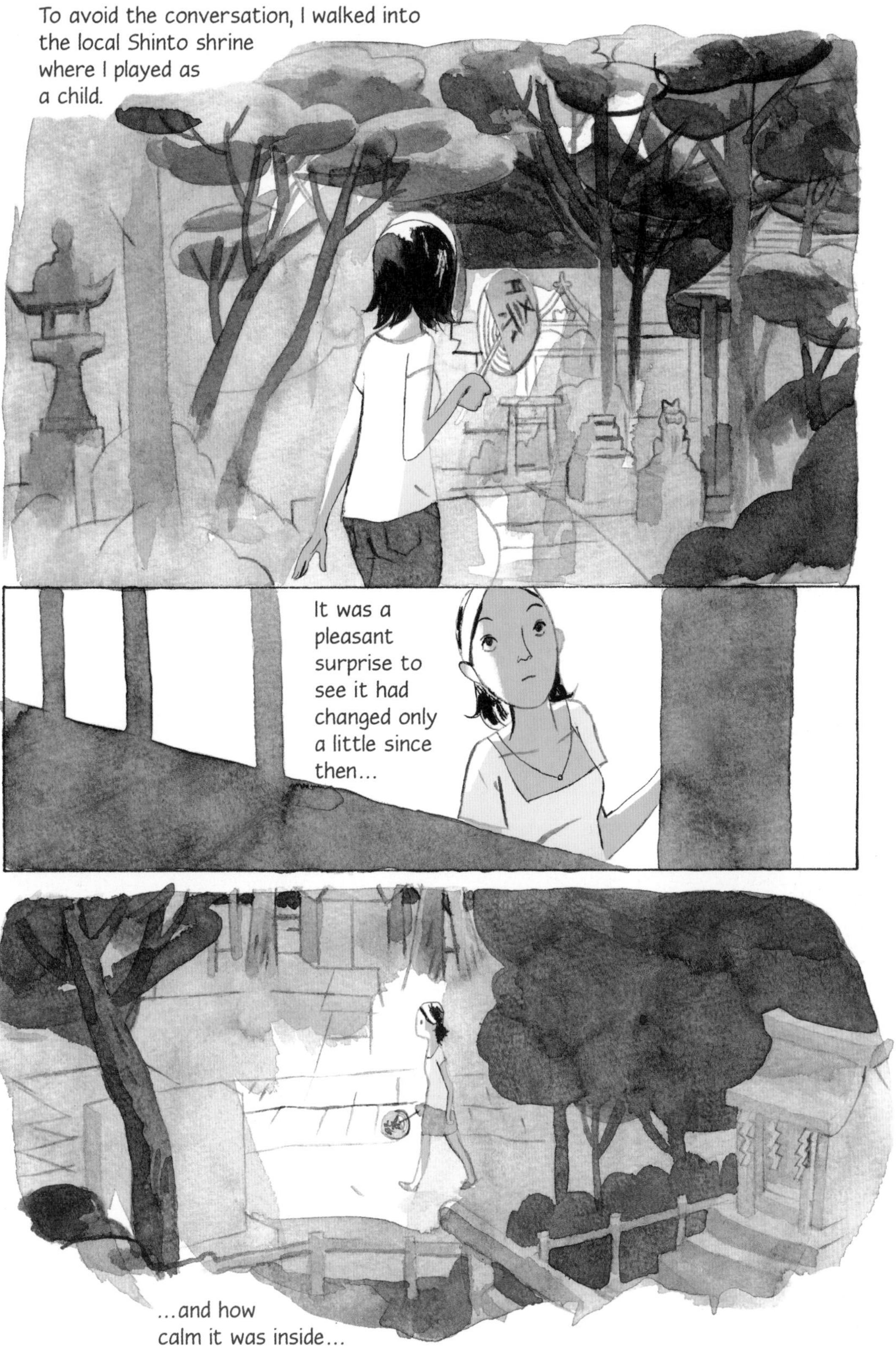

To avoid the conversation, I walked into the local Shinto shrine where I played as a child.
It was a pleasant surprise to see it had changed only a little since then...
...and how calm it was inside...

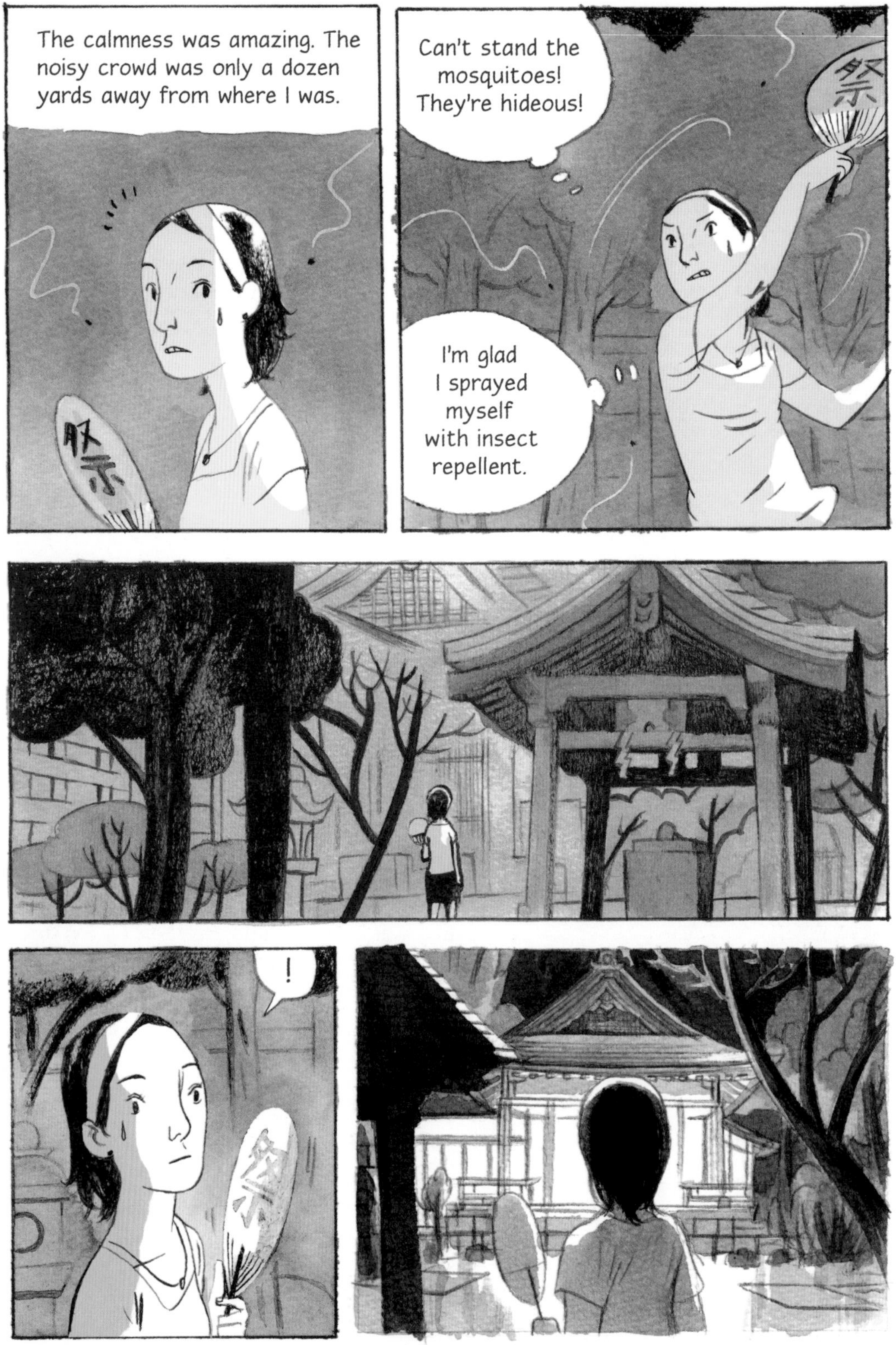
The calmness was amazing. The noisy crowd was only a dozen yards away from where I was.
Can't stand the mosquitoes! They're hideous!
祭
I'm glad I sprayed myself with insect repellent.
!

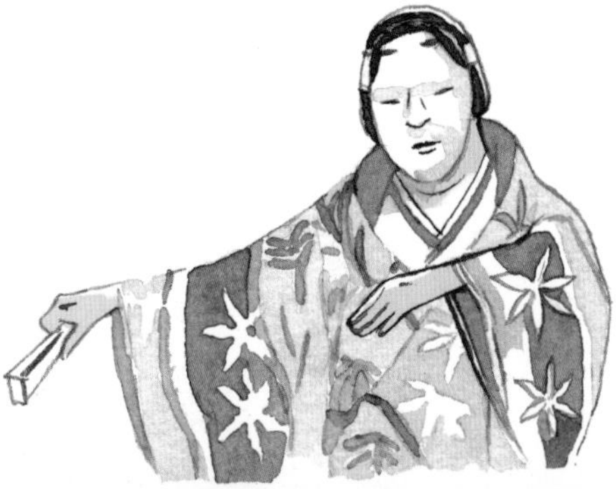

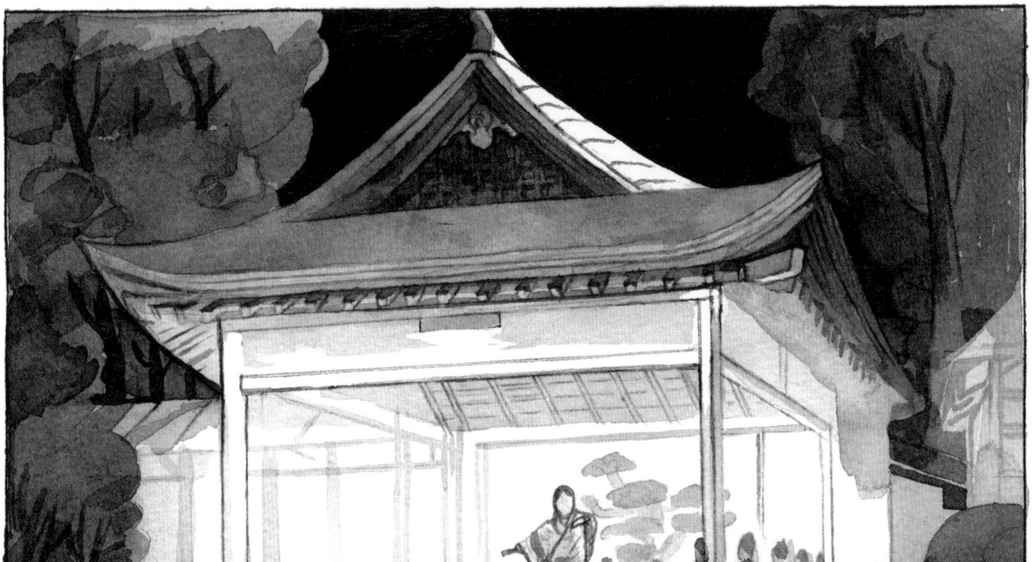

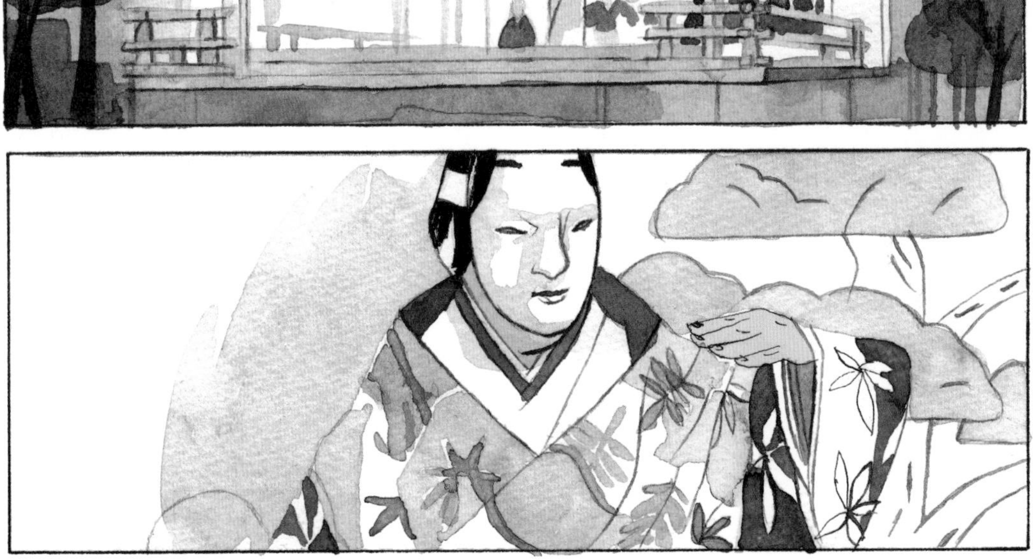

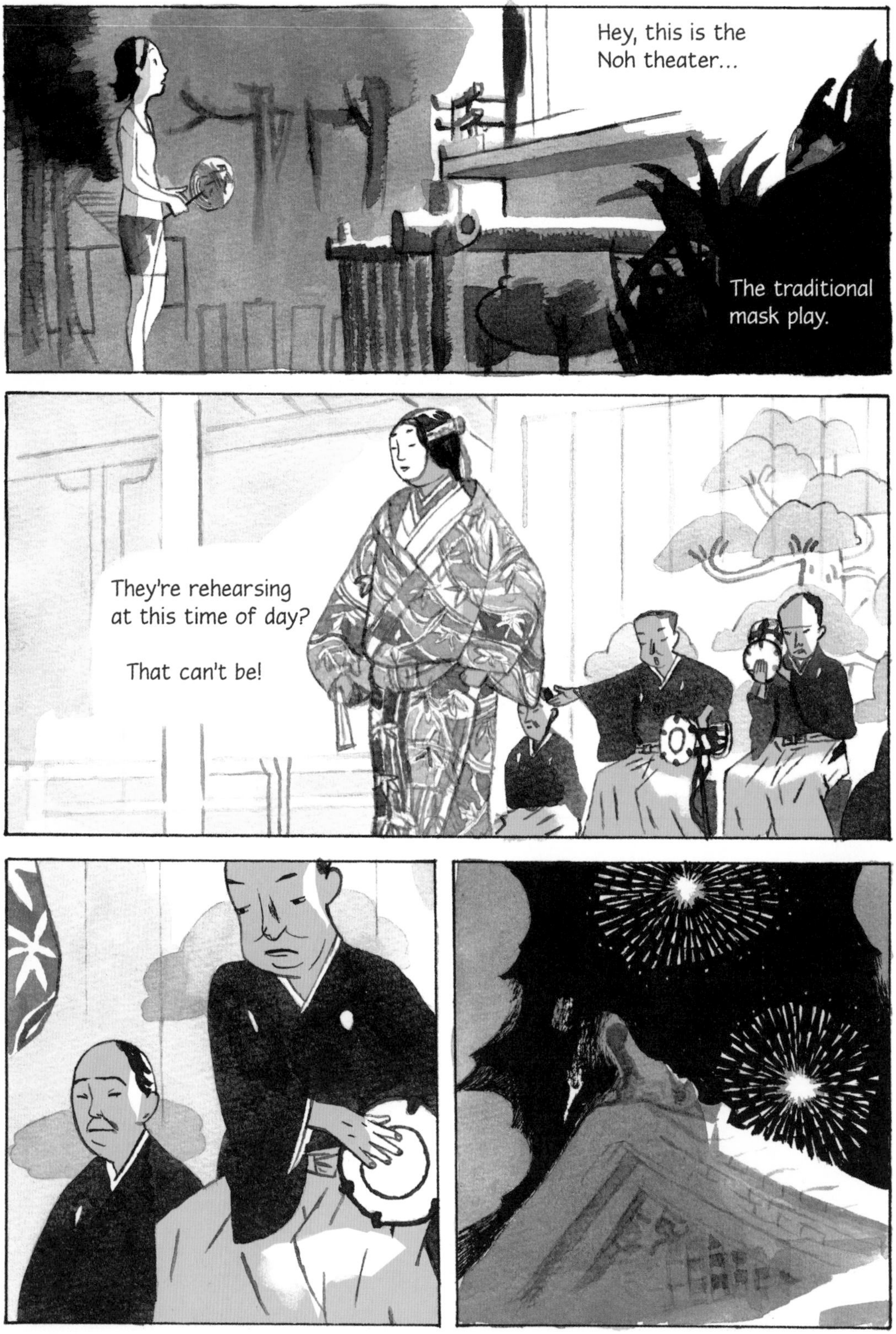

Hey, this is the Noh theater...
The traditional mask play.
They're rehearsing at this time of day?
That can't be!

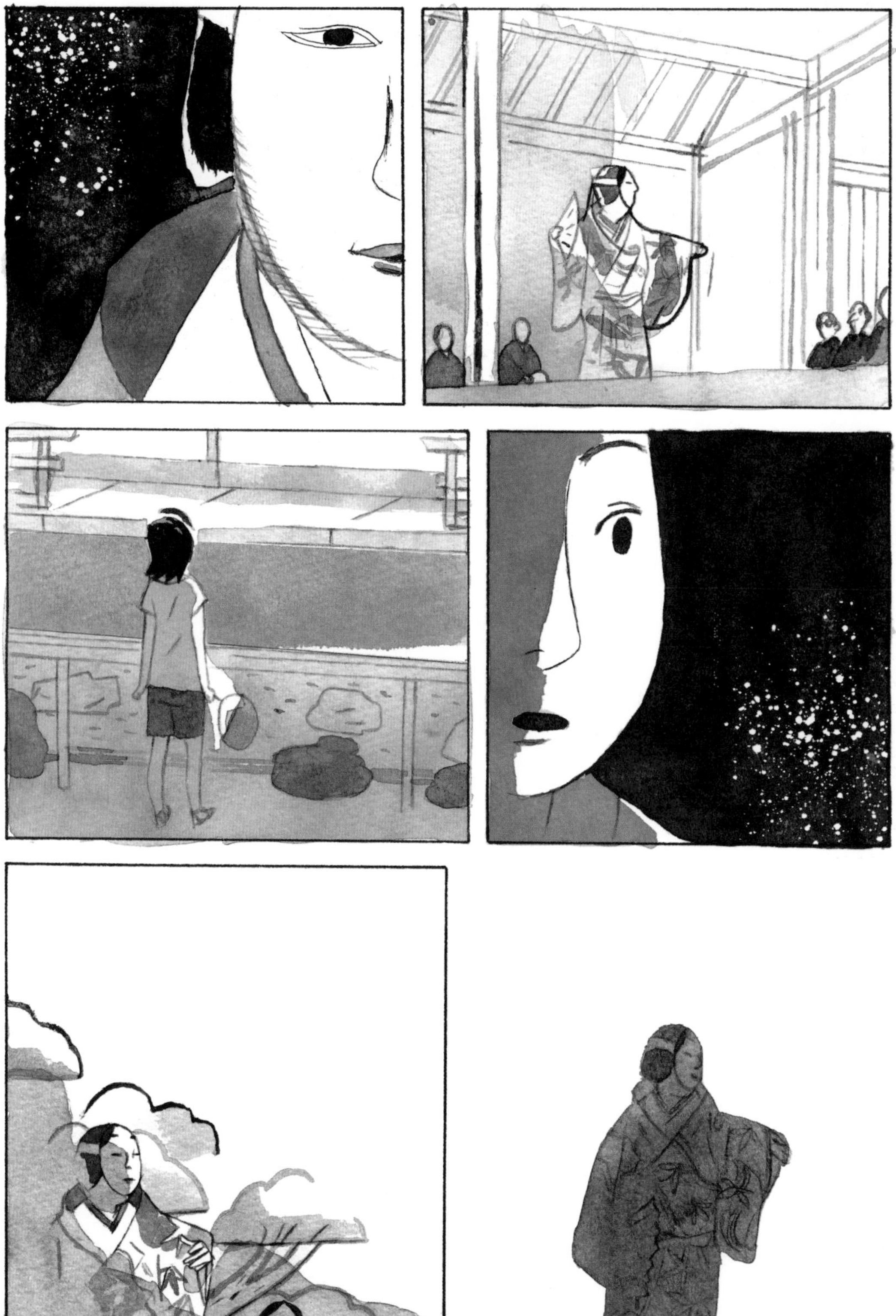

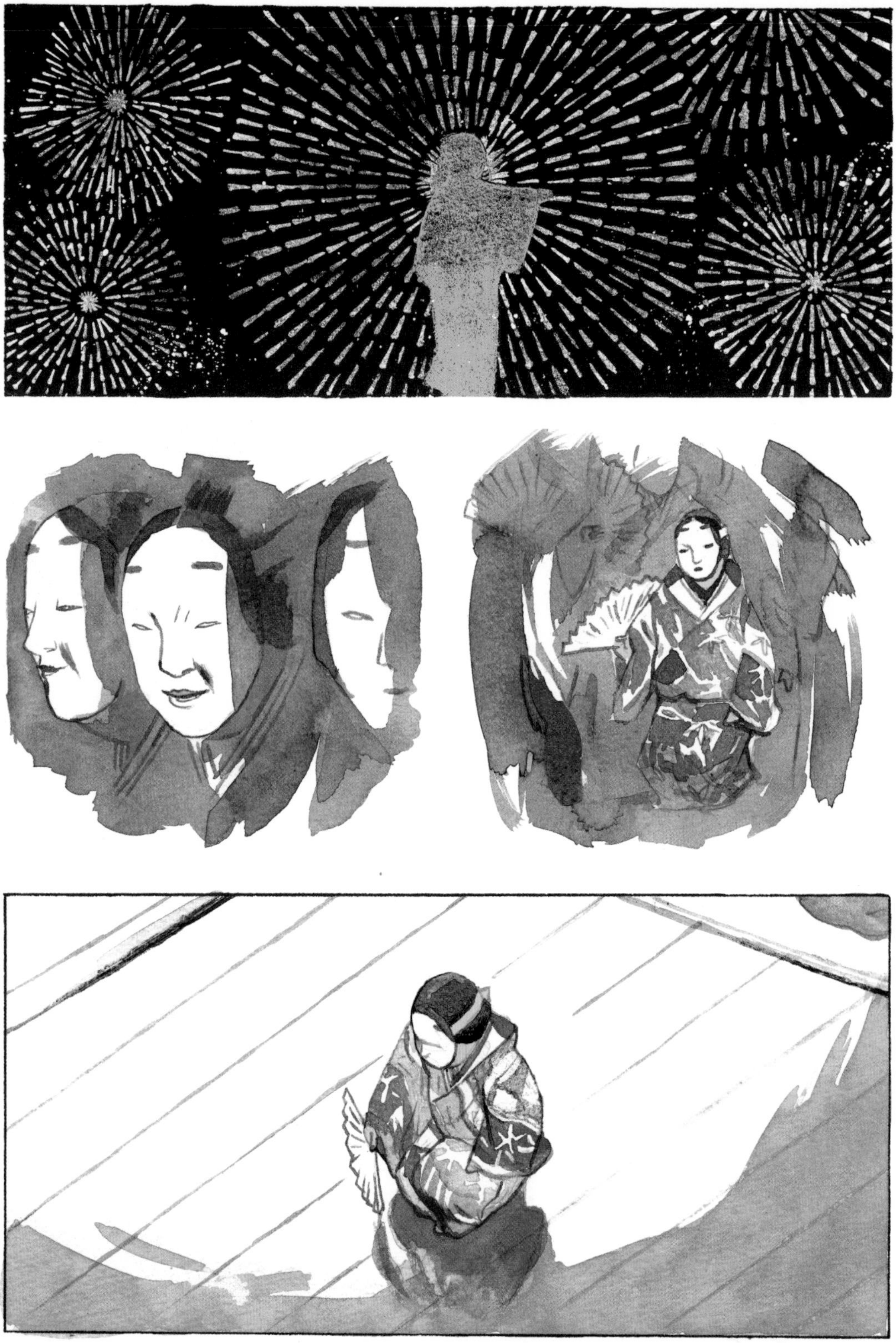

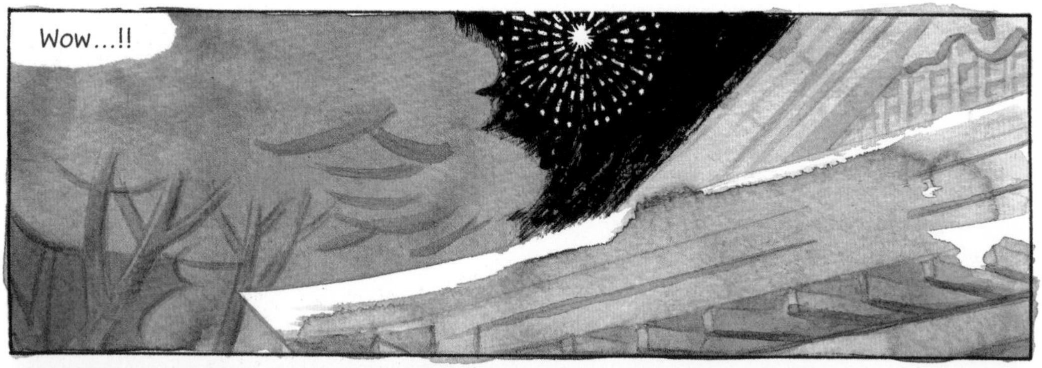
Wow...!!

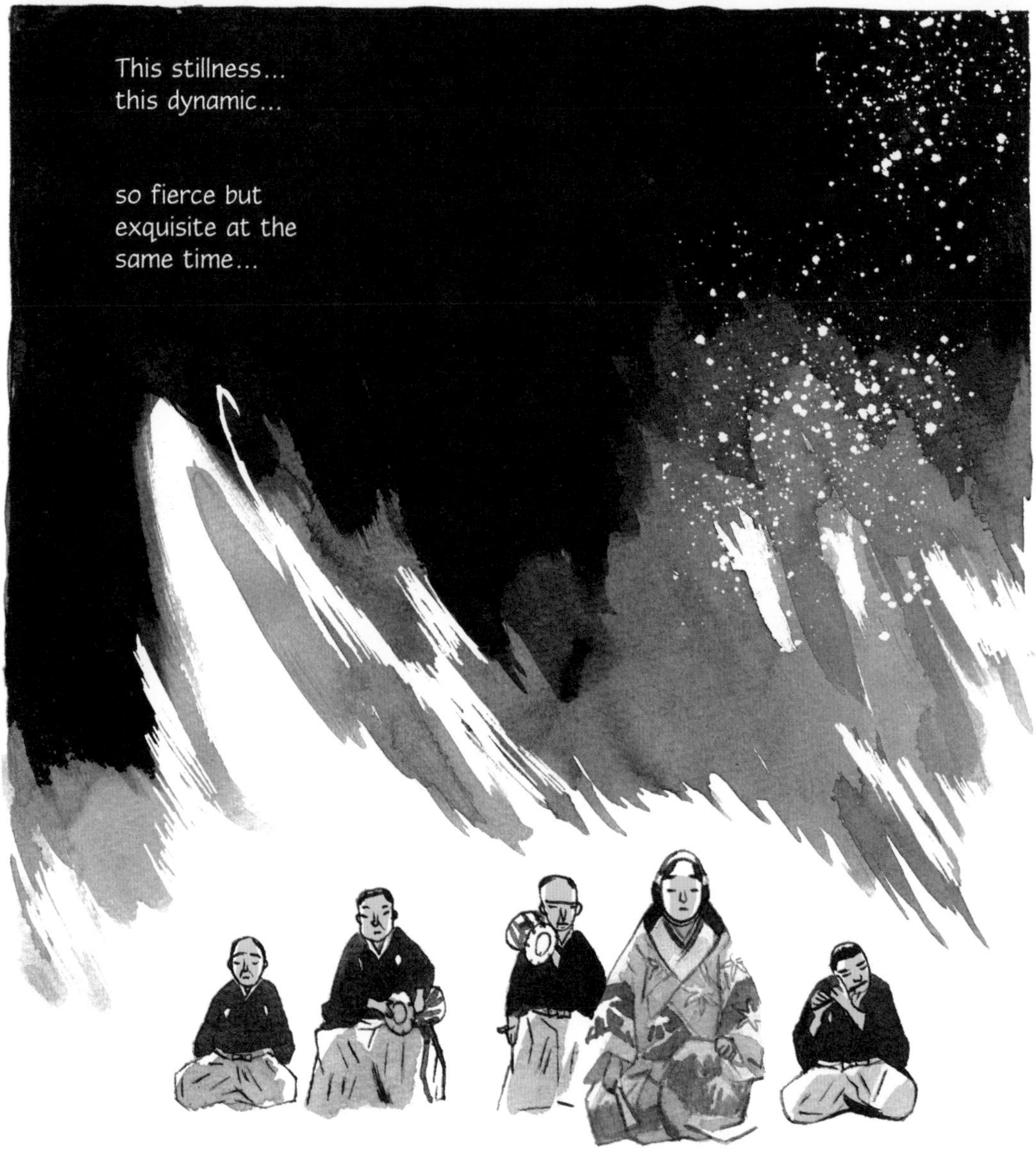
This stillness...
this dynamic...
so fierce but
exquisite at the
same time...

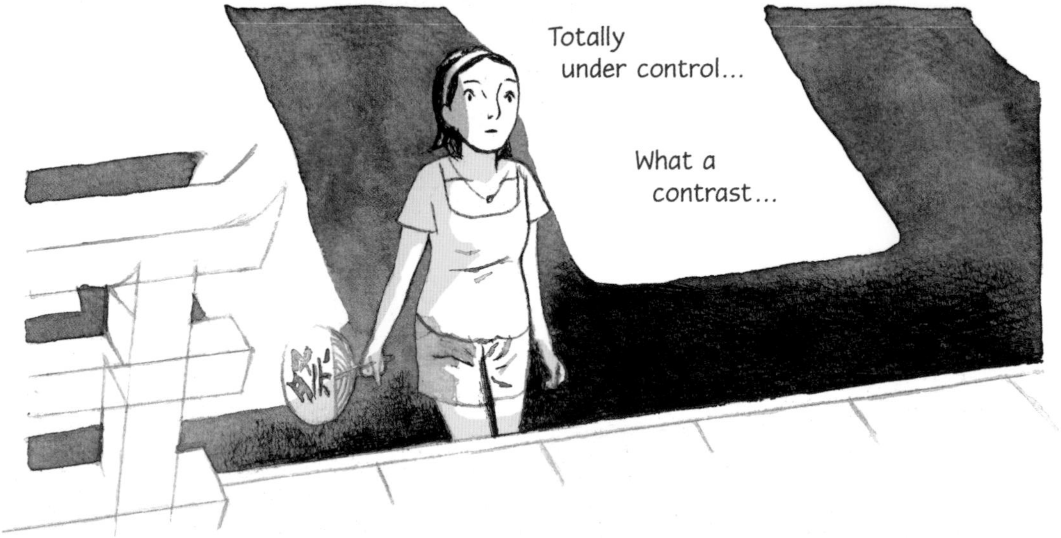
Totally under control...
What a contrast...

I just couldn't take my eyes away.

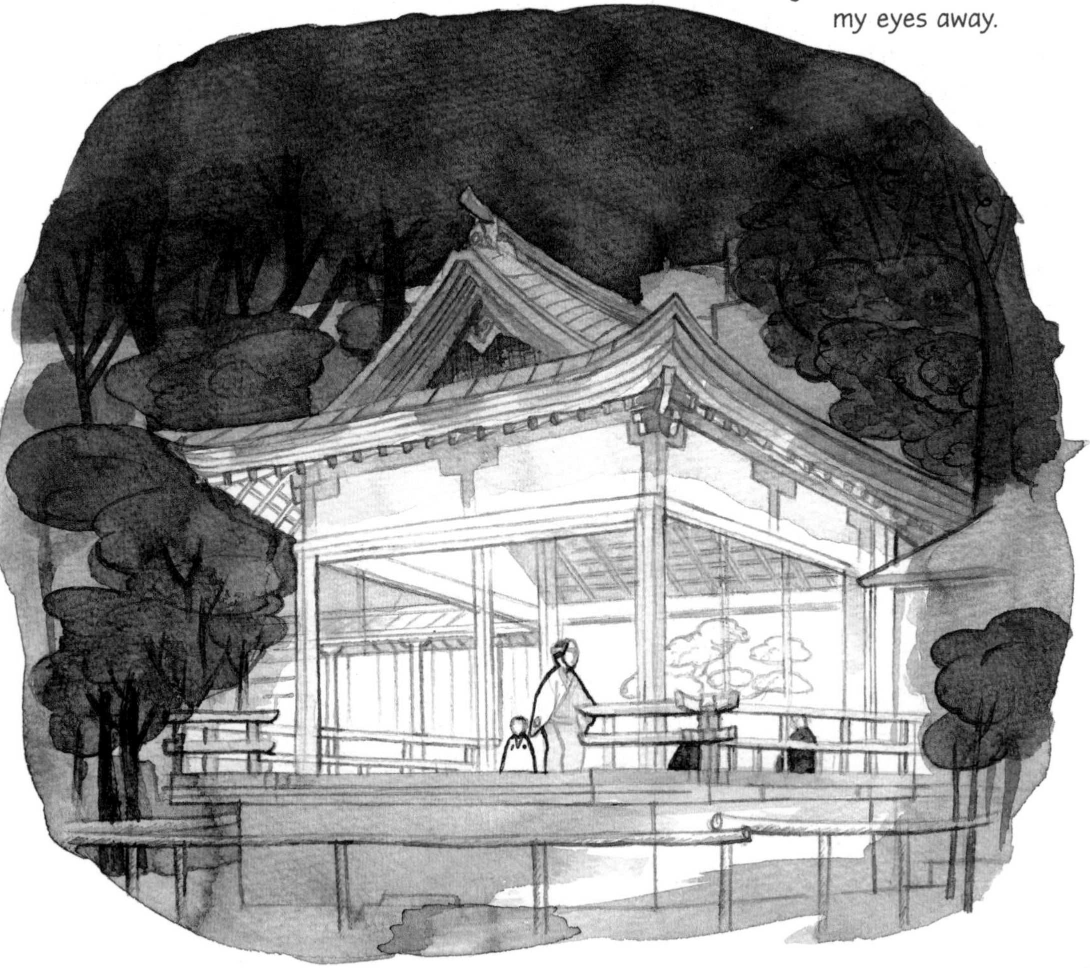

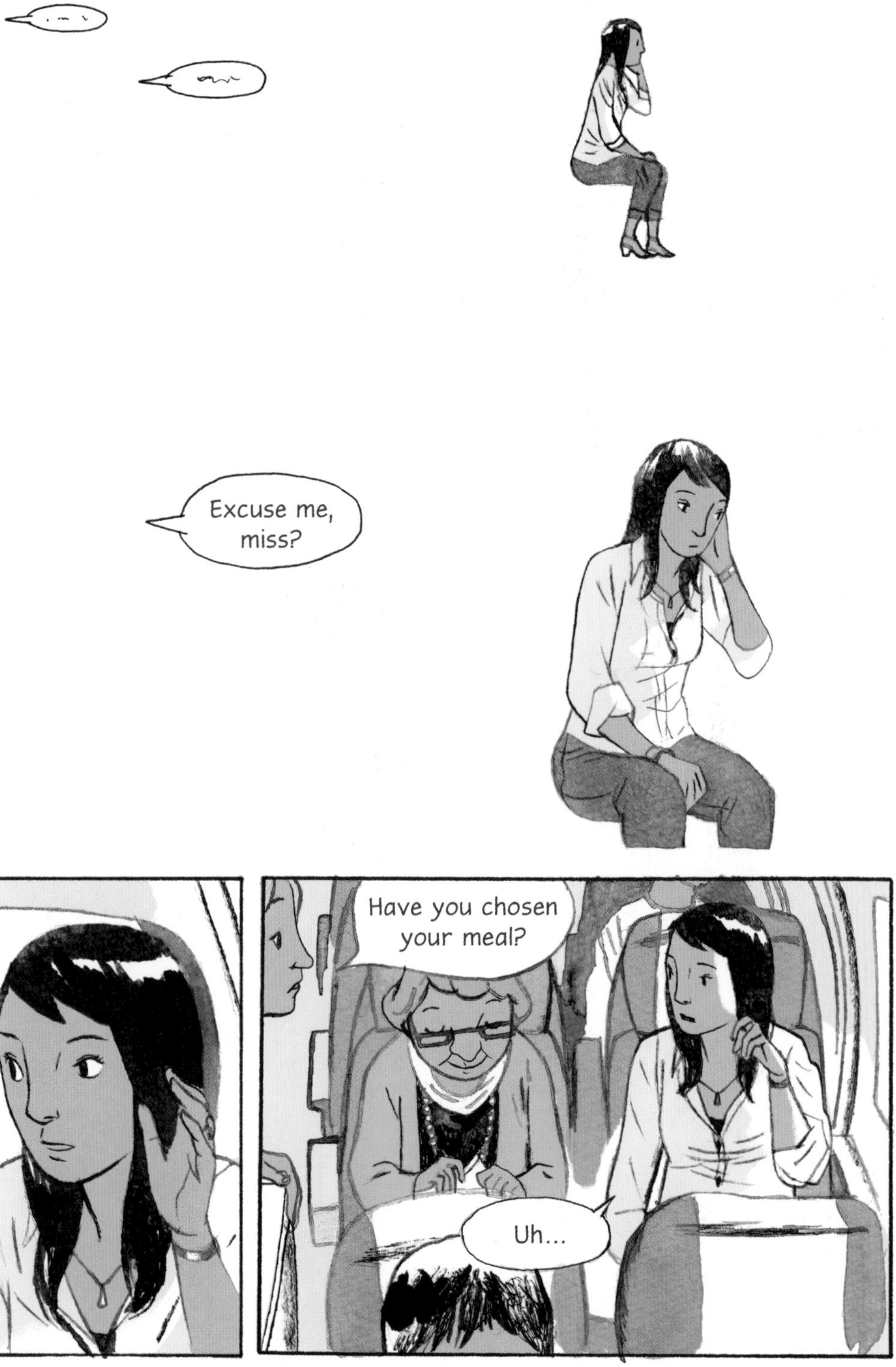
Excuse me, miss?
Have you chosen your meal?
Uh...

Would you like beef or chicken?

No...thank you. I'm not hungry.

Actually, may I have a tea with milk?

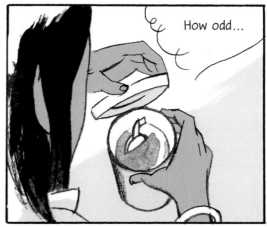

How odd...

Looking back now, that theater was so surreal, dreamlike. Did that really happen?

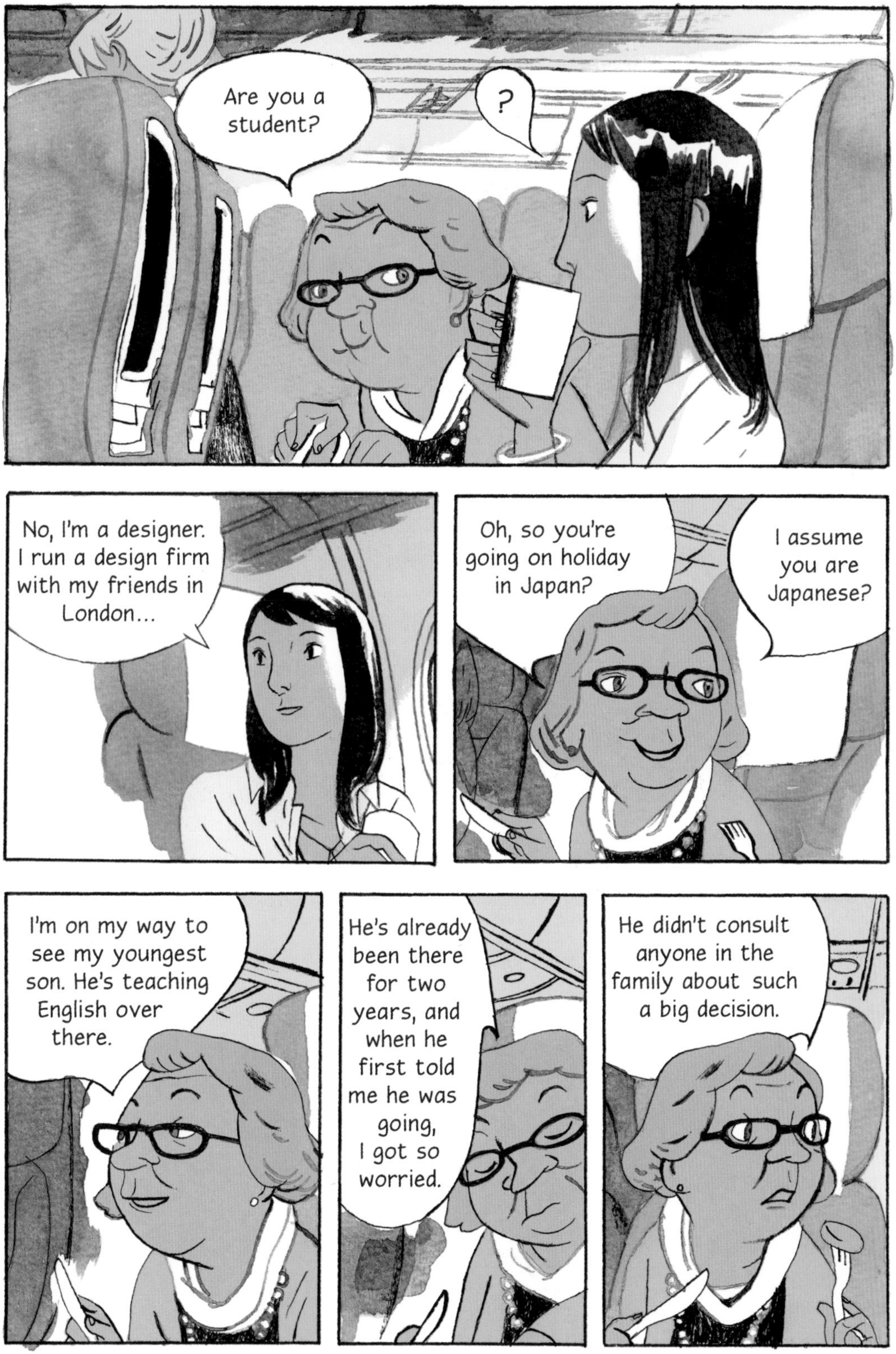
Are you a student?
?
No, I'm a designer. I run a design firm with my friends in London...
Oh, so you're going on holiday in Japan?
I assume you are Japanese?
I'm on my way to see my youngest son. He's teaching English over there.
He's already been there for two years, and when he first told me he was going, I got so worried.
He didn't consult anyone in the family about such a big decision.

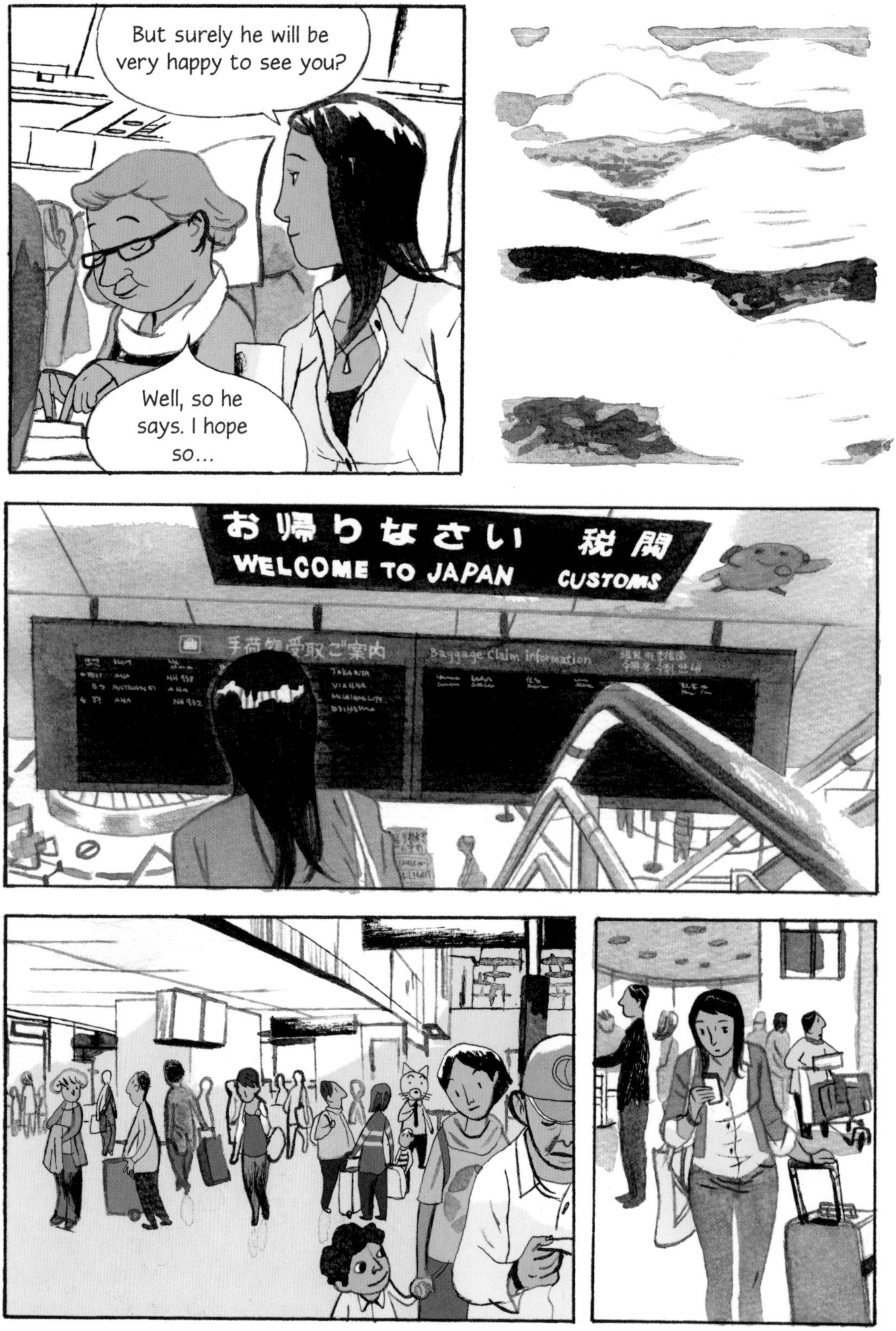
But surely he will be very happy to see you?
Well, so he says. I hope so...
お帰りなさい
WELCOME TO JAPAN
税関
CUSTOMS
手荷物受取ご案内
Baggage Claim information

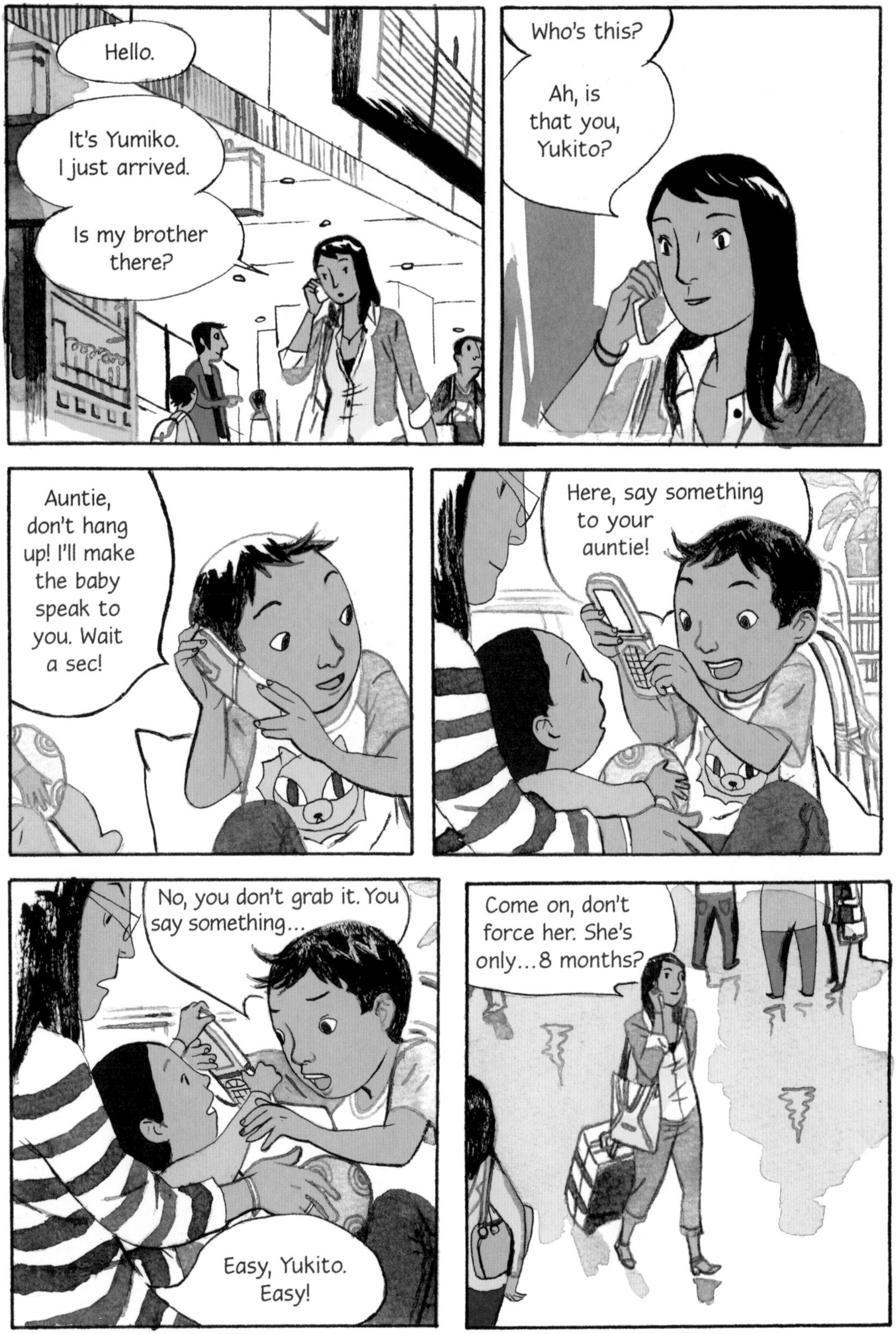
Hello.
It's Yumiko. I just arrived.
Is my brother there?
Who's this?
Ah, is that you, Yukito?
Auntie, don't hang up! I'll make the baby speak to you. Wait a sec!
Here, say something to your auntie!
No, you don't grab it. You say something...
Easy, Yukito. Easy!
Come on, don't force her. She's only...8 months?

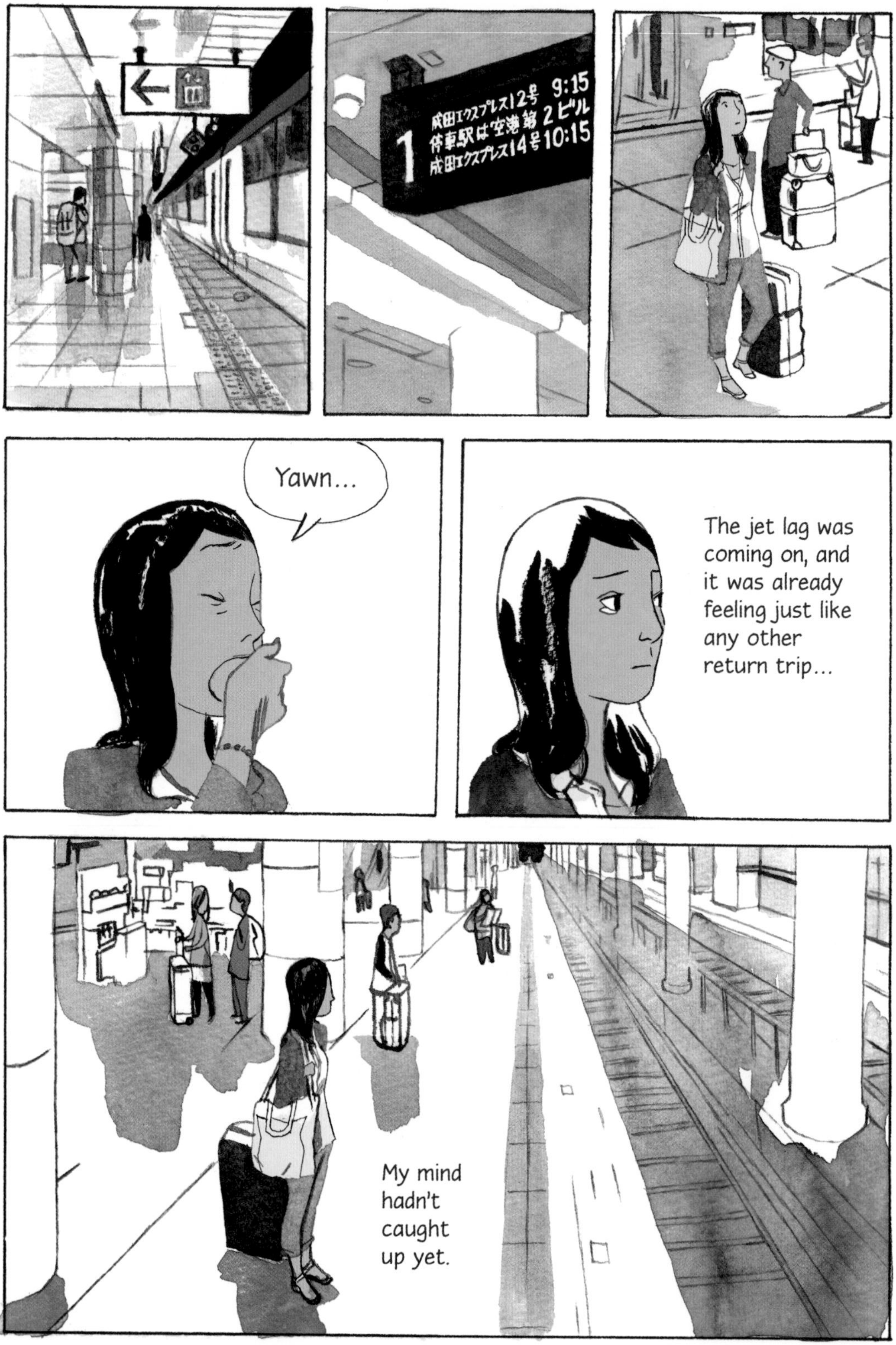
1
成田エクスプレス12号 9:15
停車駅は空港第2ビル
成田エクスプレス14号 10:15
Yawn...
The jet lag was coming on, and it was already feeling just like any other return trip...
My mind hadn't caught up yet.

II

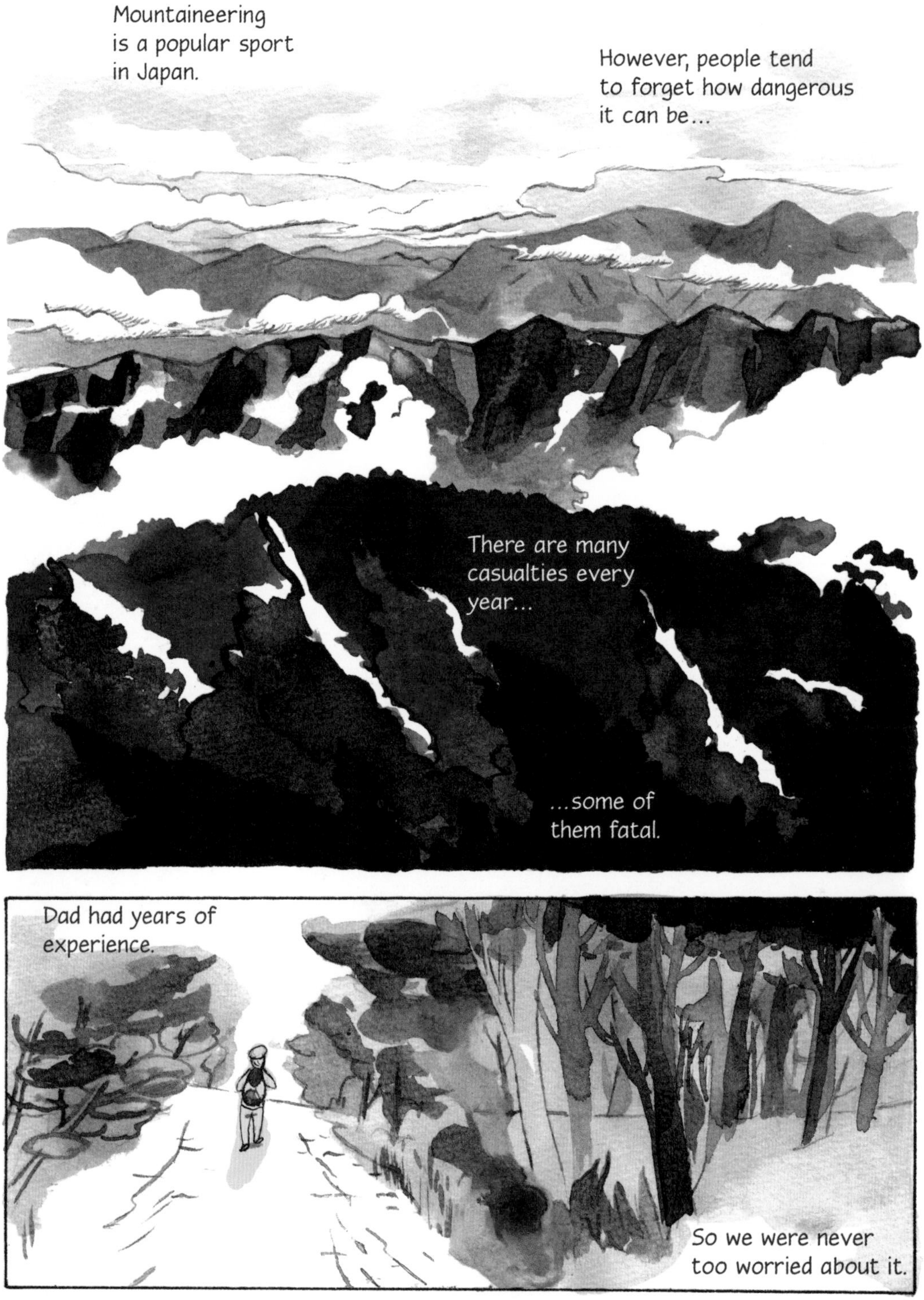
Mountaineering is a popular sport in Japan.
However, people tend to forget how dangerous it can be...
There are many casualties every year...
...some of them fatal.
Dad had years of experience.
So we were never too worried about it.

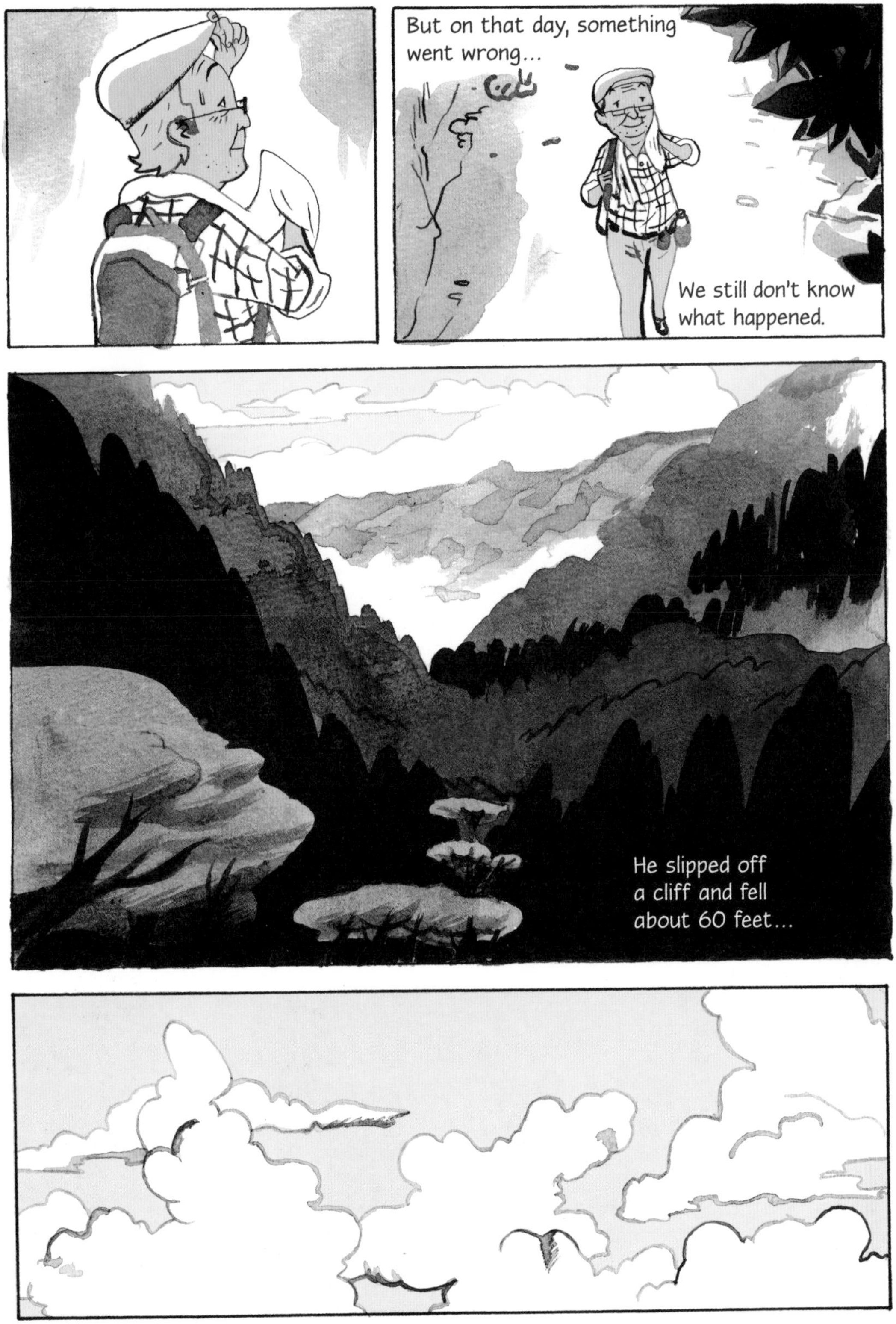
But on that day, something went wrong...
We still don't know what happened.
He slipped off a cliff and fell about 60 feet...

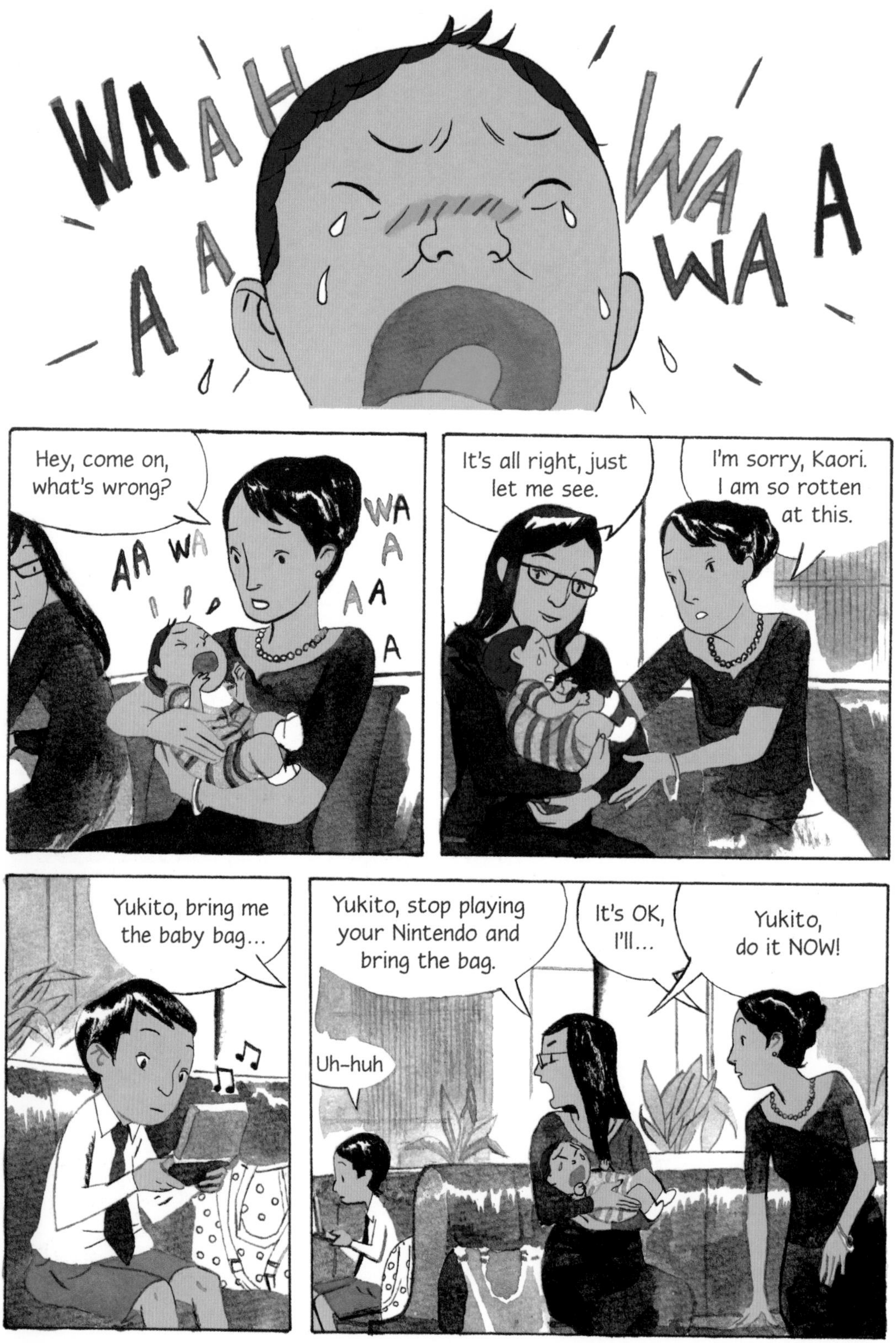
WAAAH
AAA
WAWAWAA
Hey, come on, what's wrong?
AA WA
WA A A A A
It's all right, just let me see.
I'm sorry, Kaori. I am so rotten at this.
Yukito, bring me the baby bag…
Yukito, stop playing your Nintendo and bring the bag.
Uh-huh
It's OK, I'll…
Yukito, do it NOW!

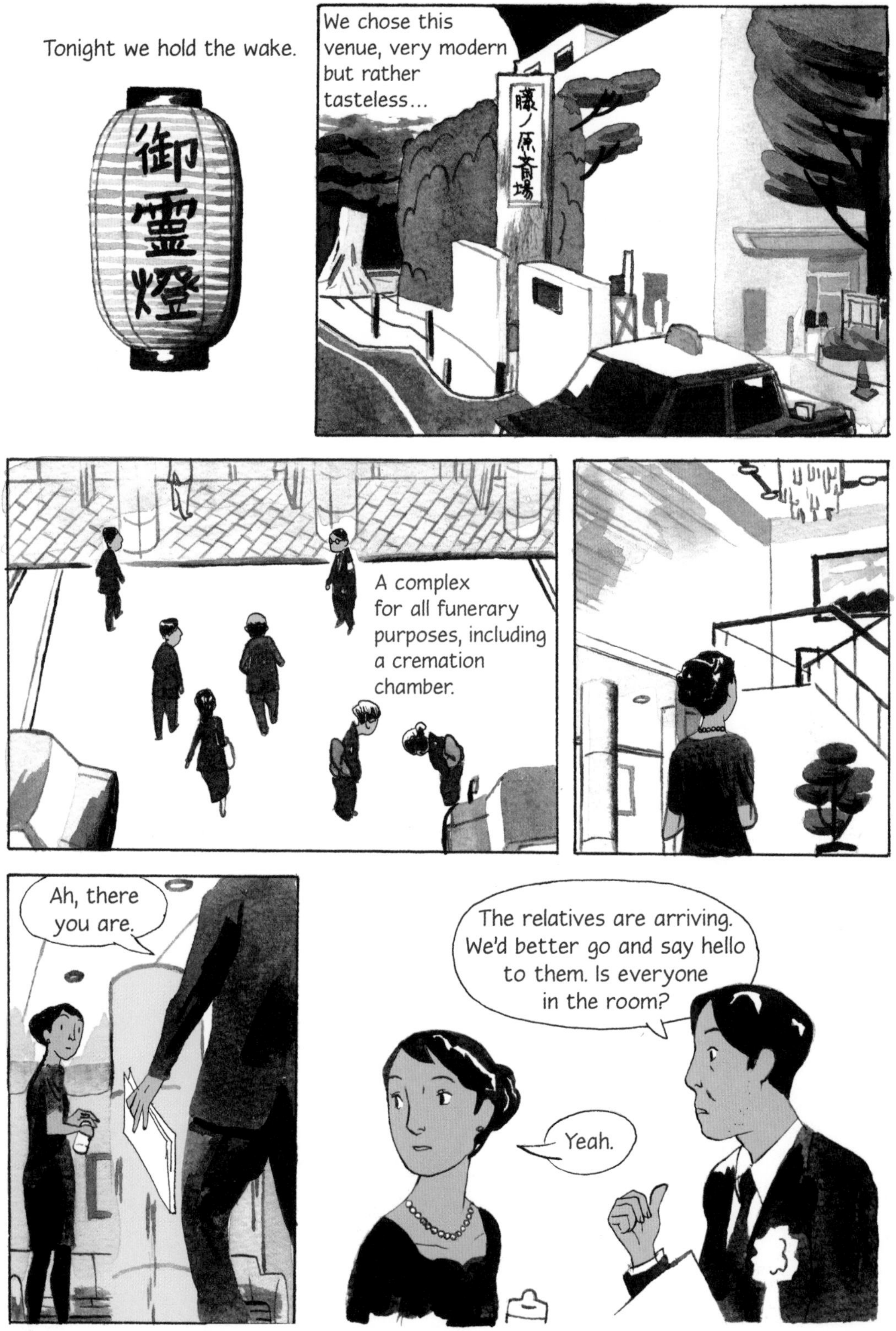
Tonight we hold the wake.
御霊燈
We chose this venue, very modern but rather tasteless...
A complex for all funerary purposes, including a cremation chamber.
Ah, there you are.
The relatives are arriving. We'd better go and say hello to them. Is everyone in the room?
Yeah.

It was totally unexpected...

The painful thing is that there was no chance to say a final farewell.

I am so sorry...

And your niece, has she come back from...is it London?

You mean Yumiko? Yes, she's back already. Thank God.

I am worried about his children. They must be very upset...

Well, I can be around for them. Since their mother can't be here.

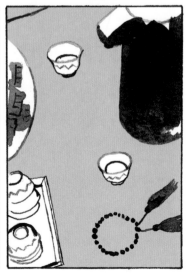

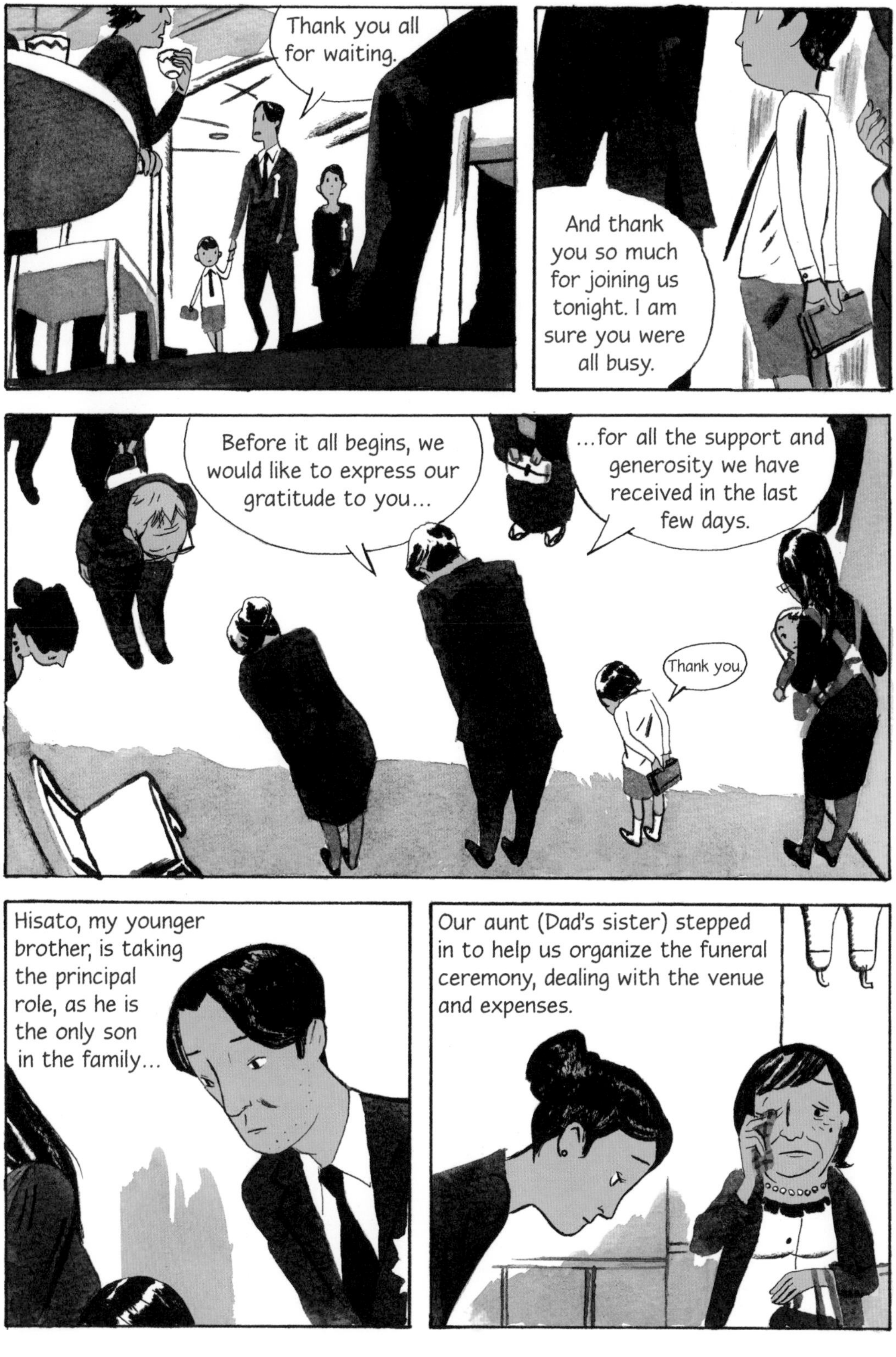
Thank you all for waiting.
And thank you so much for joining us tonight. I am sure you were all busy.
Before it all begins, we would like to express our gratitude to you...
...for all the support and generosity we have received in the last few days.
Thank you.
Hisato, my younger brother, is taking the principal role, as he is the only son in the family...
Our aunt (Dad's sister) stepped in to help us organize the funeral ceremony, dealing with the venue and expenses.

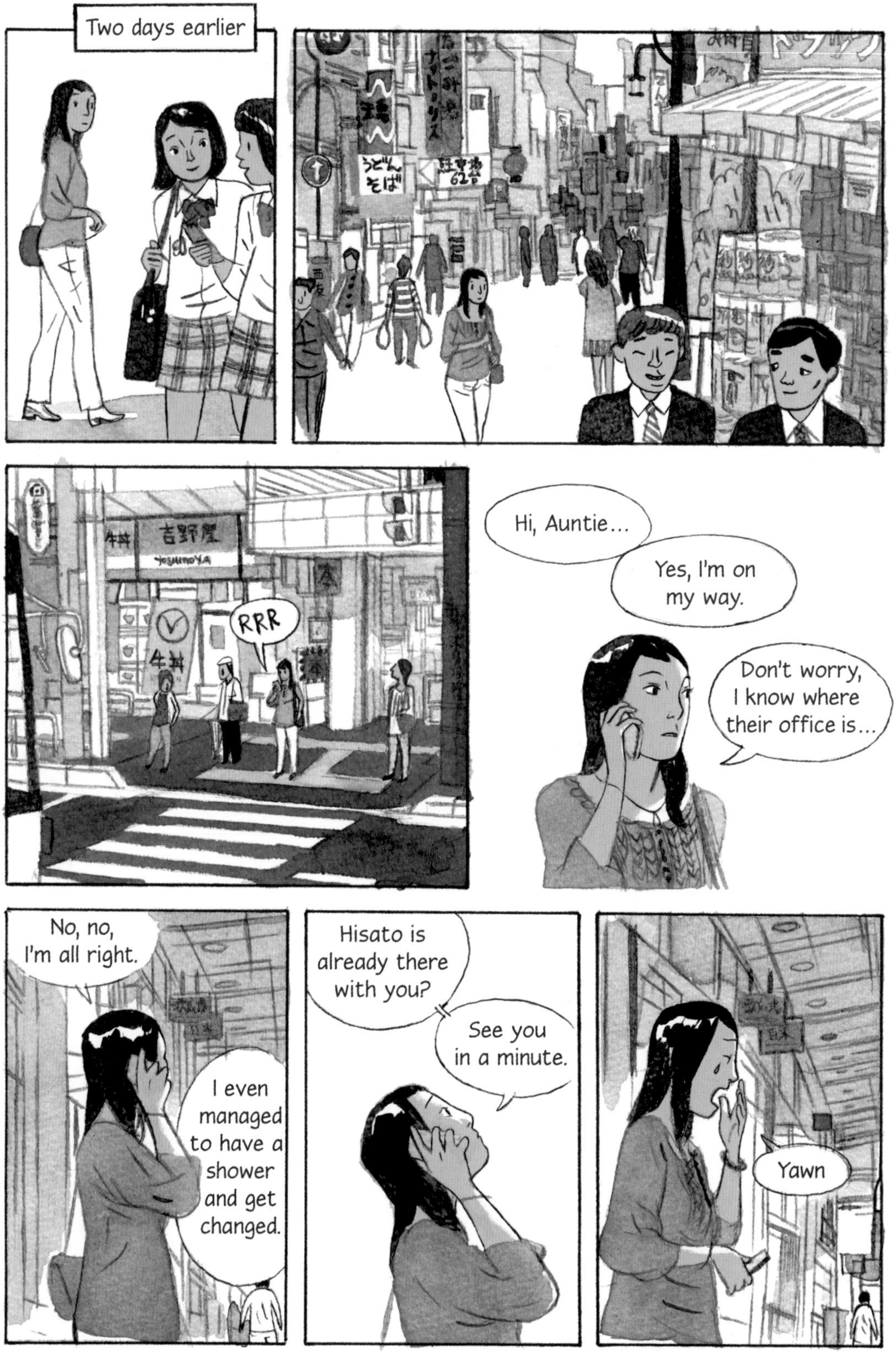
Two days earlier
うどん そば
吉野屋
YOSHINOYA
RRR
Hi, Auntie…
Yes, I'm on my way.
Don't worry, I know where their office is…
No, no, I'm all right.
I even managed to have a shower and get changed.
Hisato is already there with you?
See you in a minute.
Yawn

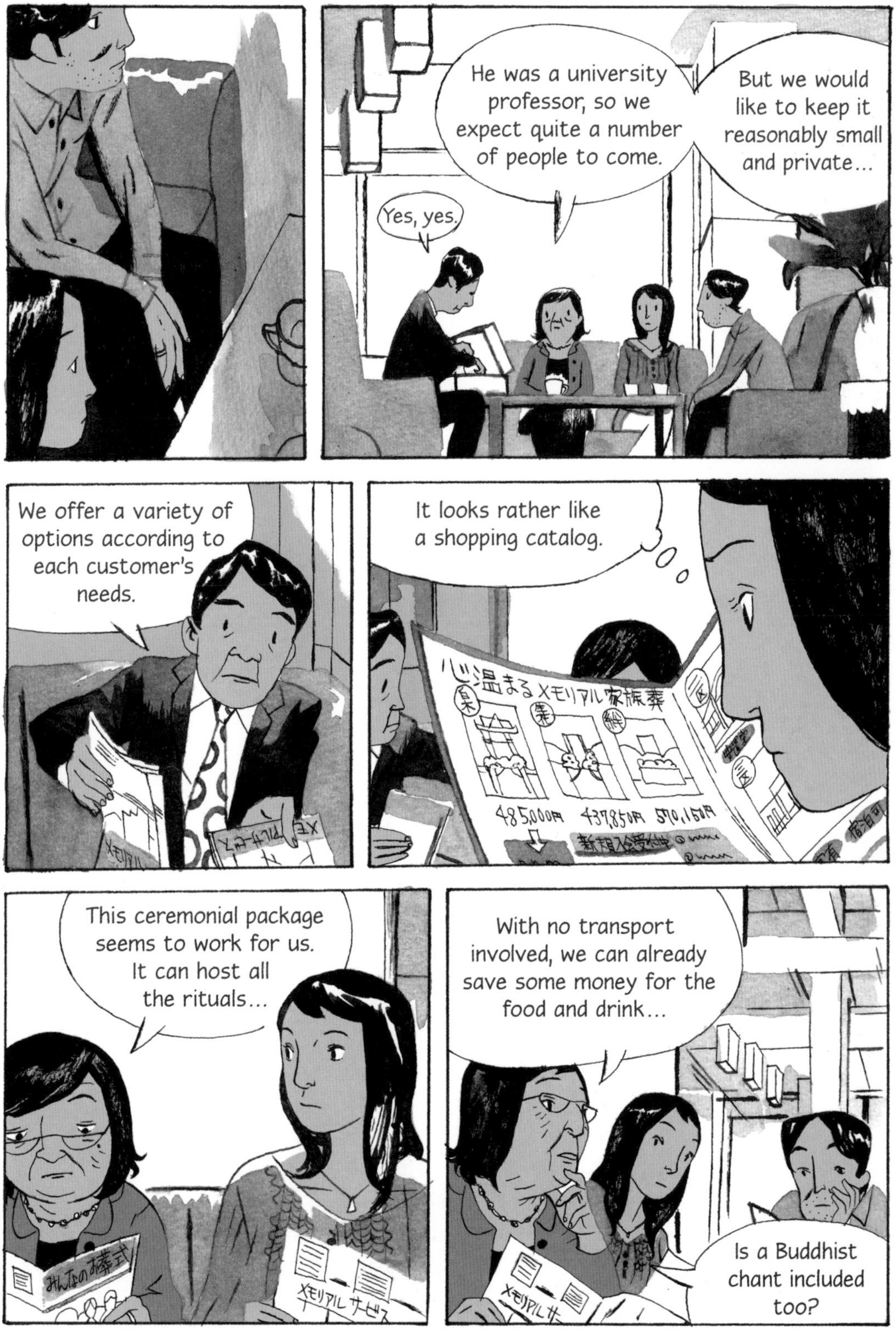
He was a university professor, so we expect quite a number of people to come.
But we would like to keep it reasonably small and private...
Yes, yes.
We offer a variety of options according to each customer's needs.
It looks rather like a shopping catalog.
This ceremonial package seems to work for us. It can host all the rituals...
With no transport involved, we can already save some money for the food and drink...
Is a Buddhist chant included too?

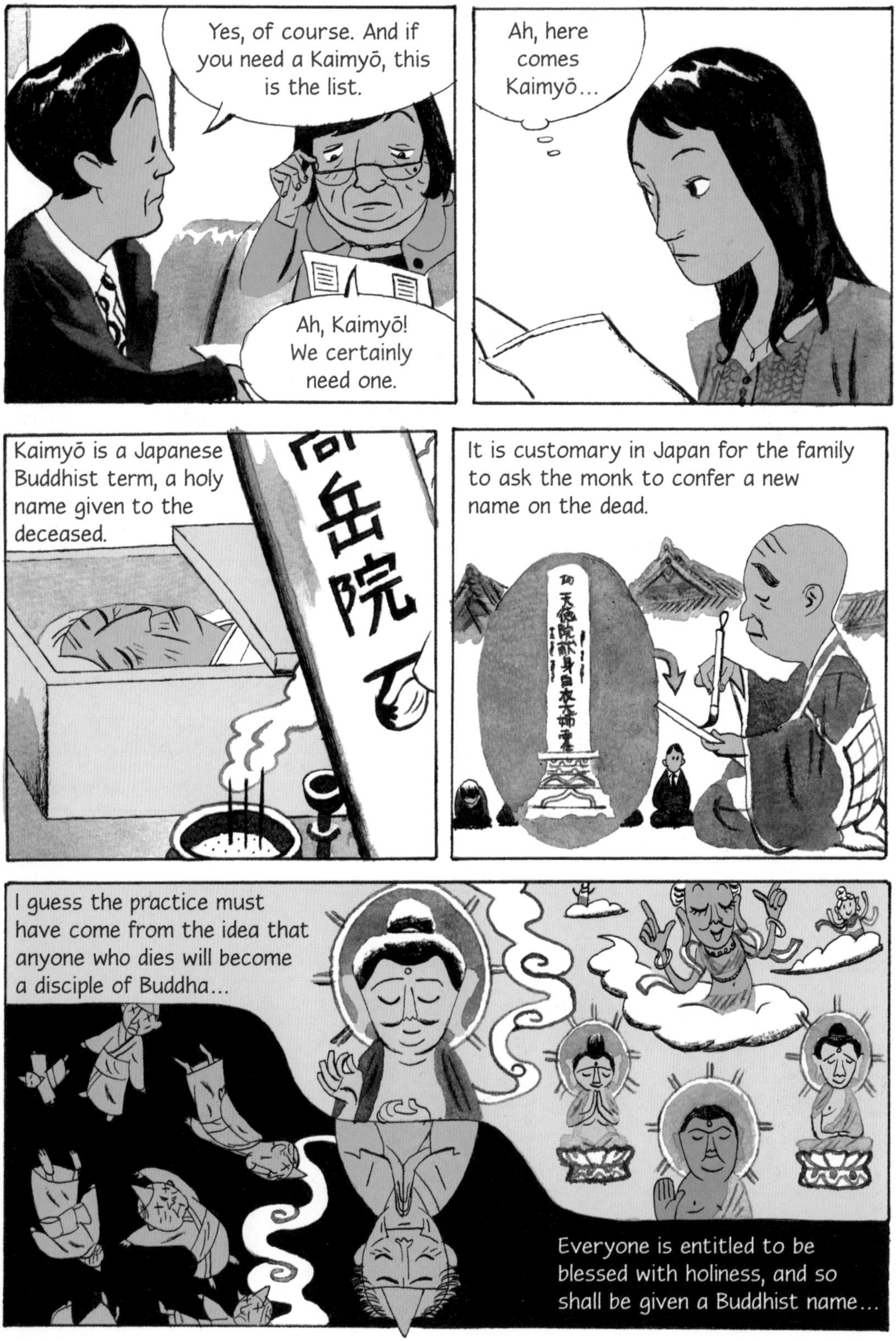
Yes, of course. And if you need a Kaimyō, this is the list.
Ah, Kaimyō! We certainly need one.
Ah, here comes Kaimyō...
Kaimyō is a Japanese Buddhist term, a holy name given to the deceased.
It is customary in Japan for the family to ask the monk to confer a new name on the dead.
I guess the practice must have come from the idea that anyone who dies will become a disciple of Buddha...
Everyone is entitled to be blessed with holiness, and so shall be given a Buddhist name...

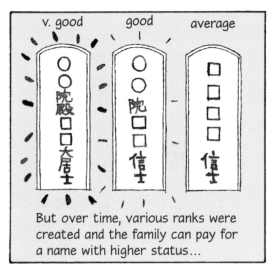

v. good   good   average

○○院殿□□大居士   ○○院□□信士   □□□□信士

But over time, various ranks were created and the family can pay for a name with higher status...

But what difference does it make?

So with this package, Kaimyō isn't included?

I'm afraid not.

To honor the dead is understandable.

But buying it seems wrong to me.

It's all for the sake of saving face...

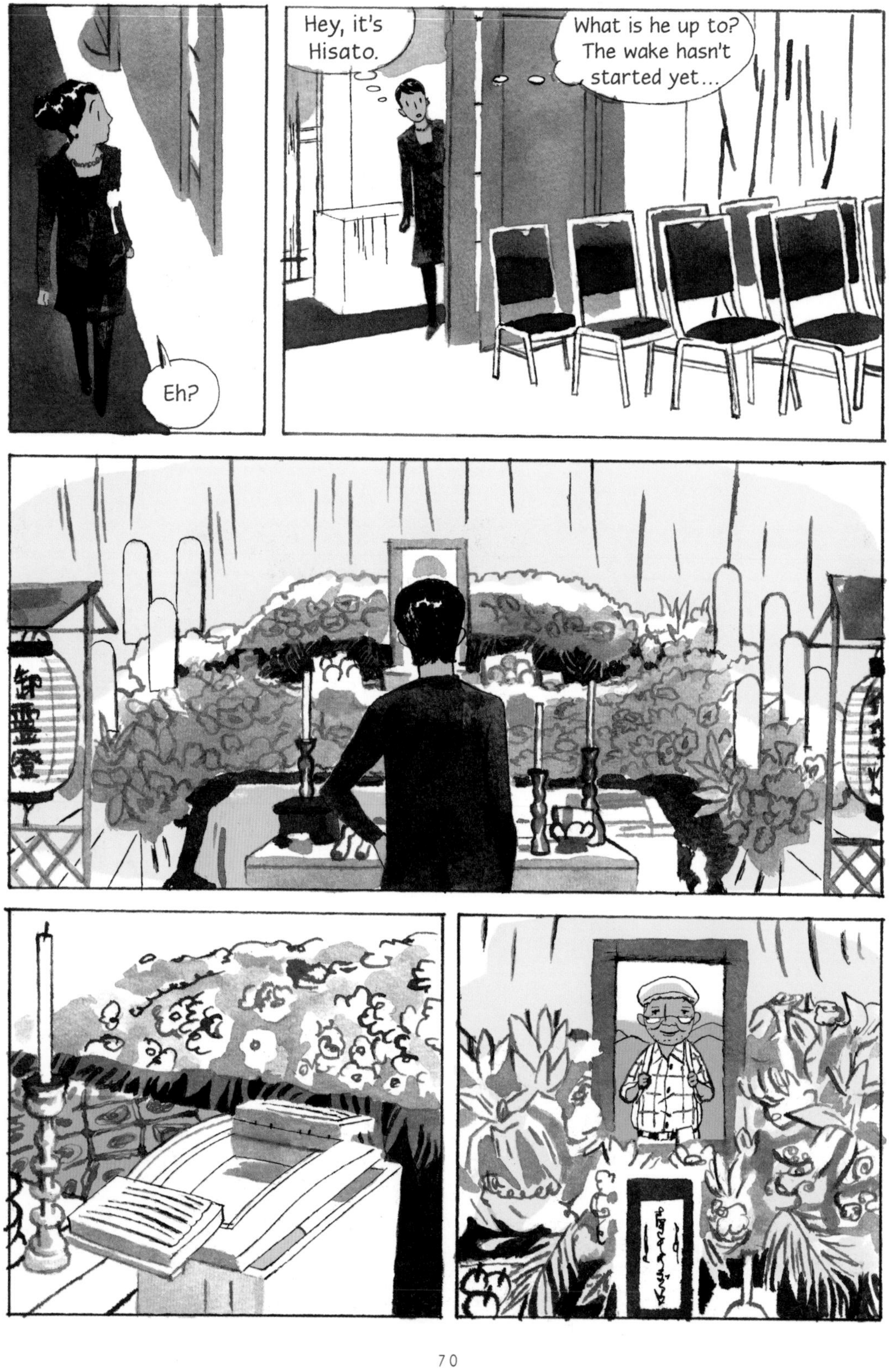
Eh?
Hey, it's Hisato.
What is he up to? The wake hasn't started yet...
御霊燈

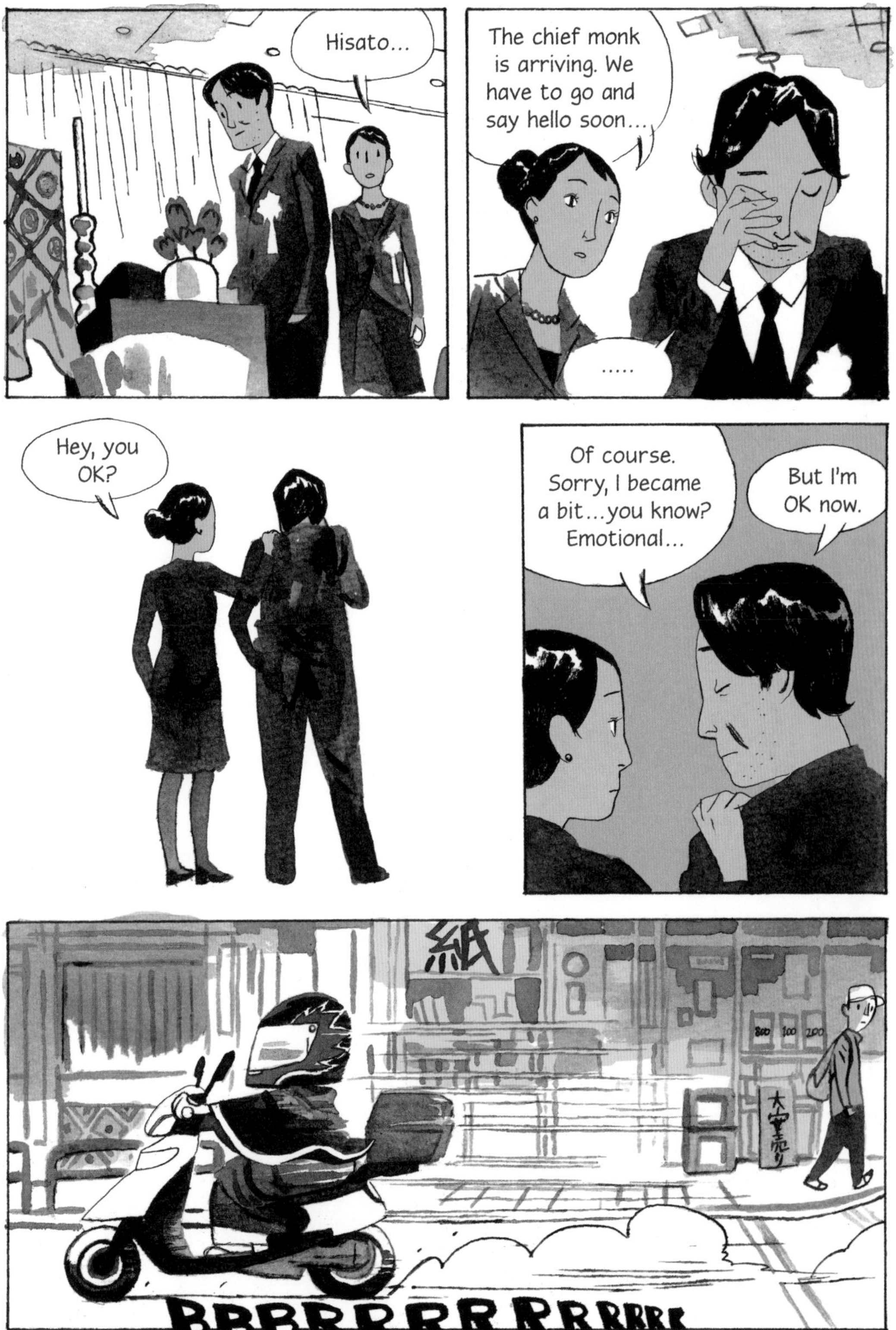
Hisato...
The chief monk is arriving. We have to go and say hello soon...
.....
Hey, you OK?
Of course. Sorry, I became a bit...you know? Emotional...
But I'm OK now.
BBBRRRRRRRRRR

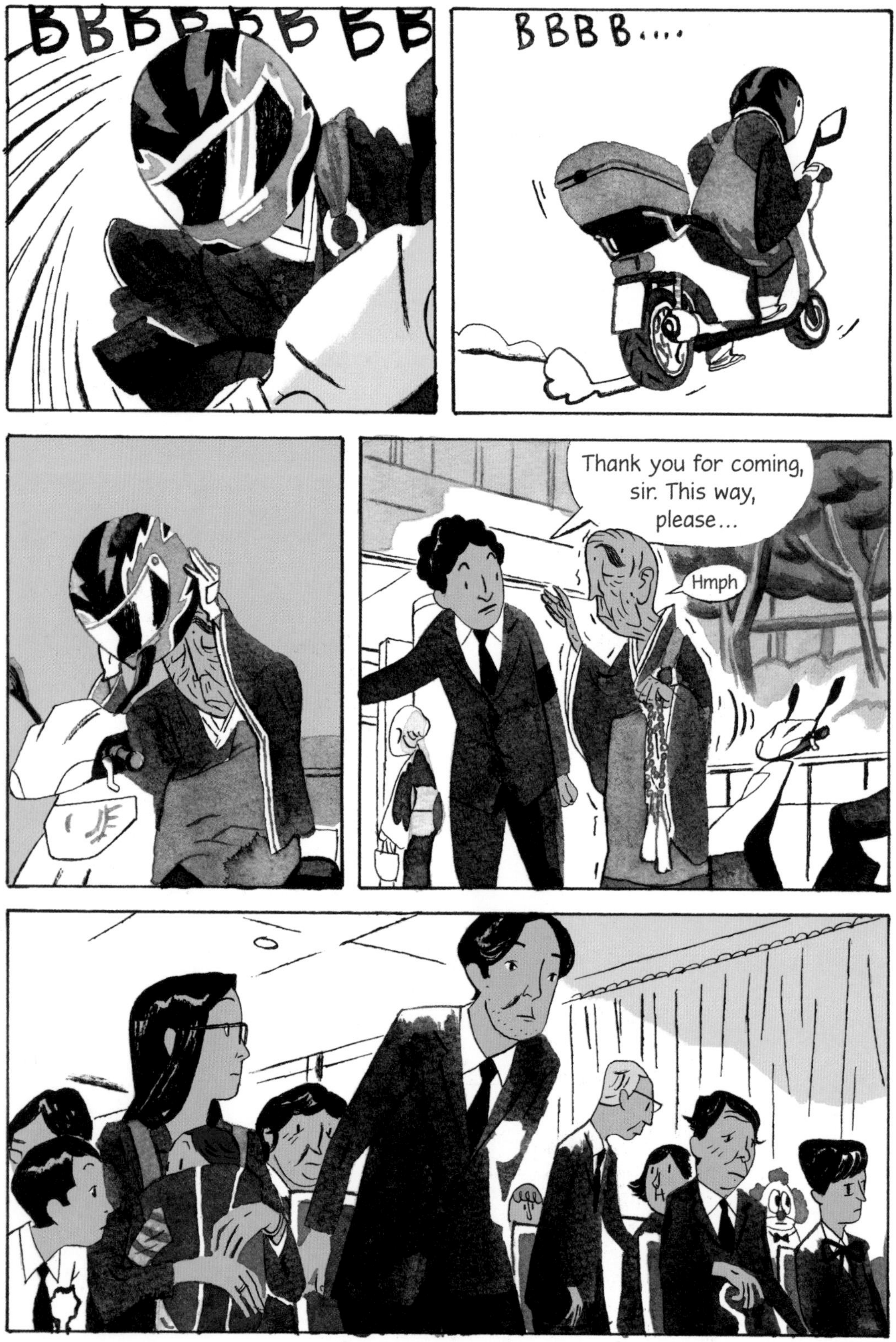
BBBBBBBBB
BBBB....
Thank you for coming, sir. This way, please...
Hmph

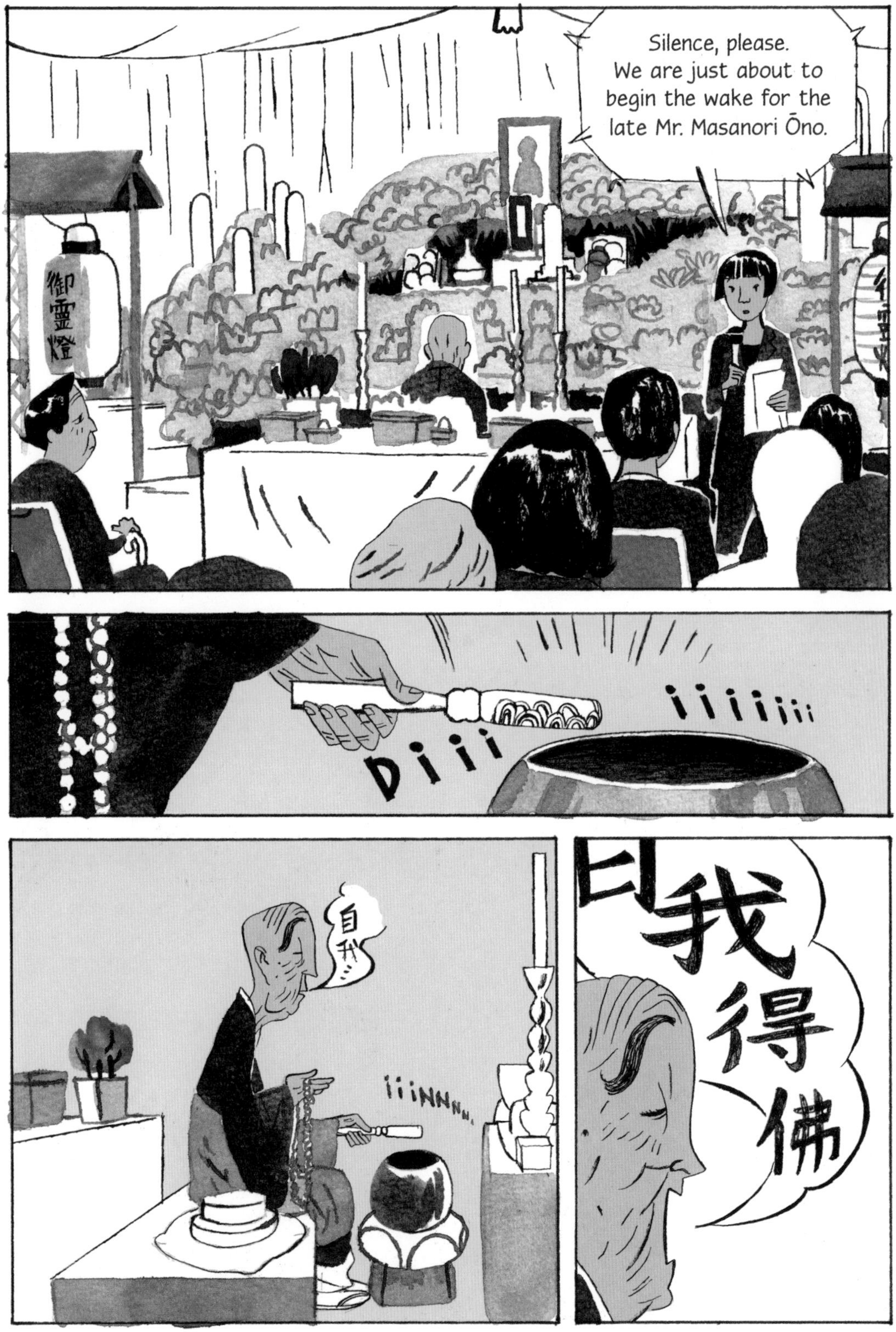
Silence, please. We are just about to begin the wake for the late Mr. Masanori Ōno.
御霊燈
Diii
iiiiiii
自我…
iiiNNN..
我得佛

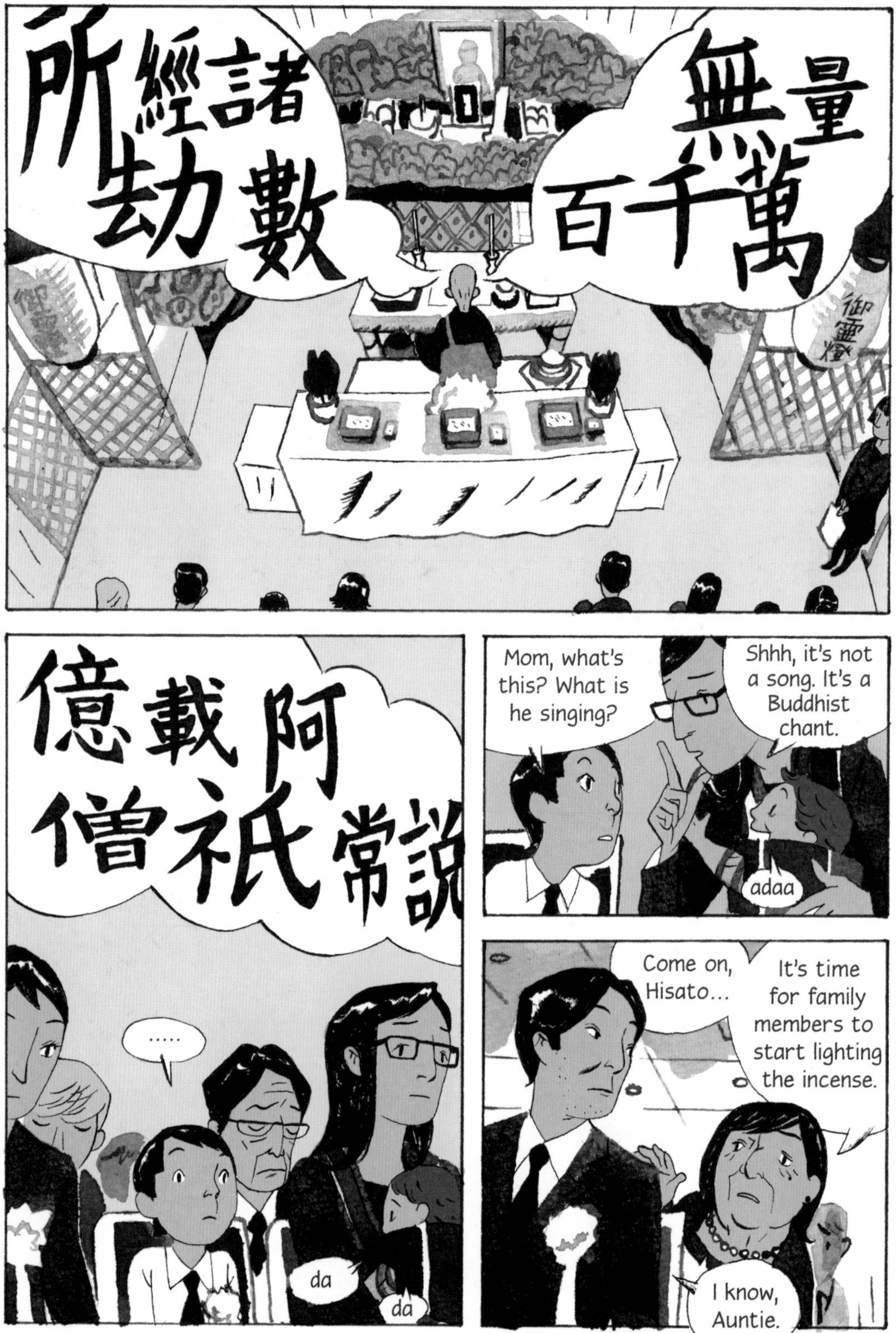
所經諸劫數
無量百千萬
億載阿僧祇常說
Mom, what's this? What is he singing?
Shhh, it's not a song. It's a Buddhist chant.
adaa
.....
da
da
Come on, Hisato...
It's time for family members to start lighting the incense.
I know, Auntie.

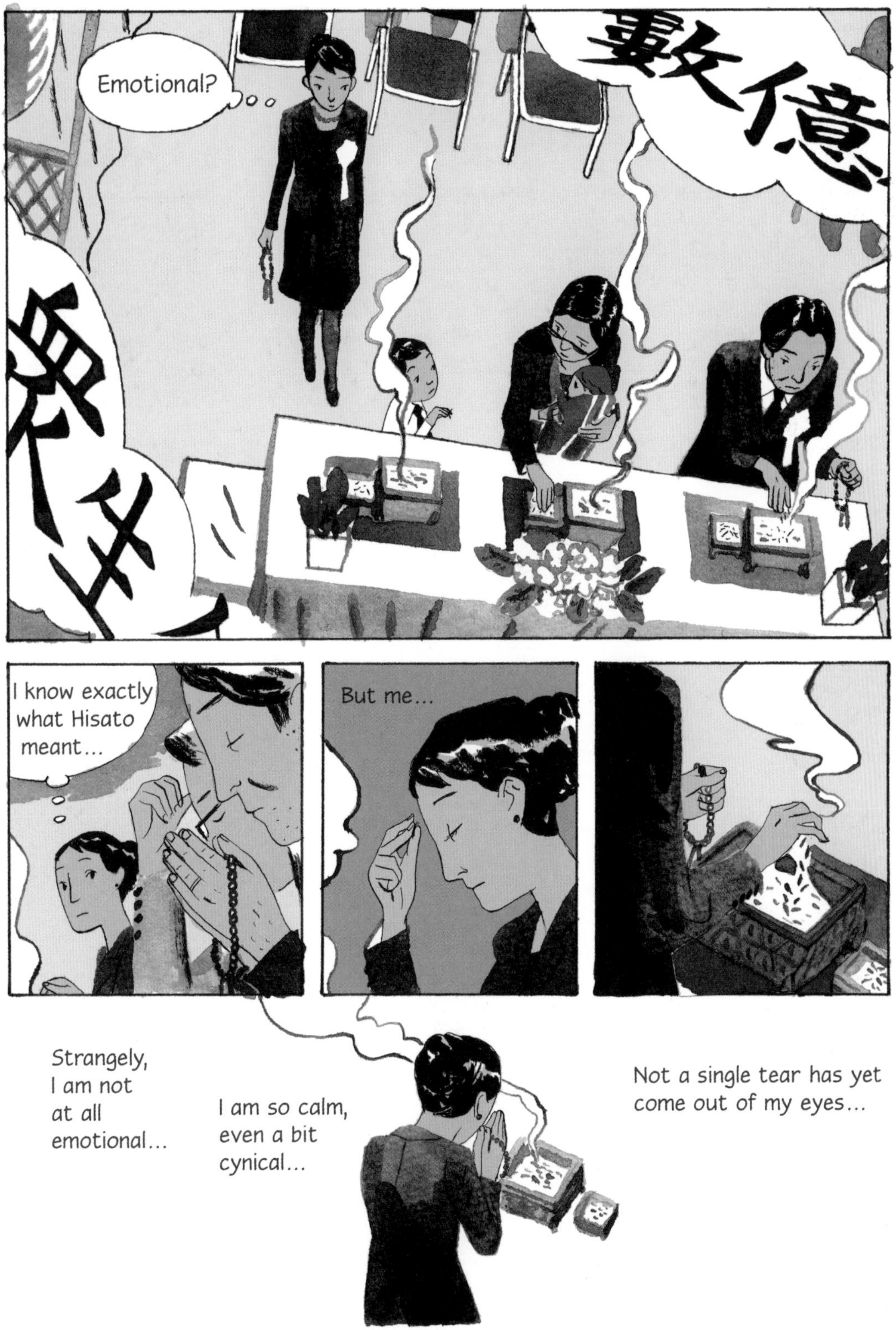
Emotional?
數億
I know exactly what Hisato meant...
But me...
Strangely, I am not at all emotional...
I am so calm, even a bit cynical...
Not a single tear has yet come out of my eyes...

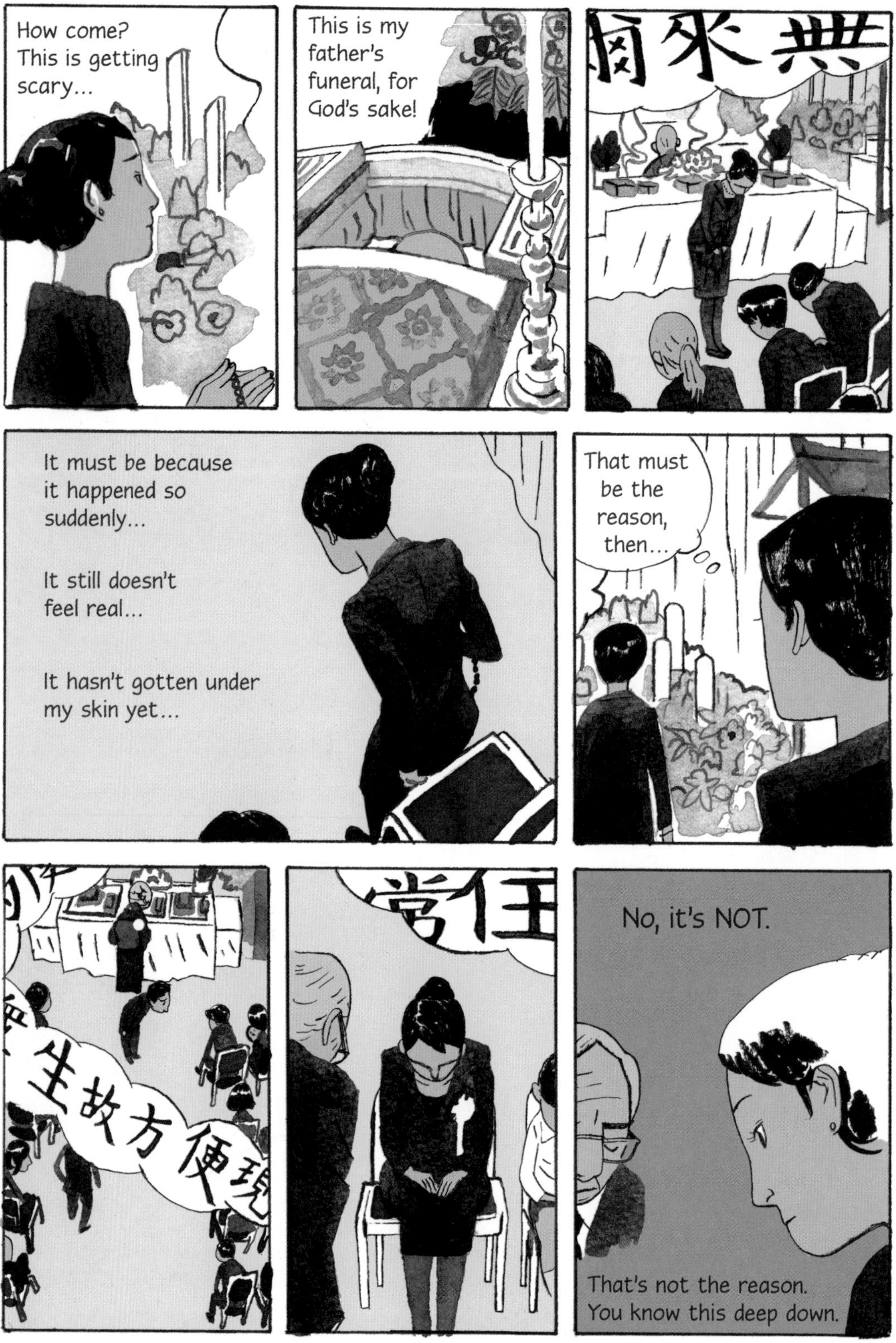
How come? This is getting scary...
This is my father's funeral, for God's sake!
It must be because it happened so suddenly...
It still doesn't feel real...
It hasn't gotten under my skin yet...
That must be the reason, then...
生故方便現
No, it's NOT.
That's not the reason. You know this deep down.

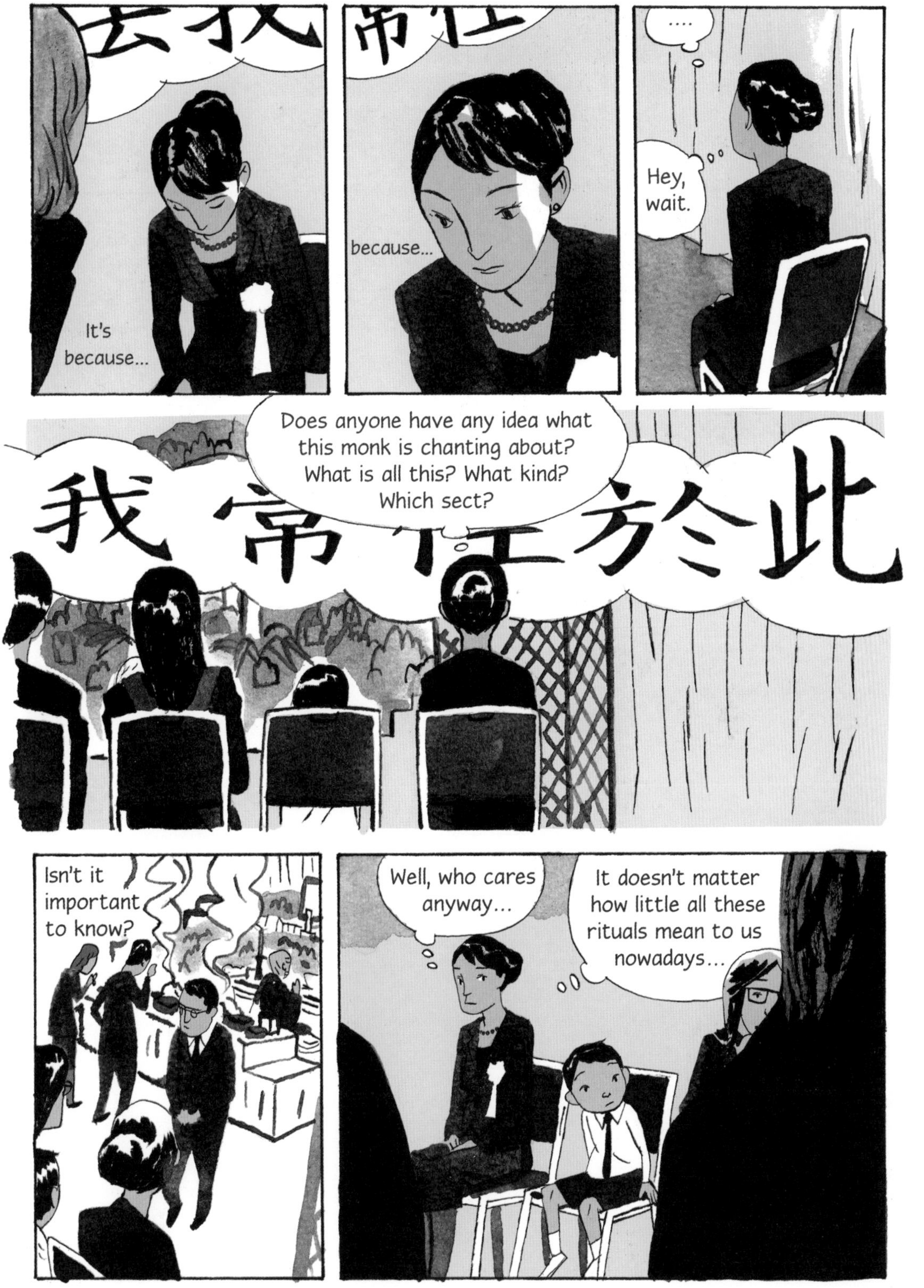
It's because...
because...
....
Hey, wait.
Does anyone have any idea what this monk is chanting about? What is all this? What kind? Which sect?
Isn't it important to know?
Well, who cares anyway...
It doesn't matter how little all these rituals mean to us nowadays...

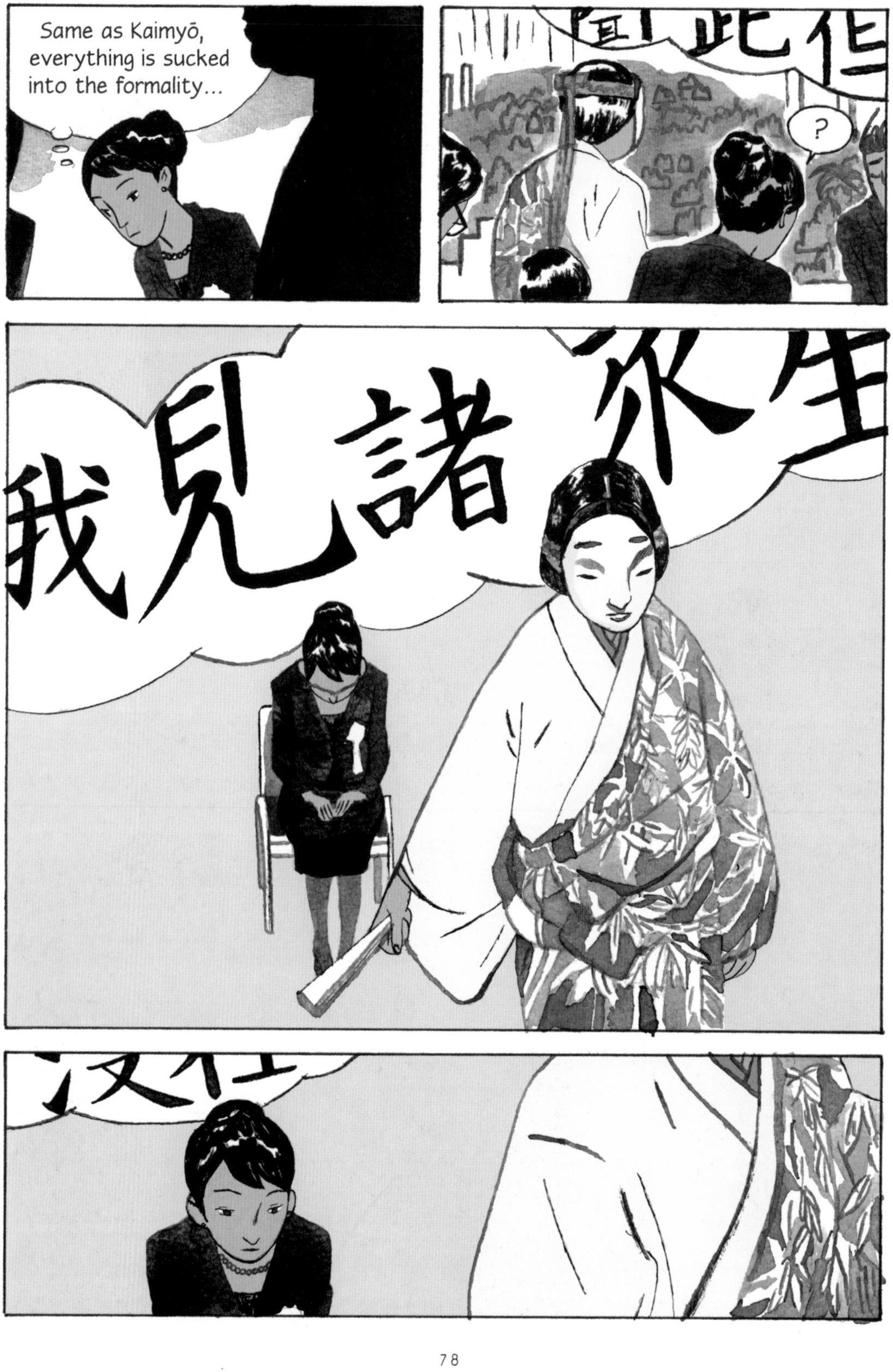
Same as Kaimyō, everything is sucked into the formality...
?
我見諸衆生

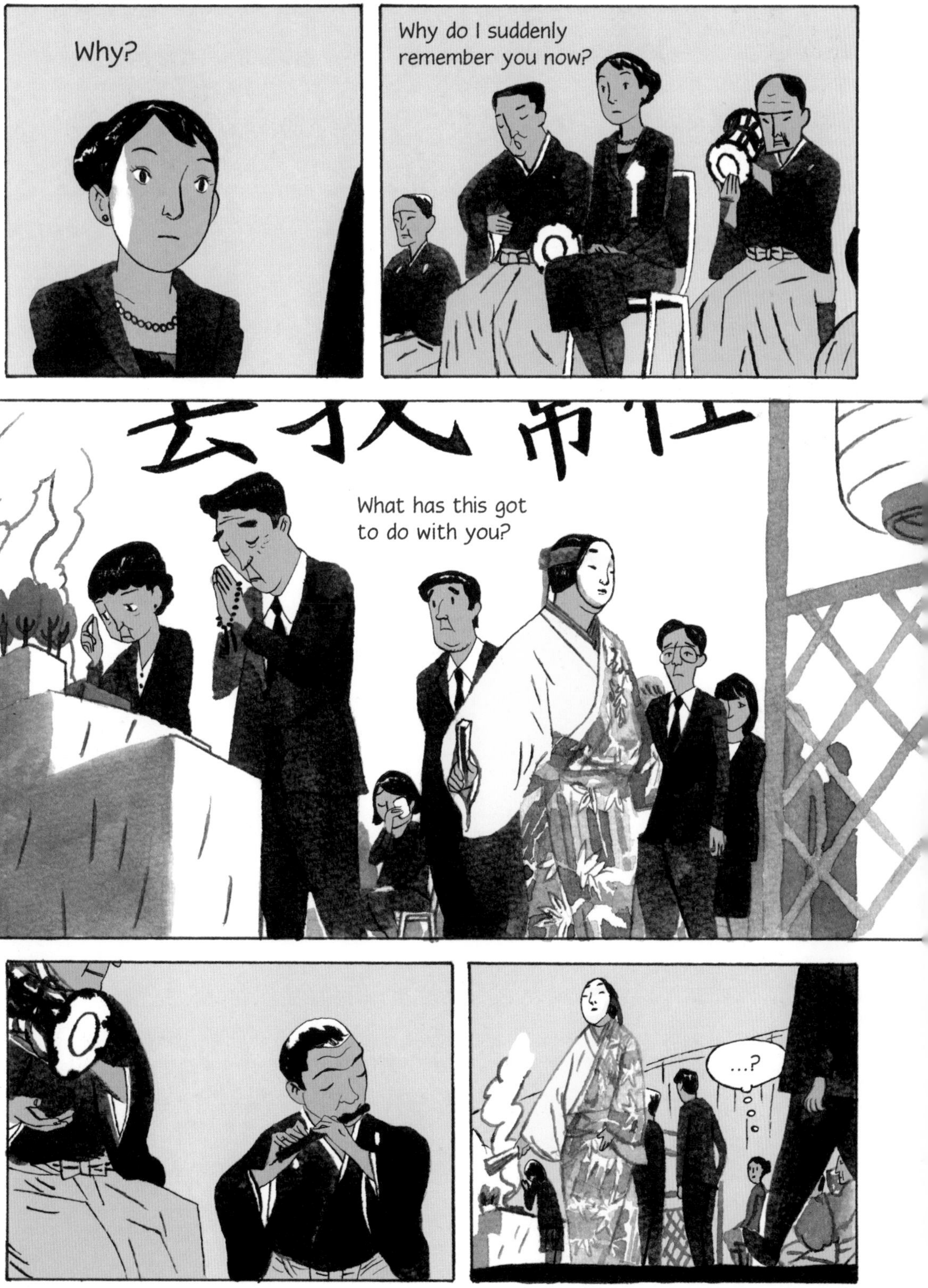
Why?
Why do I suddenly remember you now?
What has this got to do with you?
...?

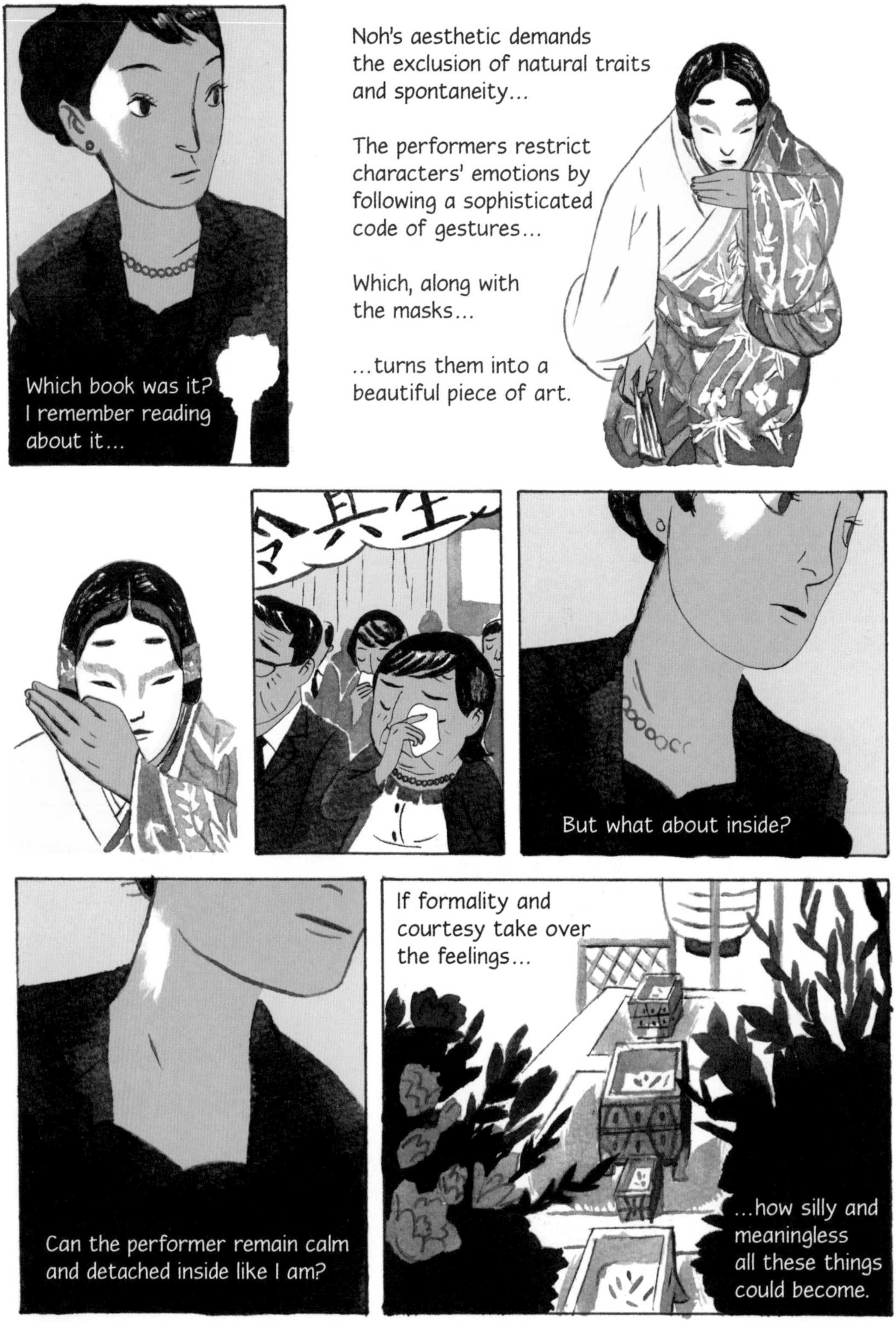
Which book was it? I remember reading about it...
Noh's aesthetic demands the exclusion of natural traits and spontaneity...
The performers restrict characters' emotions by following a sophisticated code of gestures...
Which, along with the masks...
...turns them into a beautiful piece of art.
But what about inside?
Can the performer remain calm and detached inside like I am?
If formality and courtesy take over the feelings...
...how silly and meaningless all these things could become.

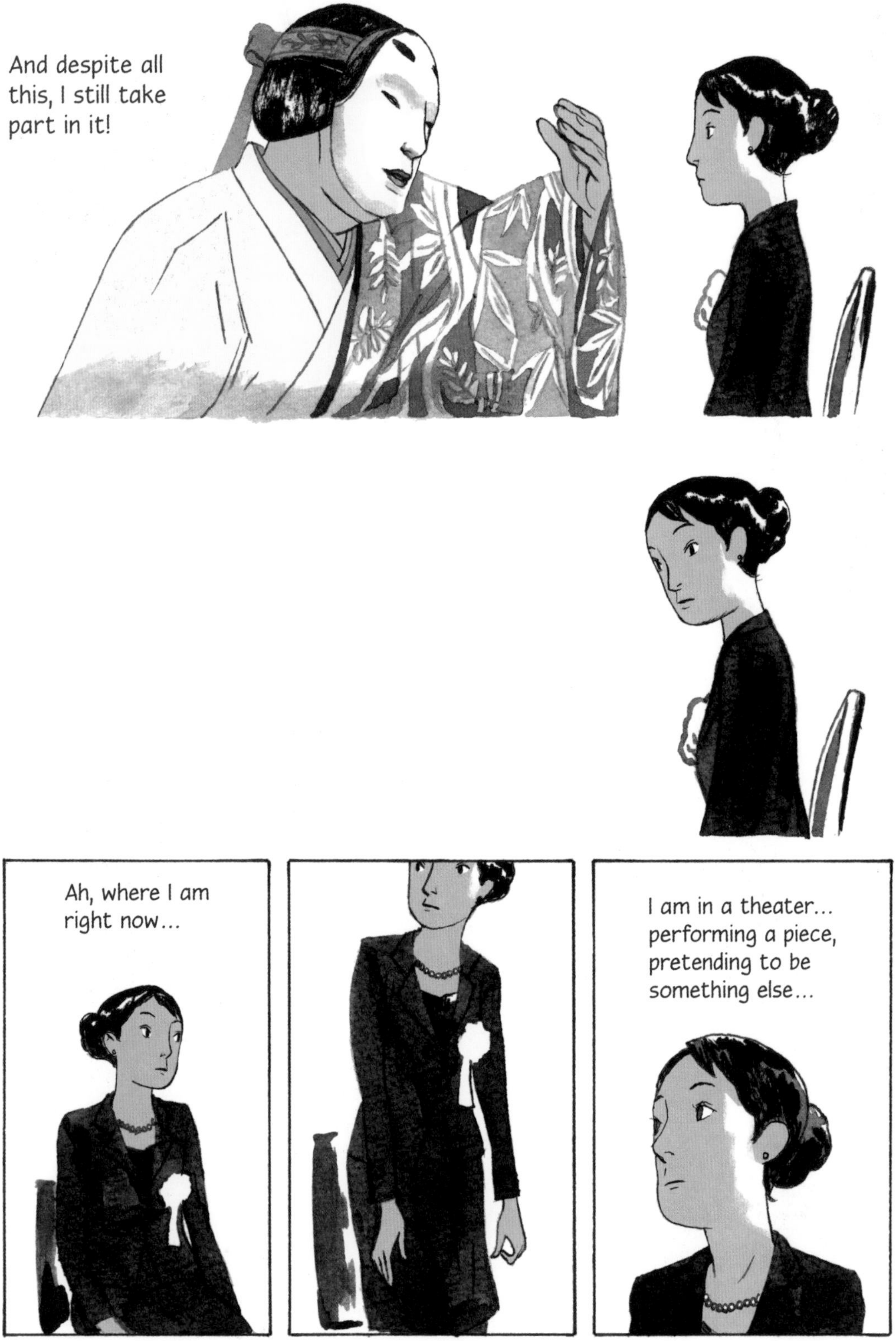
And despite all this, I still take part in it!
Ah, where I am right now...
I am in a theater... performing a piece, pretending to be something else...

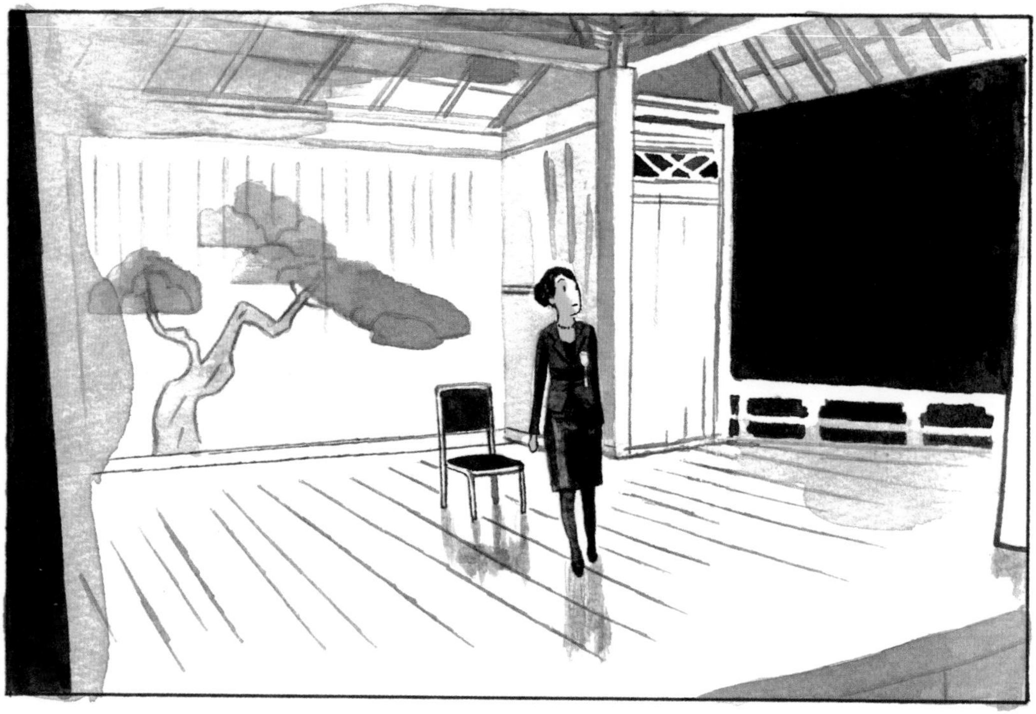

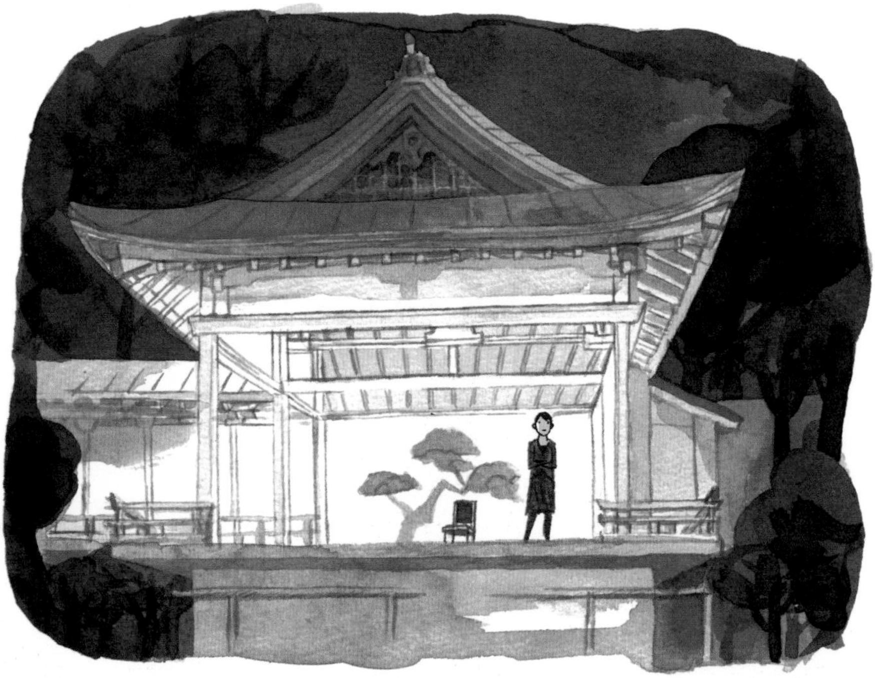

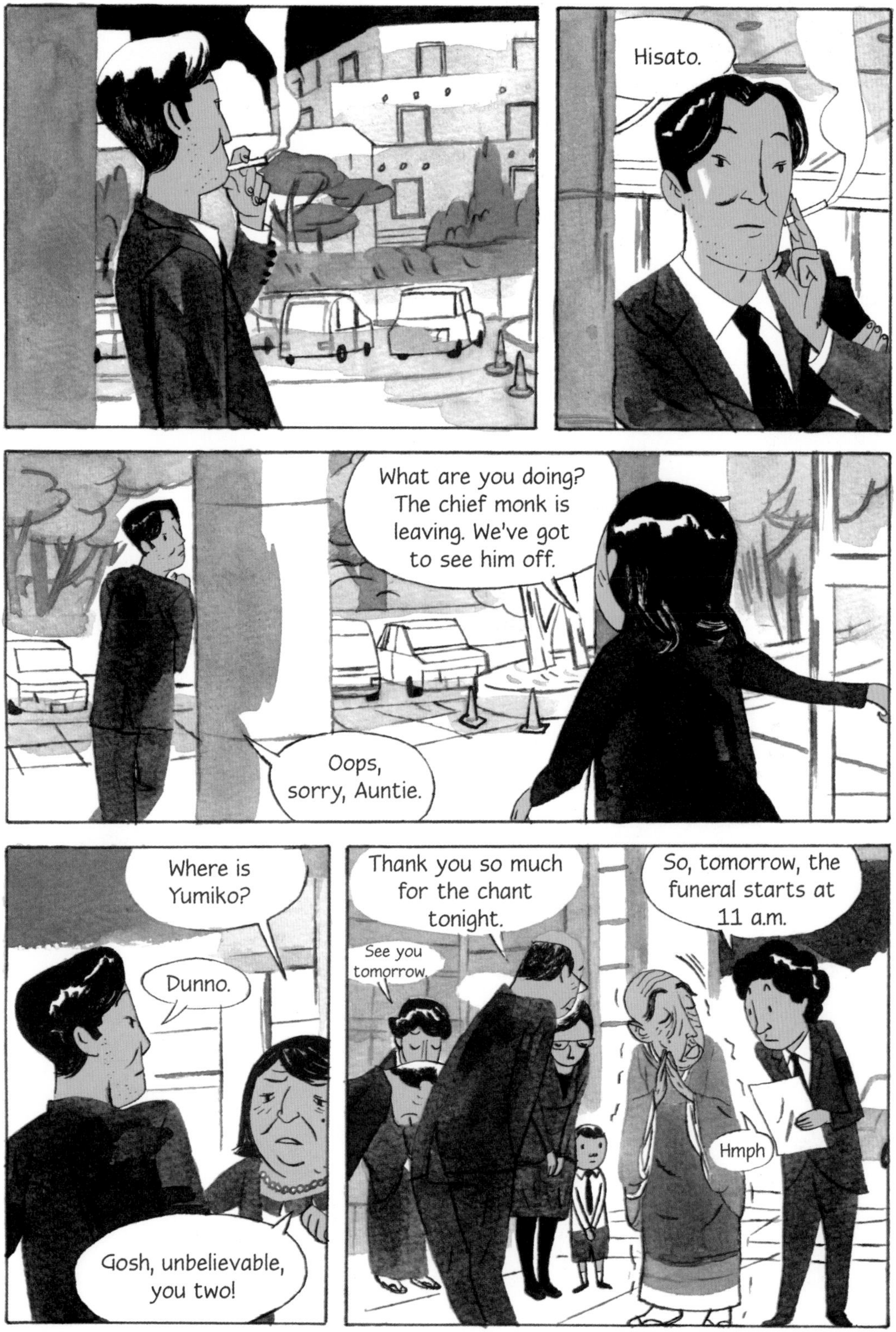
Hisato.
What are you doing? The chief monk is leaving. We've got to see him off.
Oops, sorry, Auntie.
Where is Yumiko?
Dunno.
Gosh, unbelievable, you two!
Thank you so much for the chant tonight.
See you tomorrow.
So, tomorrow, the funeral starts at 11 a.m.
Hmph

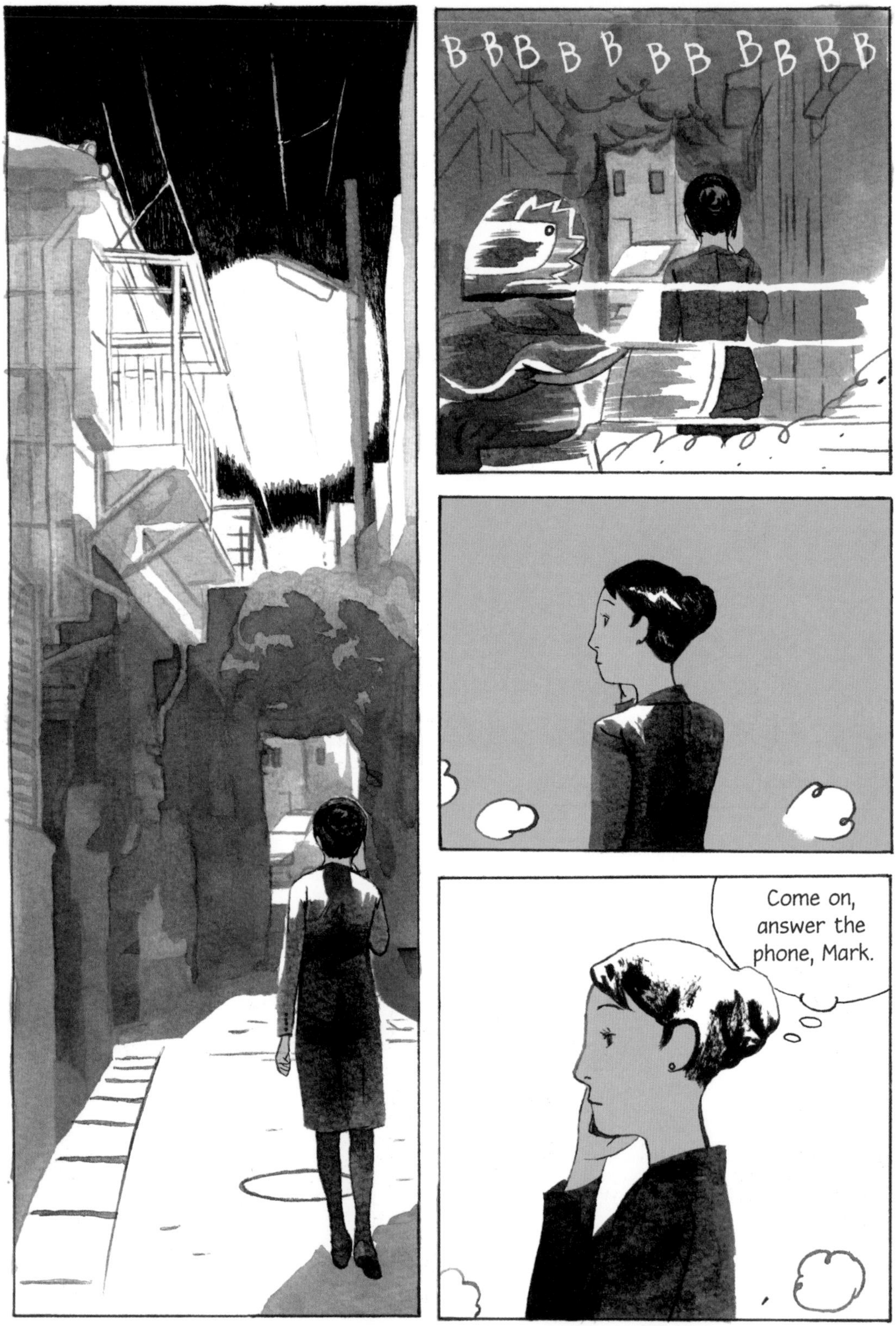
B B B B B B B B B B B
Come on, answer the phone, Mark.

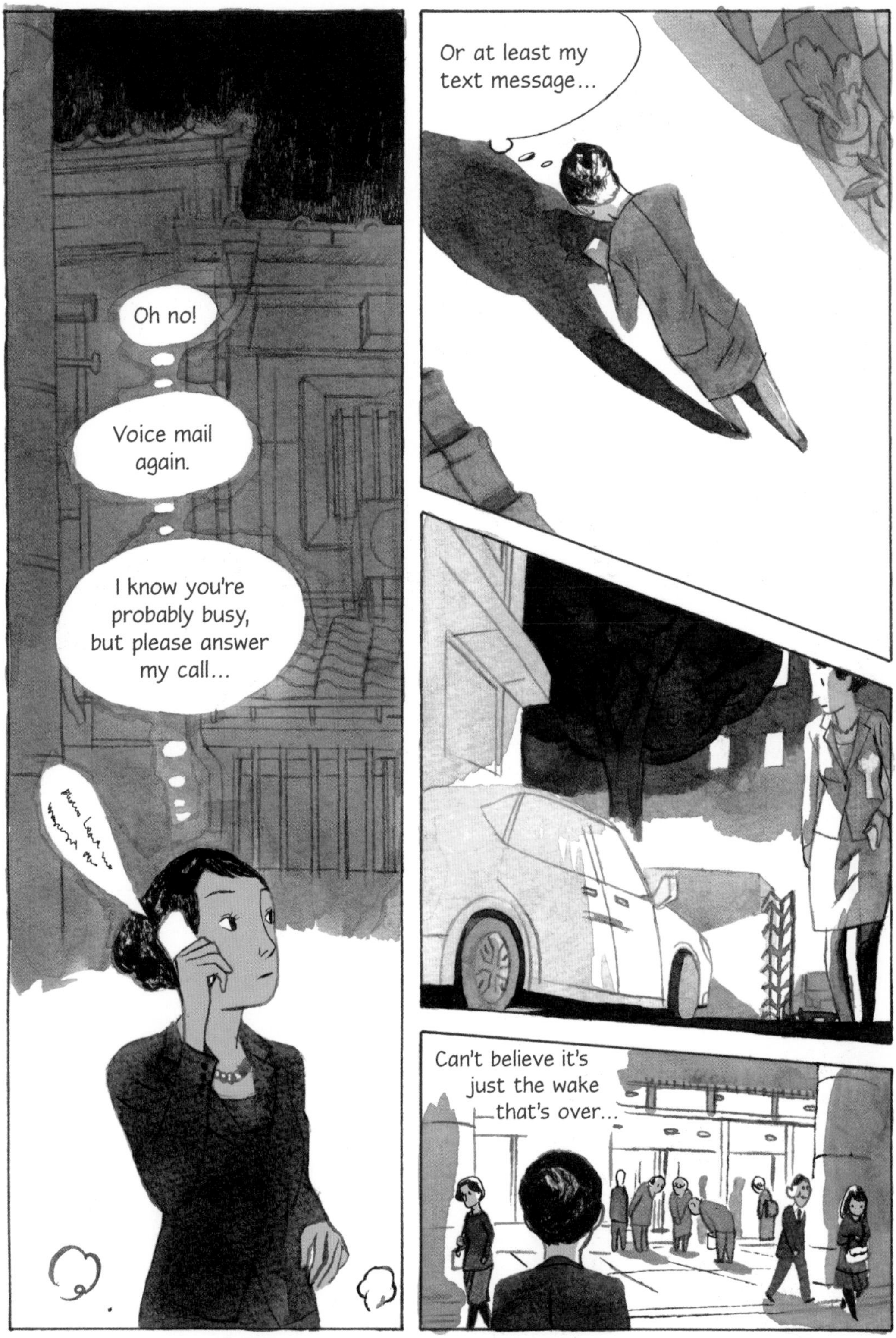
Oh no!
Voice mail again.
I know you're probably busy, but please answer my call...
Or at least my text message...
Can't believe it's just the wake that's over...

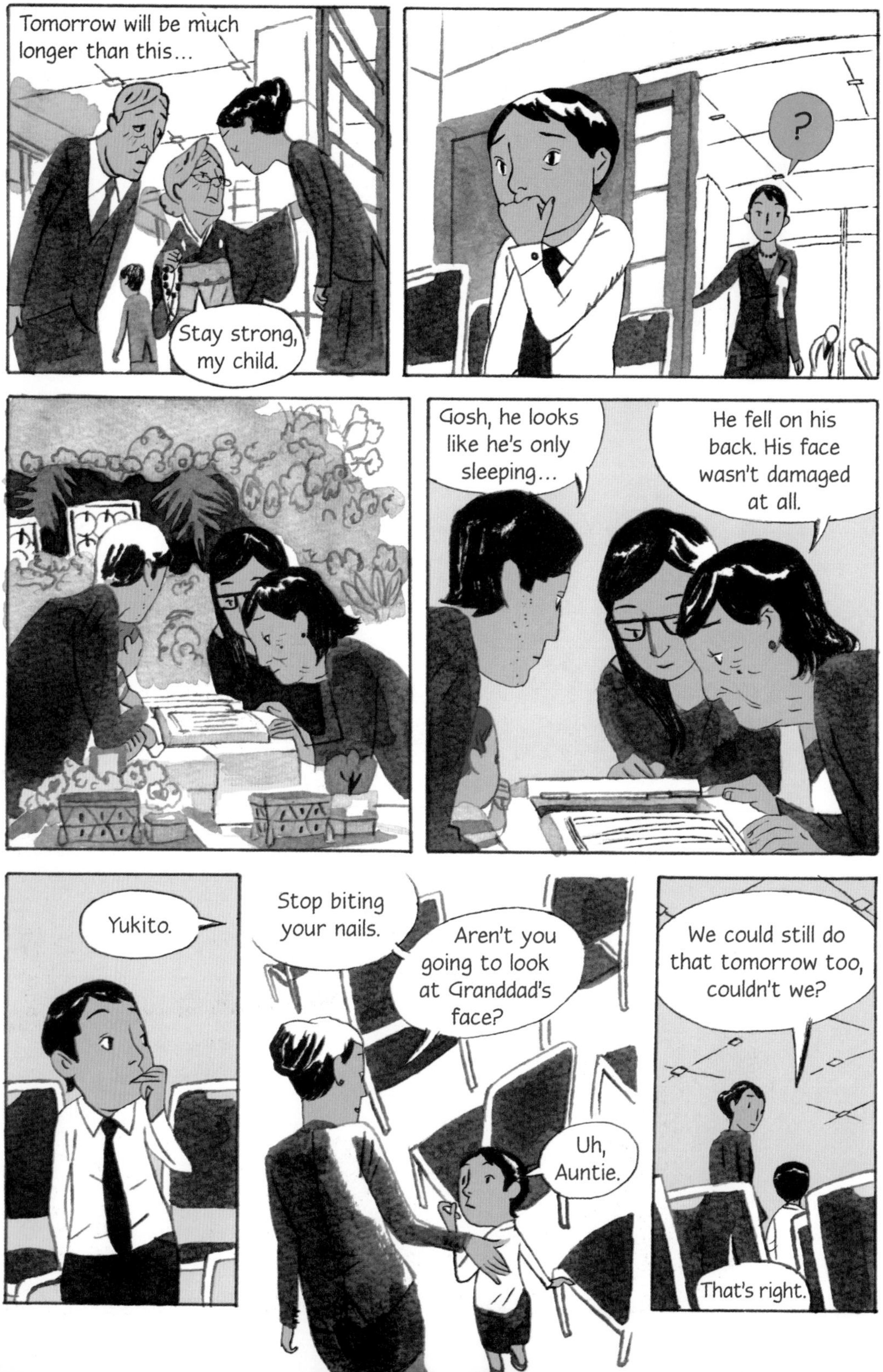
Tomorrow will be much longer than this...
Stay strong, my child.
?
Gosh, he looks like he's only sleeping...
He fell on his back. His face wasn't damaged at all.
Yukito.
Stop biting your nails.
Aren't you going to look at Granddad's face?
Uh, Auntie.
We could still do that tomorrow too, couldn't we?
That's right.

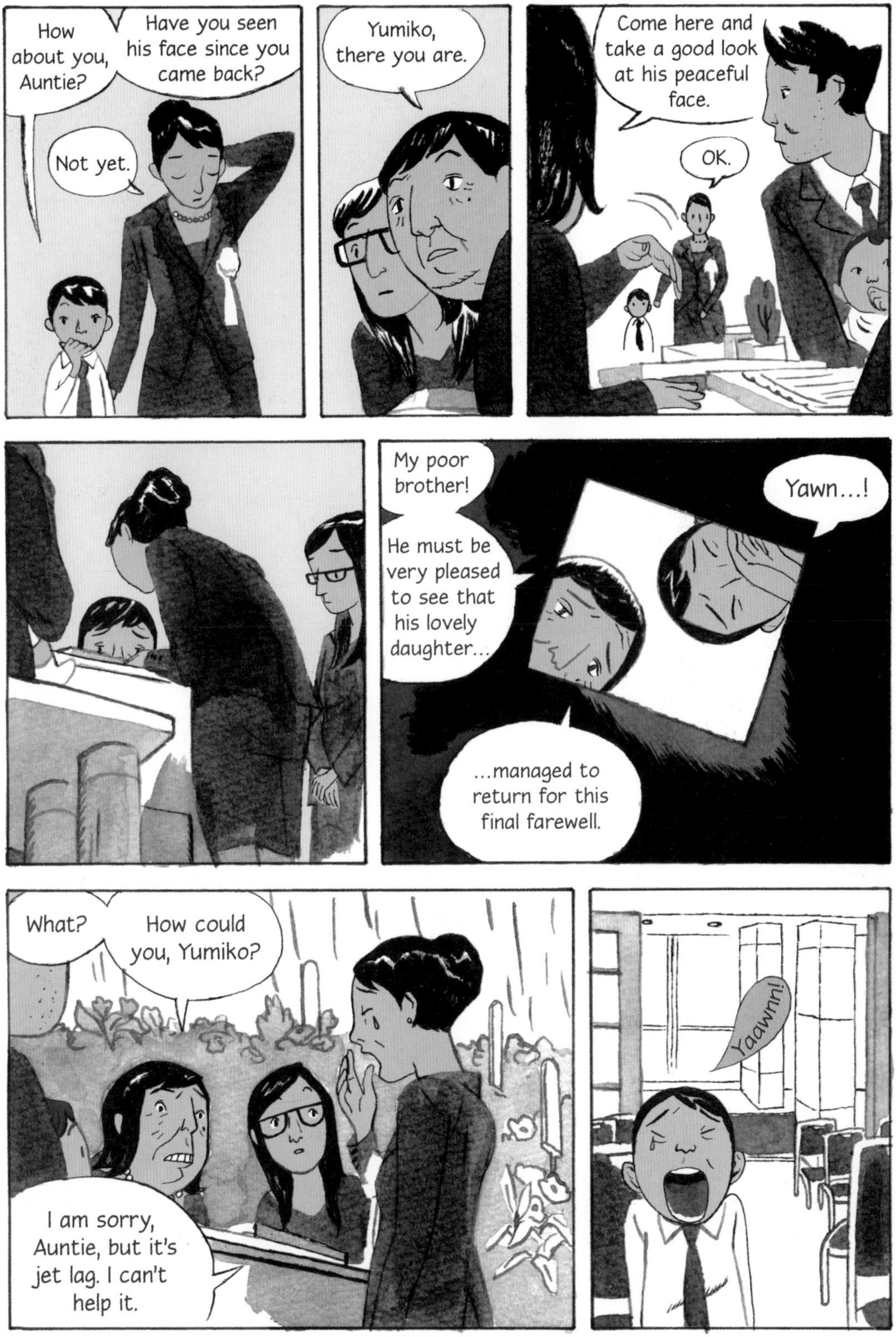
How about you, Auntie?
Have you seen his face since you came back?
Not yet.
Yumiko, there you are.
Come here and take a good look at his peaceful face.
OK.
My poor brother!
He must be very pleased to see that his lovely daughter...
Yawn...!
...managed to return for this final farewell.
What?
How could you, Yumiko?
I am sorry, Auntie, but it's jet lag. I can't help it.
Yaawnn!

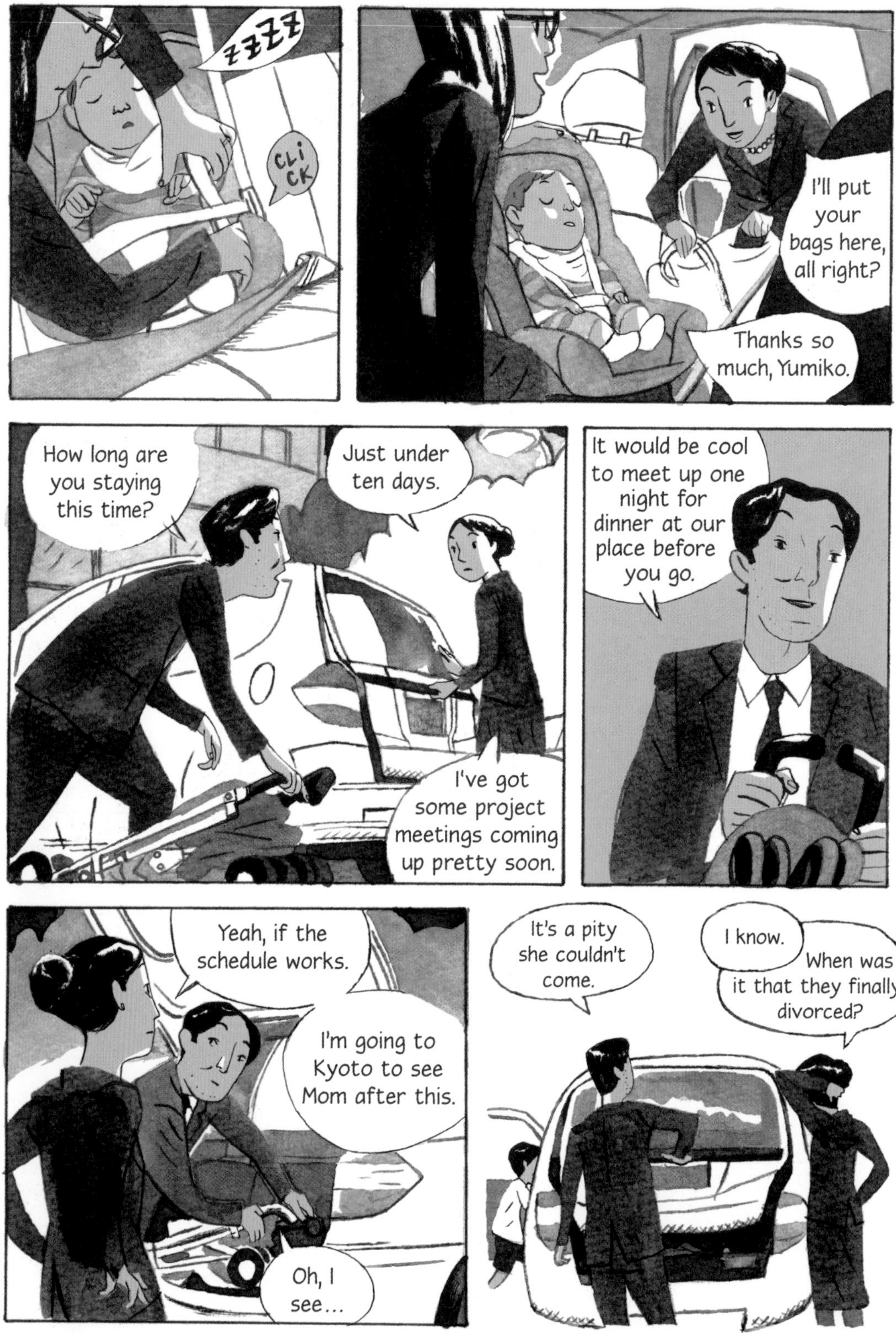
ZZZZ
CLICK
I'll put your bags here, all right?
Thanks so much, Yumiko.
How long are you staying this time?
Just under ten days.
I've got some project meetings coming up pretty soon.
It would be cool to meet up one night for dinner at our place before you go.
Yeah, if the schedule works.
I'm going to Kyoto to see Mom after this.
Oh, I see...
It's a pity she couldn't come.
I know.
When was it that they finally divorced?

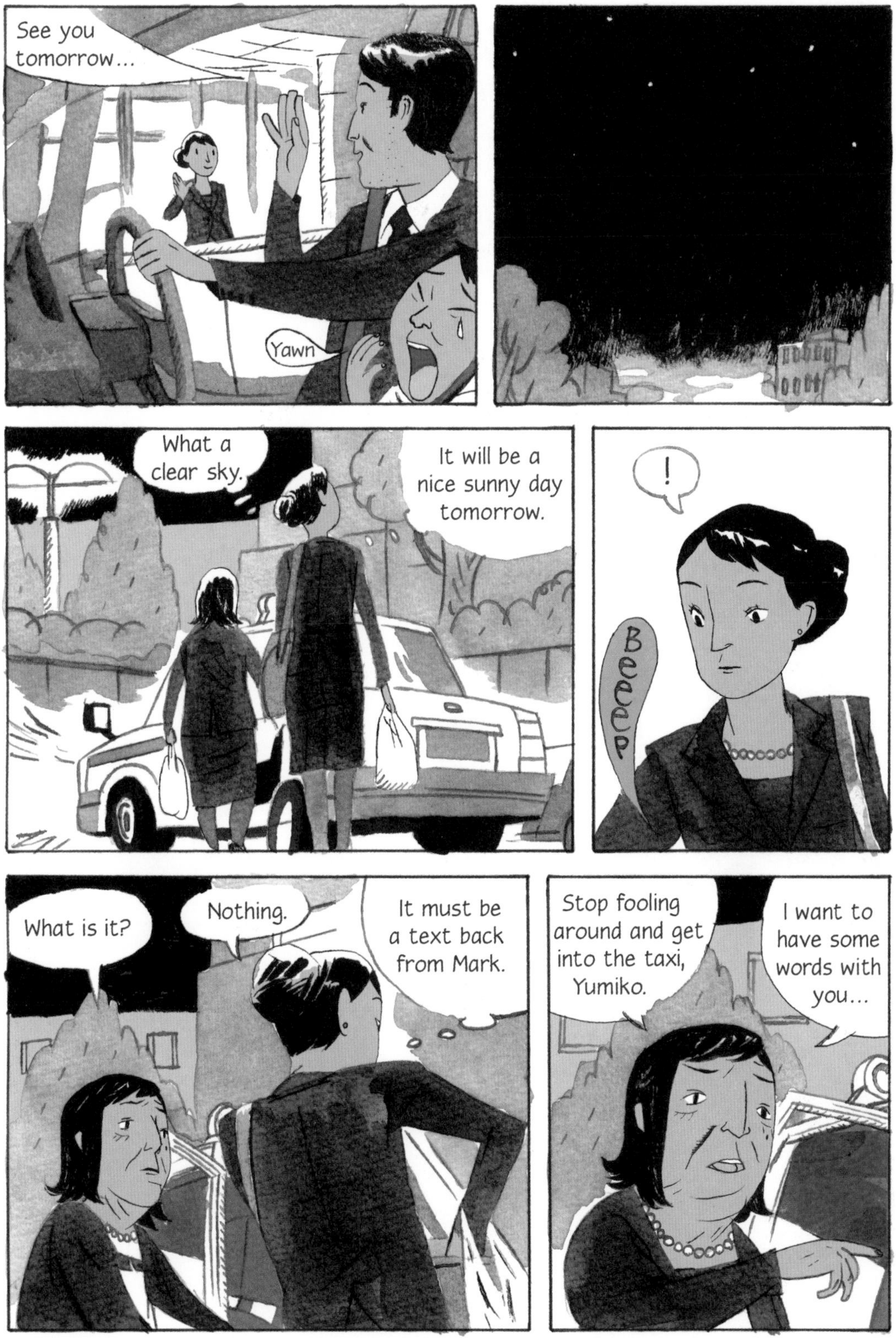
See you tomorrow...
Yawn
What a clear sky.
It will be a nice sunny day tomorrow.
!
Beeep
What is it?
Nothing.
It must be a text back from Mark.
Stop fooling around and get into the taxi, Yumiko.
I want to have some words with you...

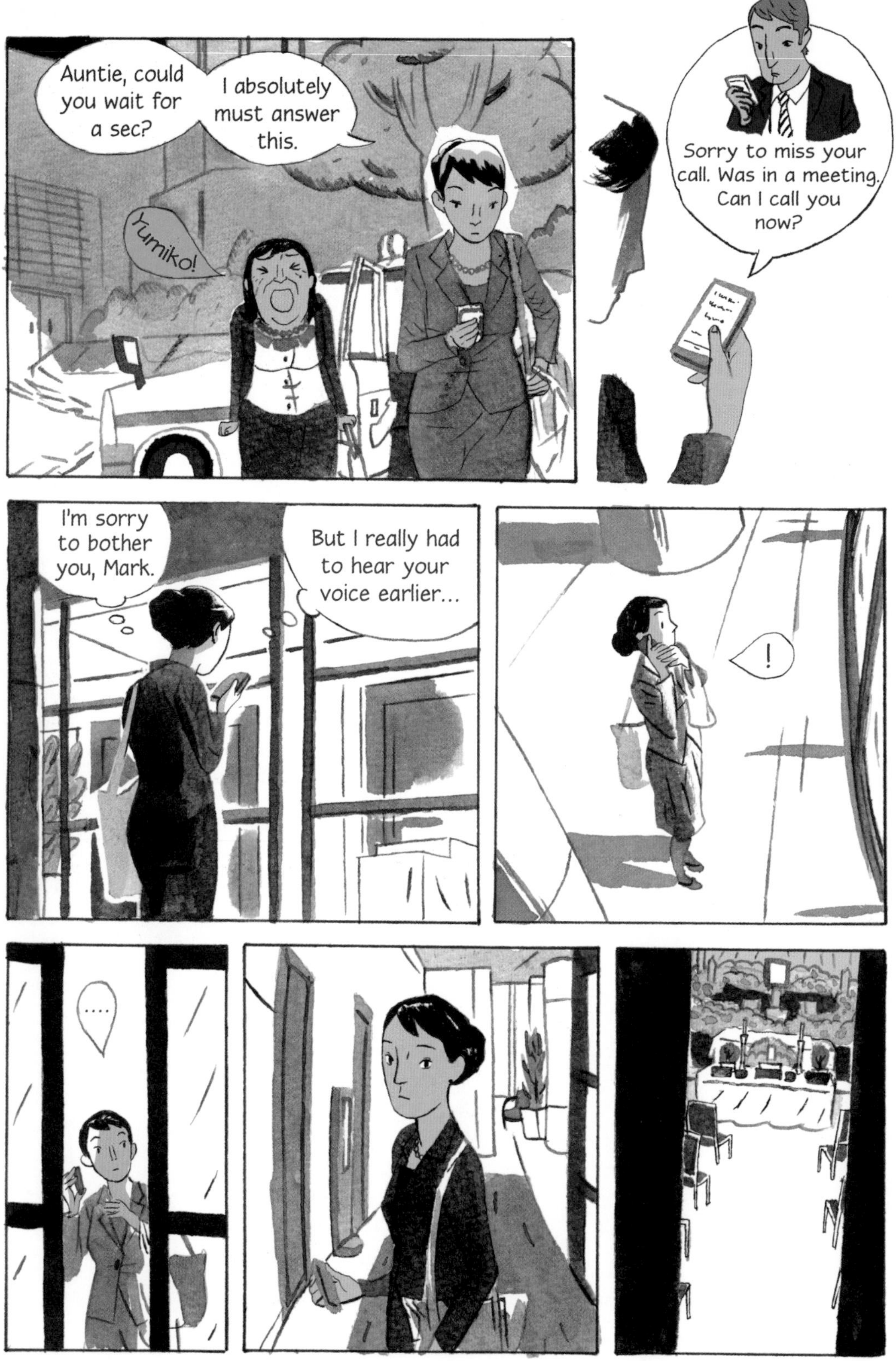
Auntie, could you wait for a sec?
I absolutely must answer this.
Yumiko!
Sorry to miss your call. Was in a meeting. Can I call you now?
I'm sorry to bother you, Mark.
But I really had to hear your voice earlier...
!
....

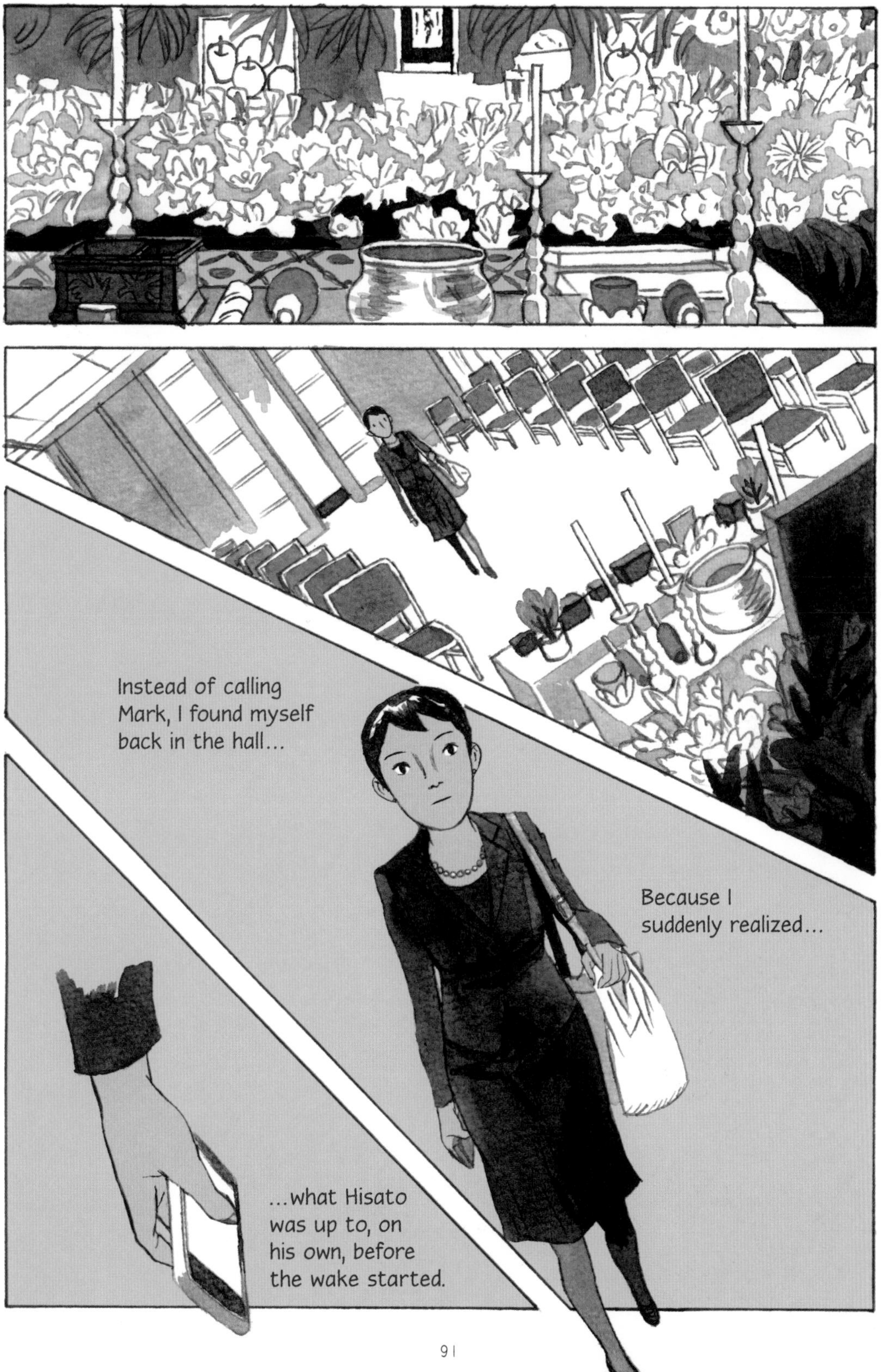
Instead of calling Mark, I found myself back in the hall...
Because I suddenly realized...
...what Hisato was up to, on his own, before the wake started.

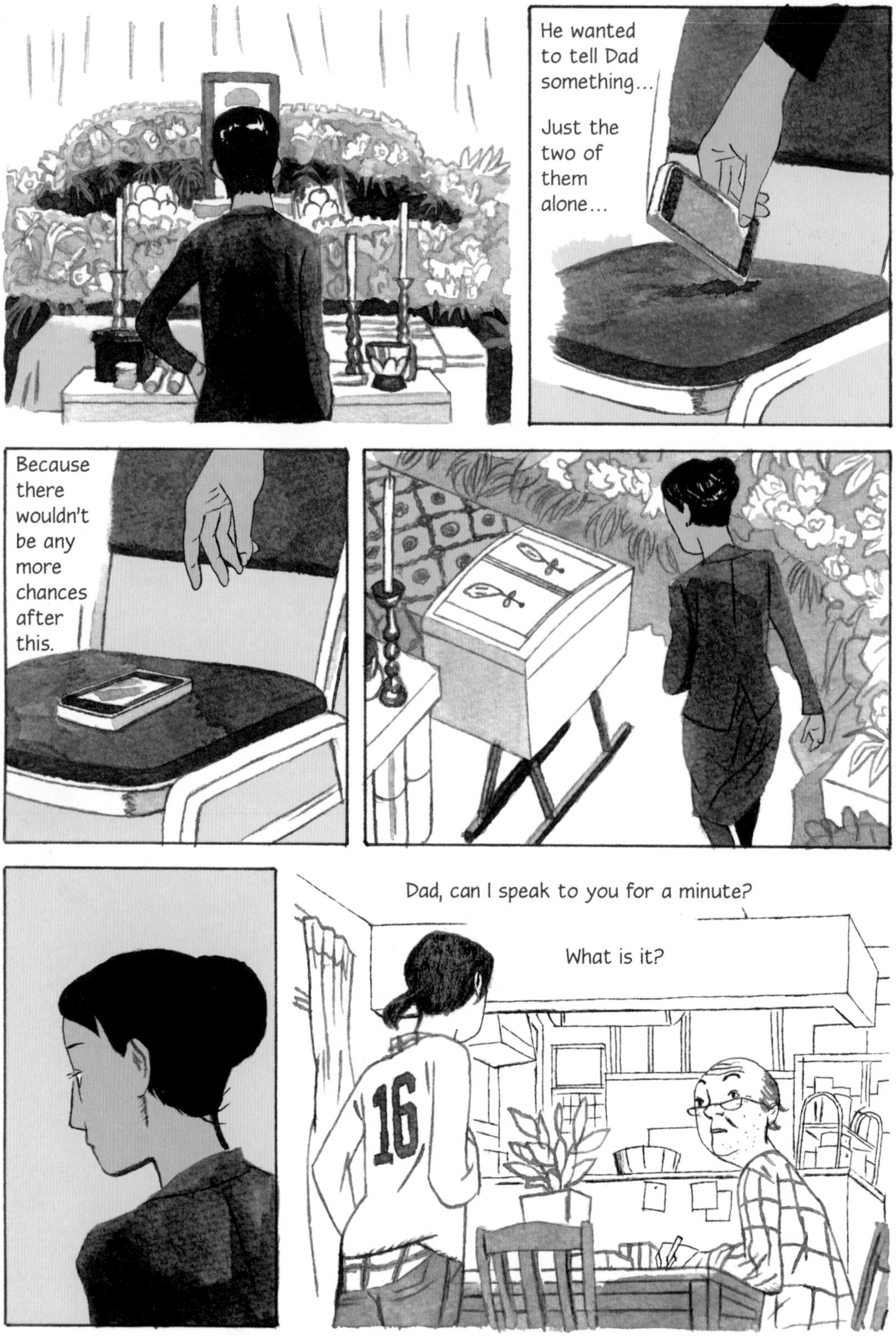

He wanted to tell Dad something…
Just the two of them alone…
Because there wouldn't be any more chances after this.
Dad, can I speak to you for a minute?
What is it?
16

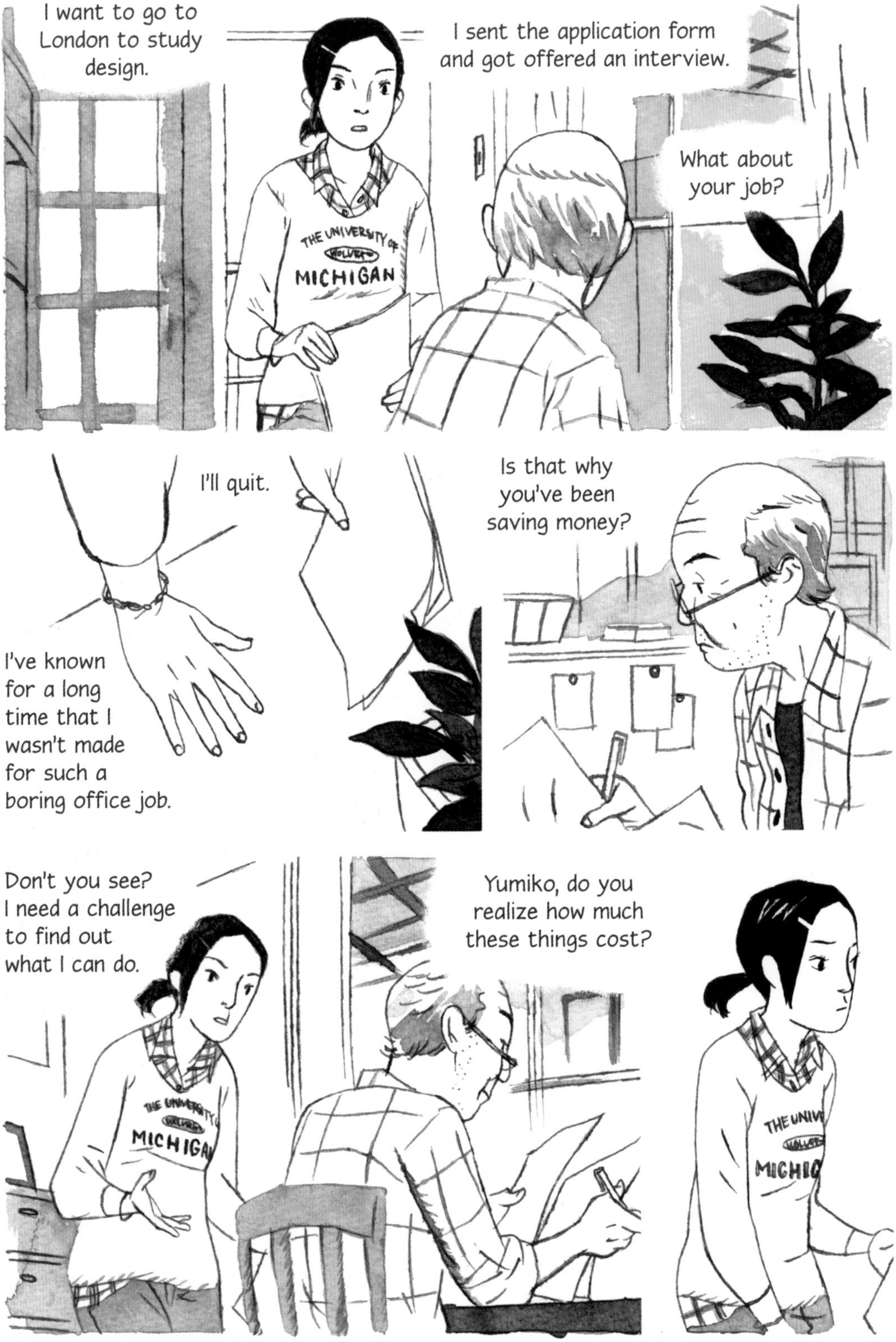
I want to go to London to study design.
I sent the application form and got offered an interview.
What about your job?
I'll quit.
I've known for a long time that I wasn't made for such a boring office job.
Is that why you've been saving money?
Don't you see? I need a challenge to find out what I can do.
Yumiko, do you realize how much these things cost?
THE UNIVERSITY OF MICHIGAN

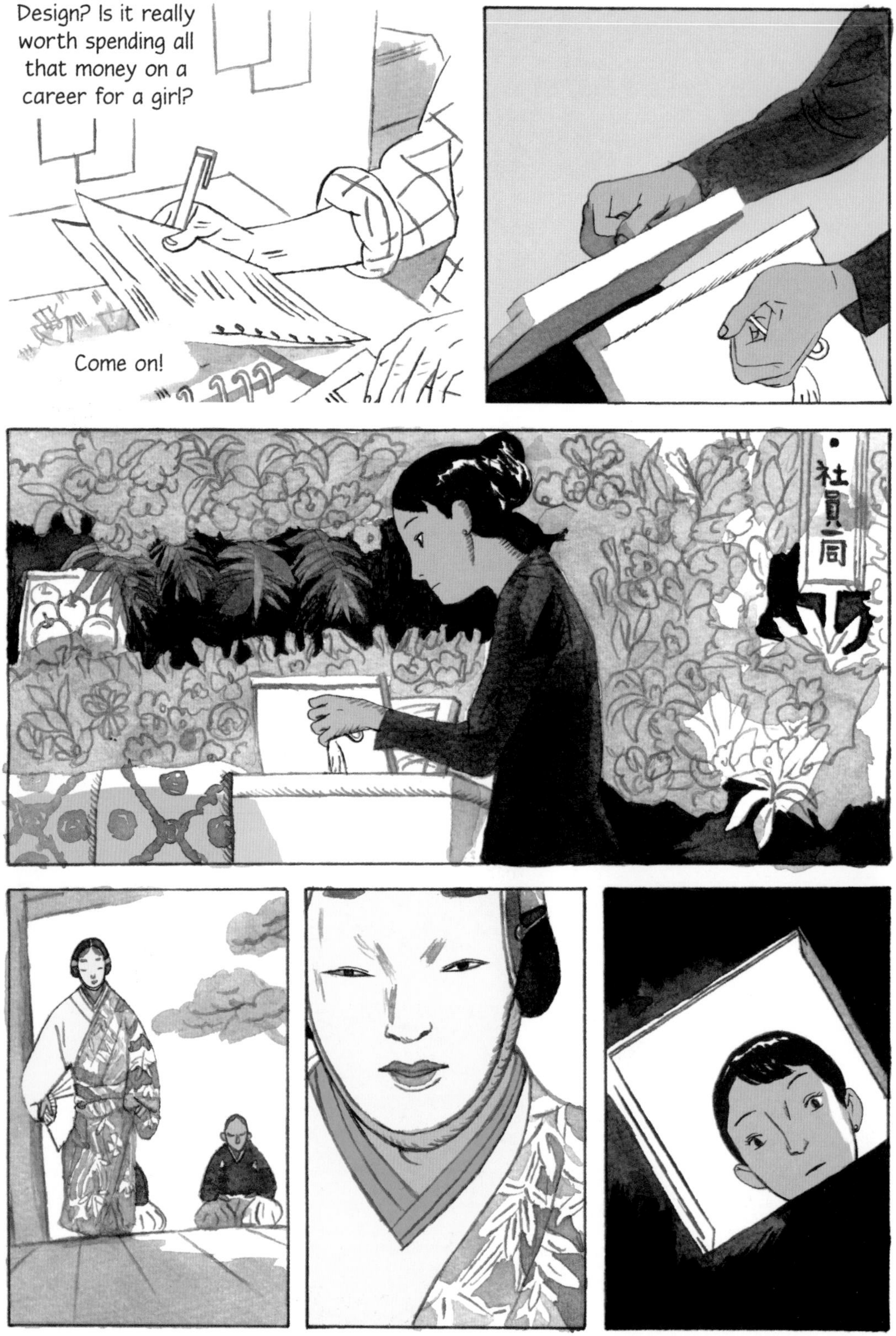
Design? Is it really worth spending all that money on a career for a girl?
Come on!
社員一同

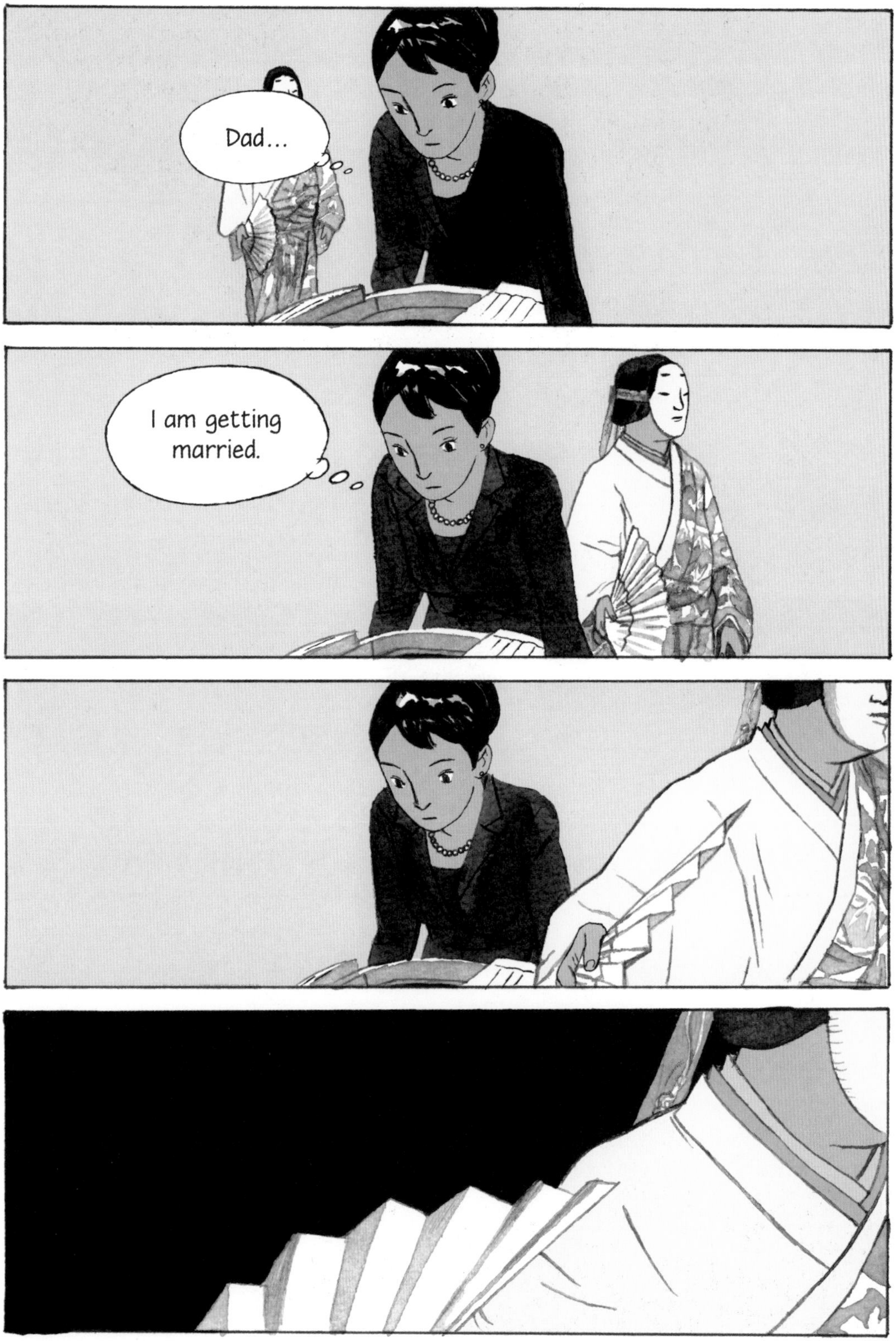
Dad...
I am getting married.

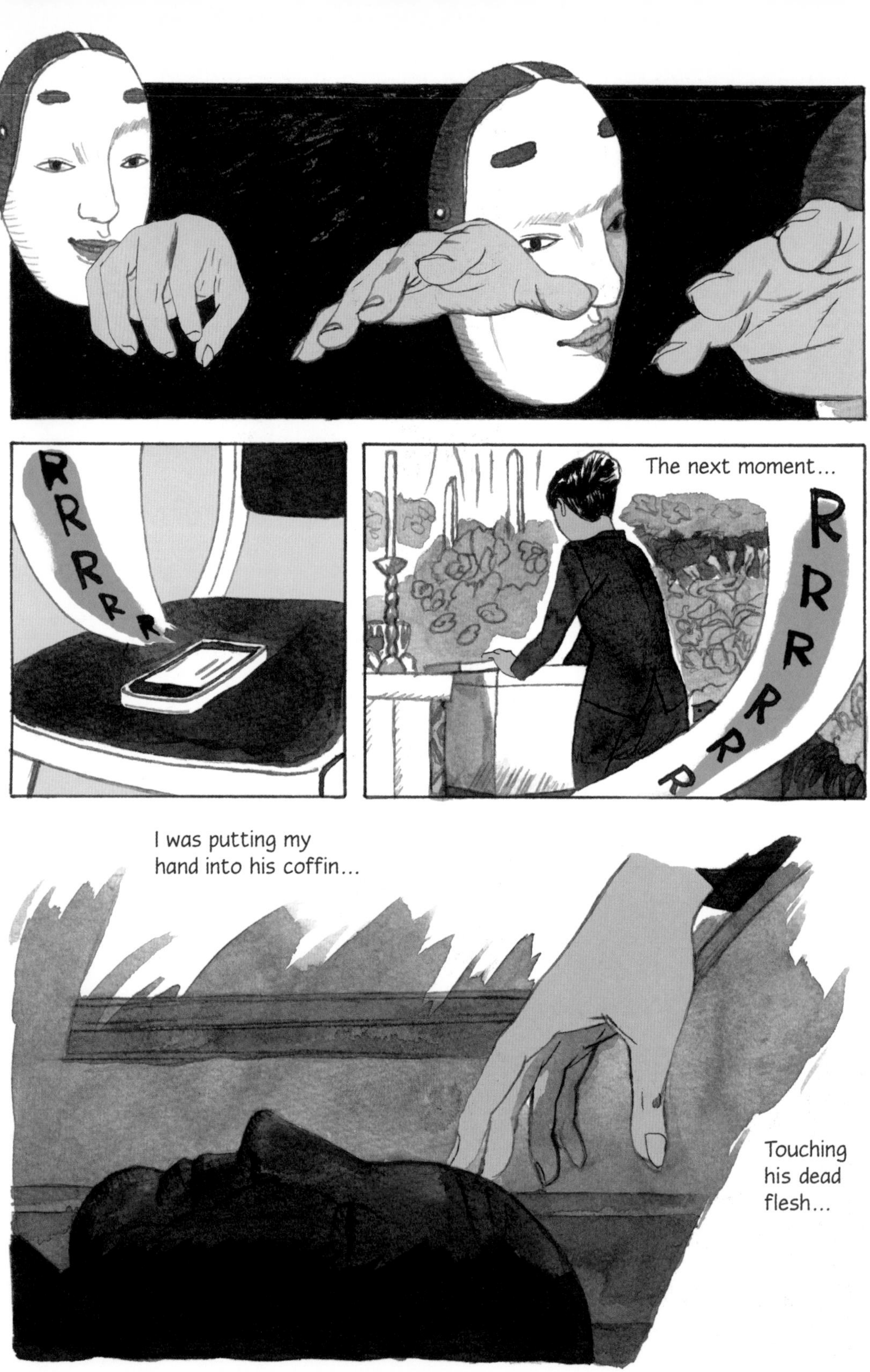
RRRRR
The next moment...
RRRRRR
I was putting my hand into his coffin...
Touching his dead flesh...

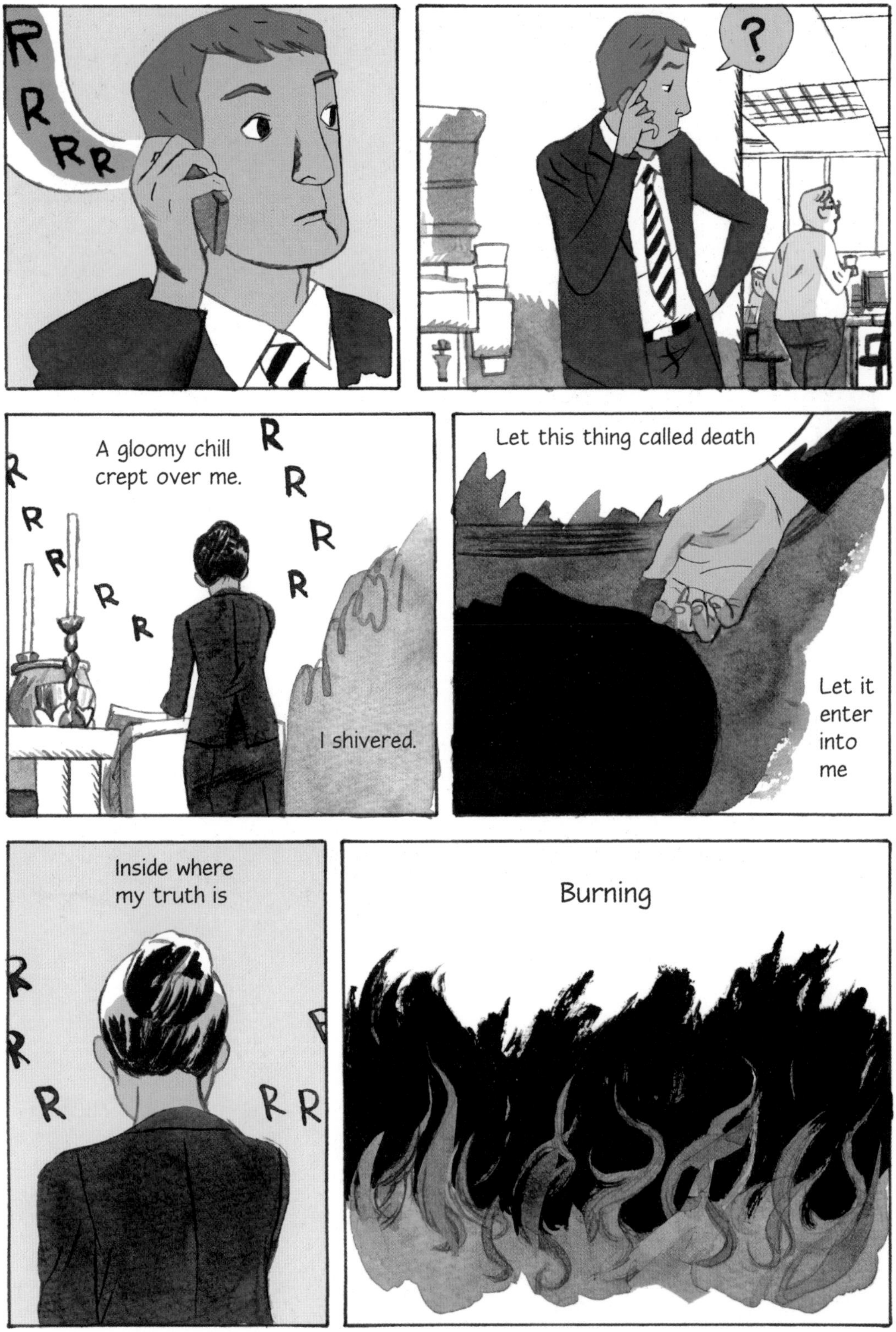
RRRRR
?
A gloomy chill crept over me.
RRRRRRRRRR
I shivered.
Let this thing called death
Let it enter into me
Inside where my truth is
RRRRR
Burning

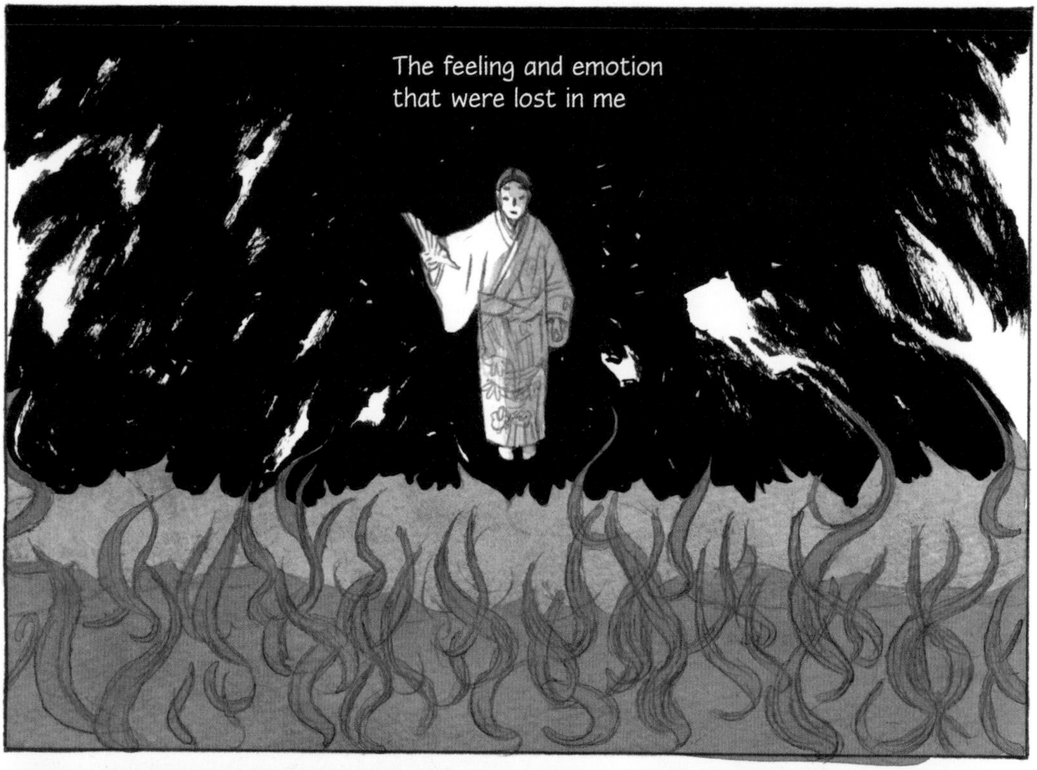
The feeling and emotion
that were lost in me

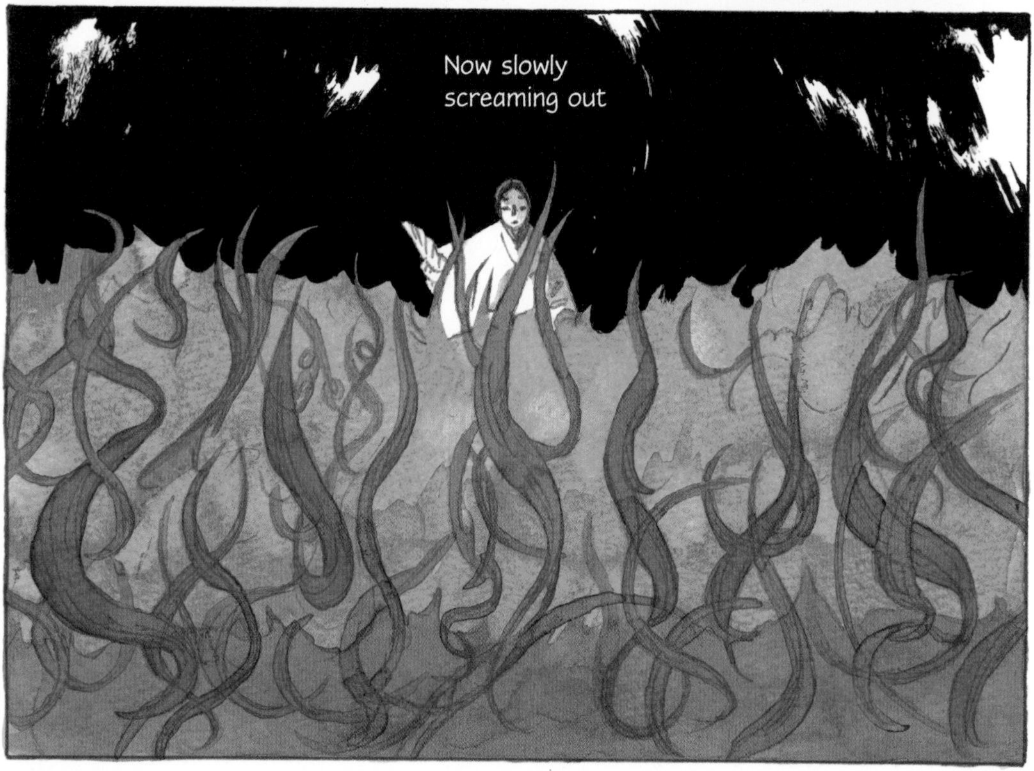
Now slowly
screaming out

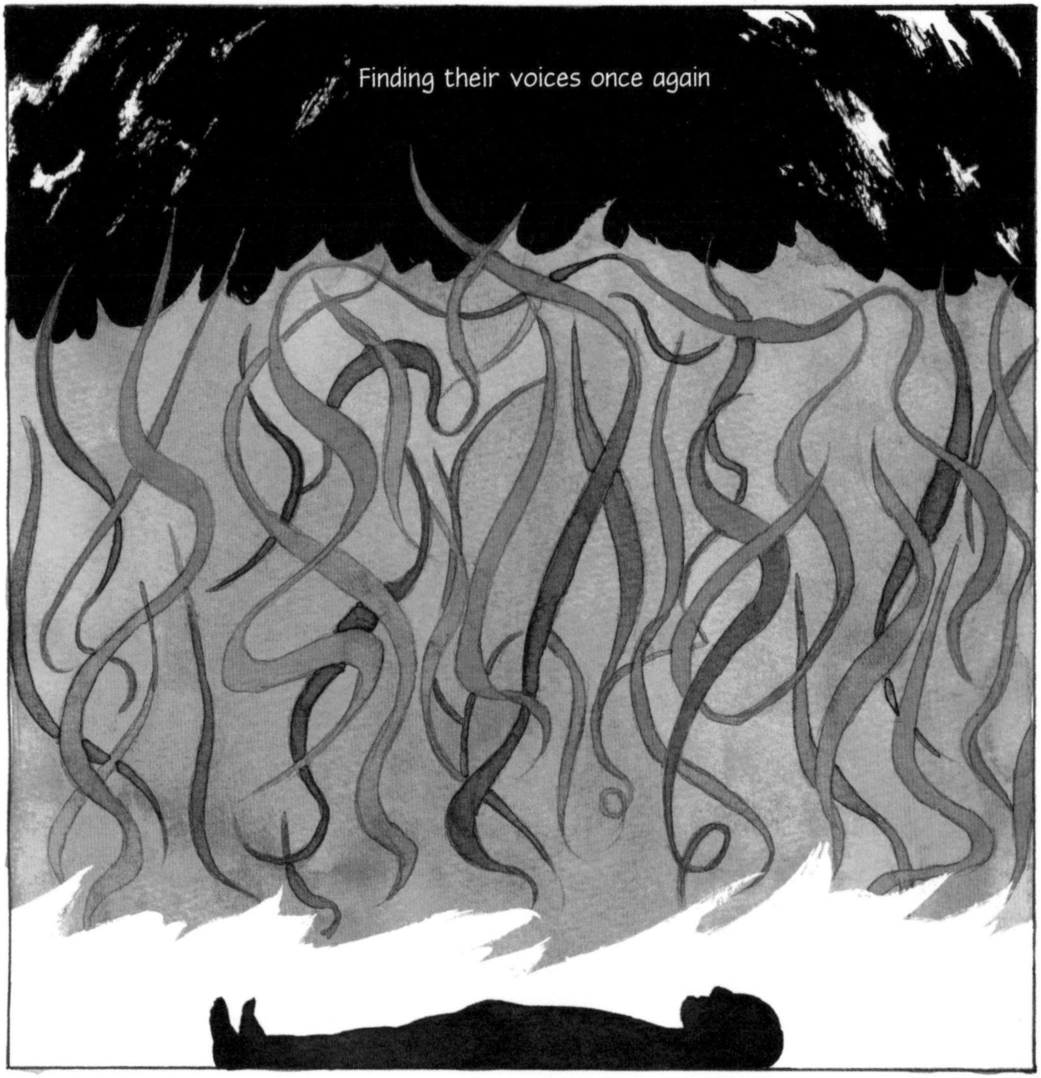
Finding their voices once again

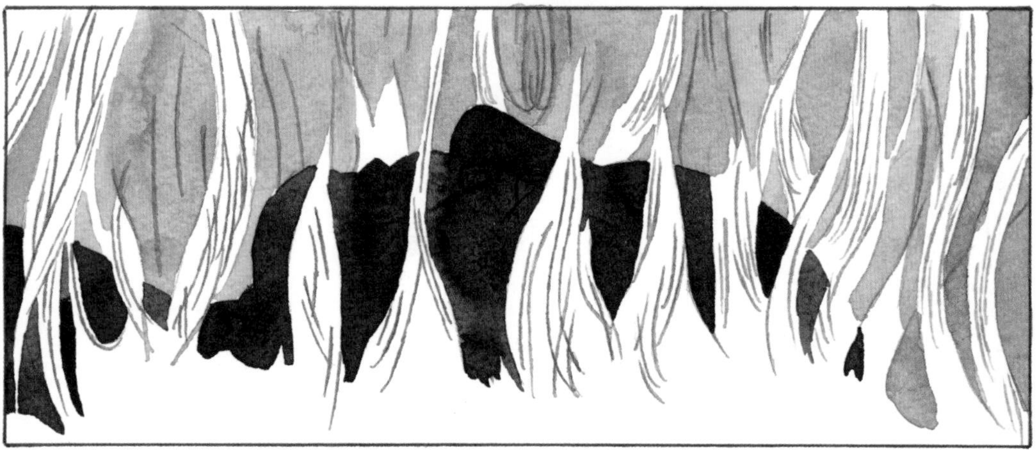

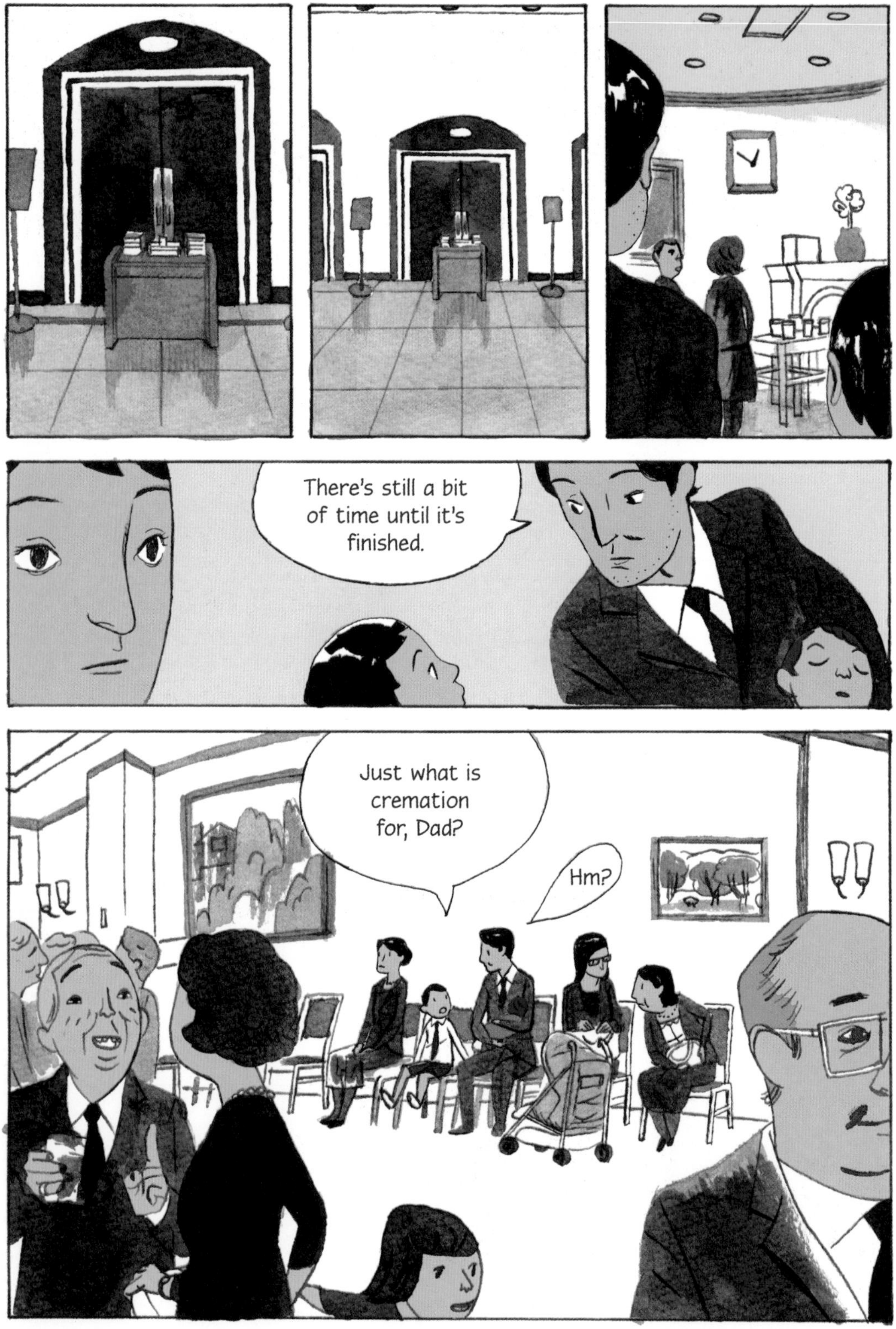
There's still a bit of time until it's finished.
Just what is cremation for, Dad?
Hm?

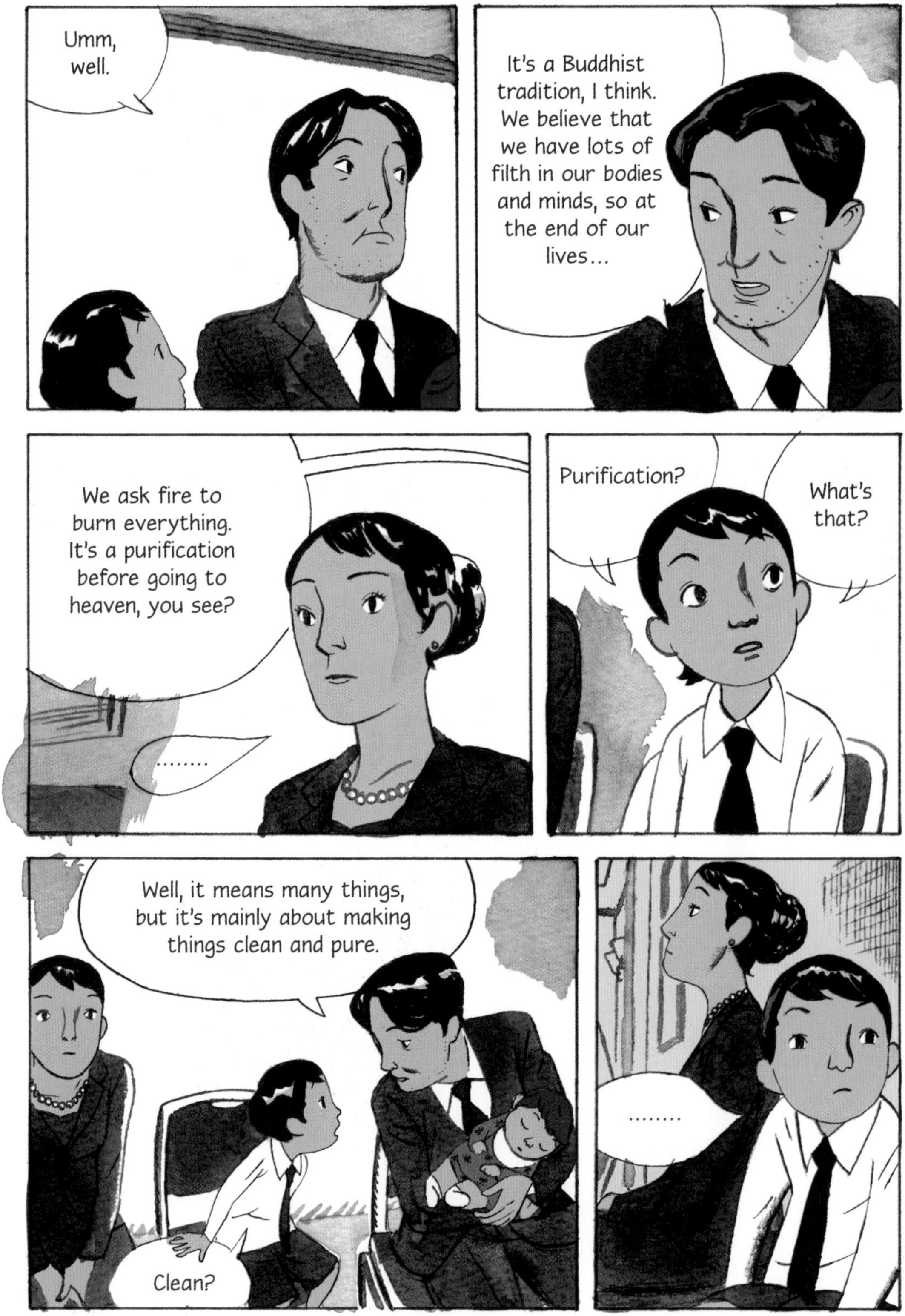

Umm, well.
It's a Buddhist tradition, I think. We believe that we have lots of filth in our bodies and minds, so at the end of our lives...
We ask fire to burn everything. It's a purification before going to heaven, you see?
....
Purification?
What's that?
Well, it means many things, but it's mainly about making things clean and pure.
Clean?
....

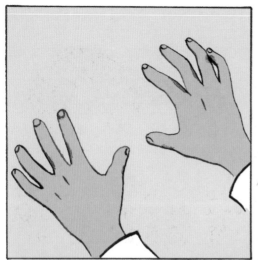

So, we're not very clean?

Are we?

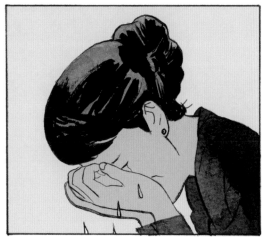

Yumiko...

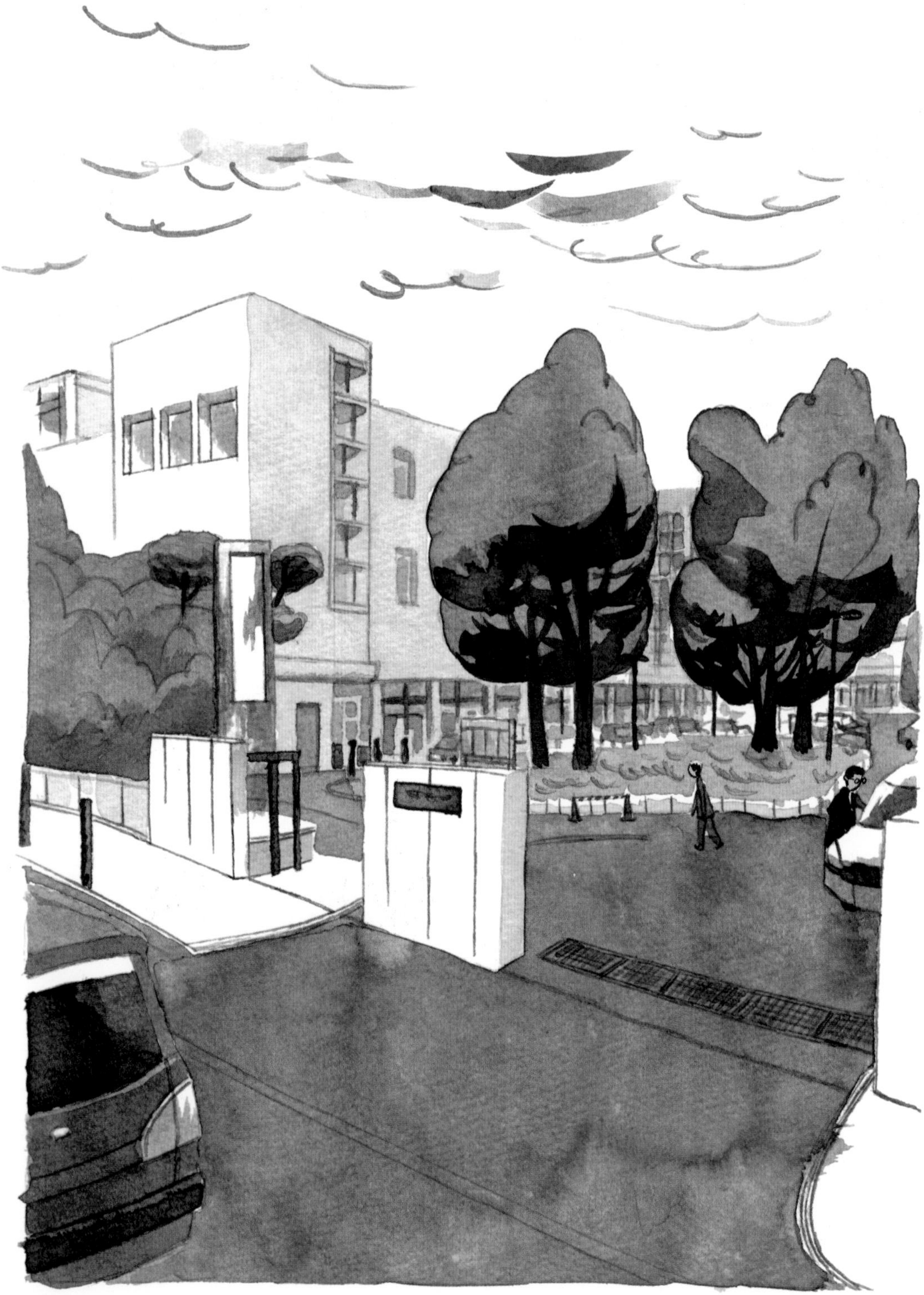

III

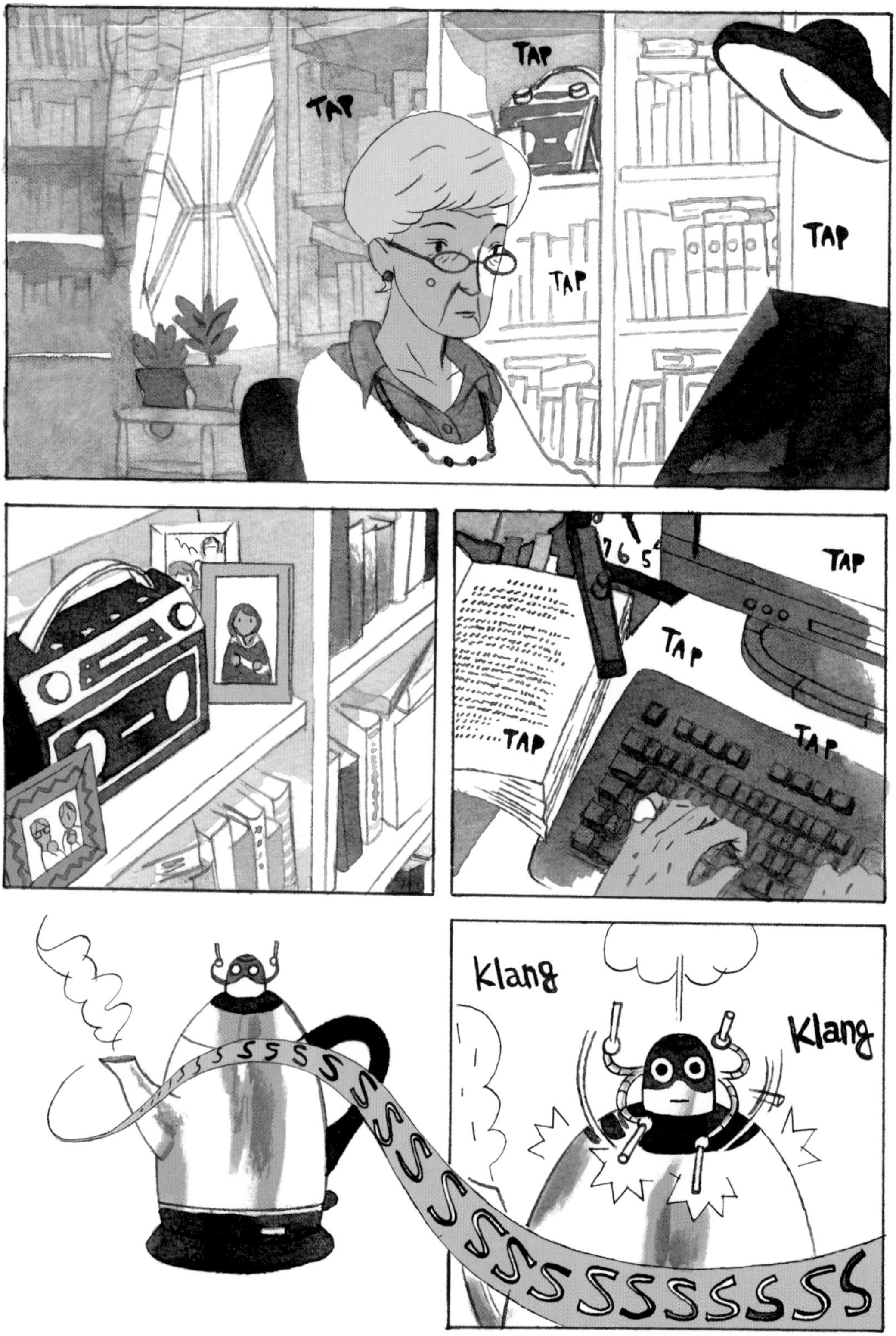
TAP
TAP
TAP
TAP
TAP
TAP
TAP
TAP
Klang
Klang
SSSSSSSSSSSSSSSSSSSSSS

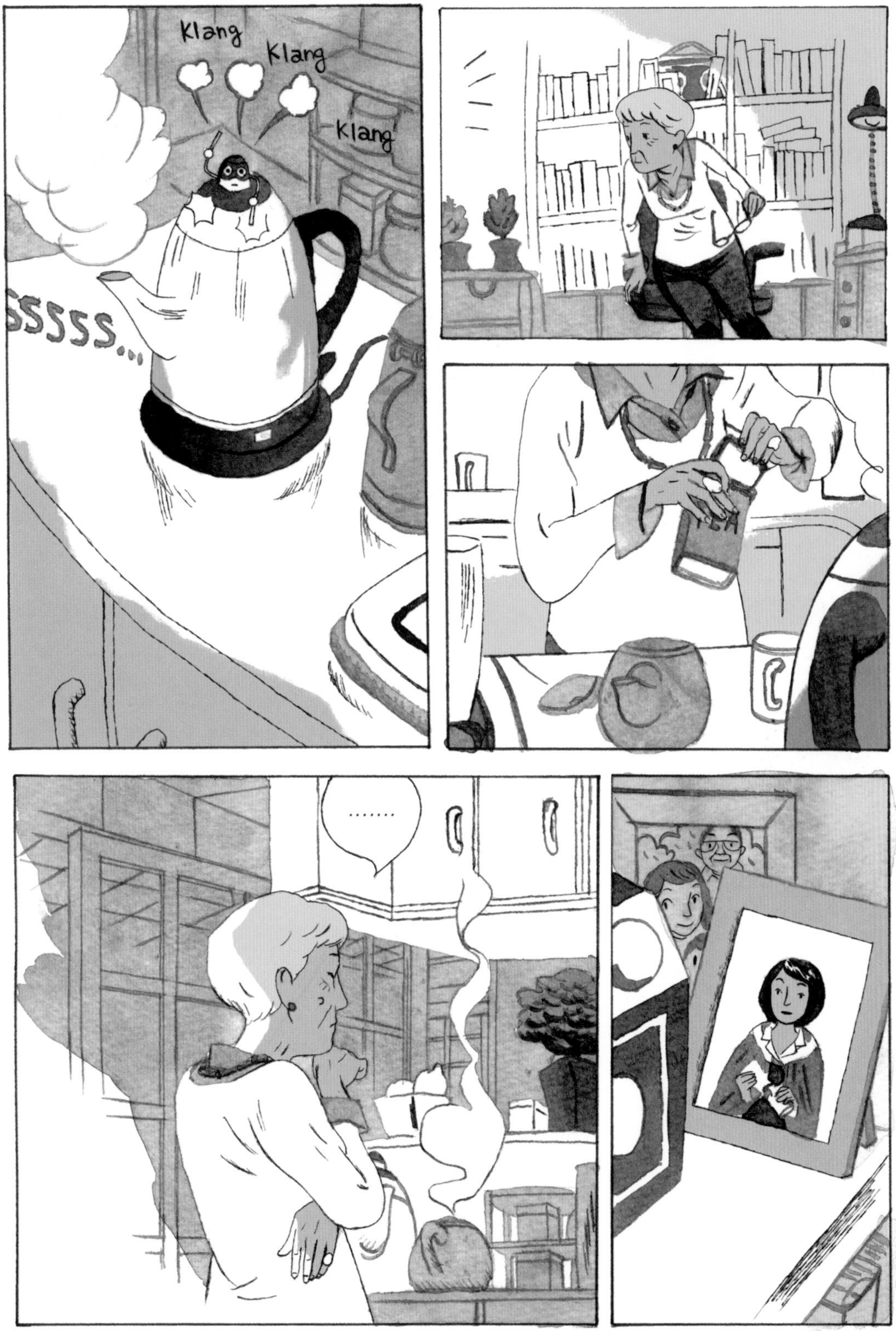
Klang
Klang
Klang
SSSSS...
TEA
....

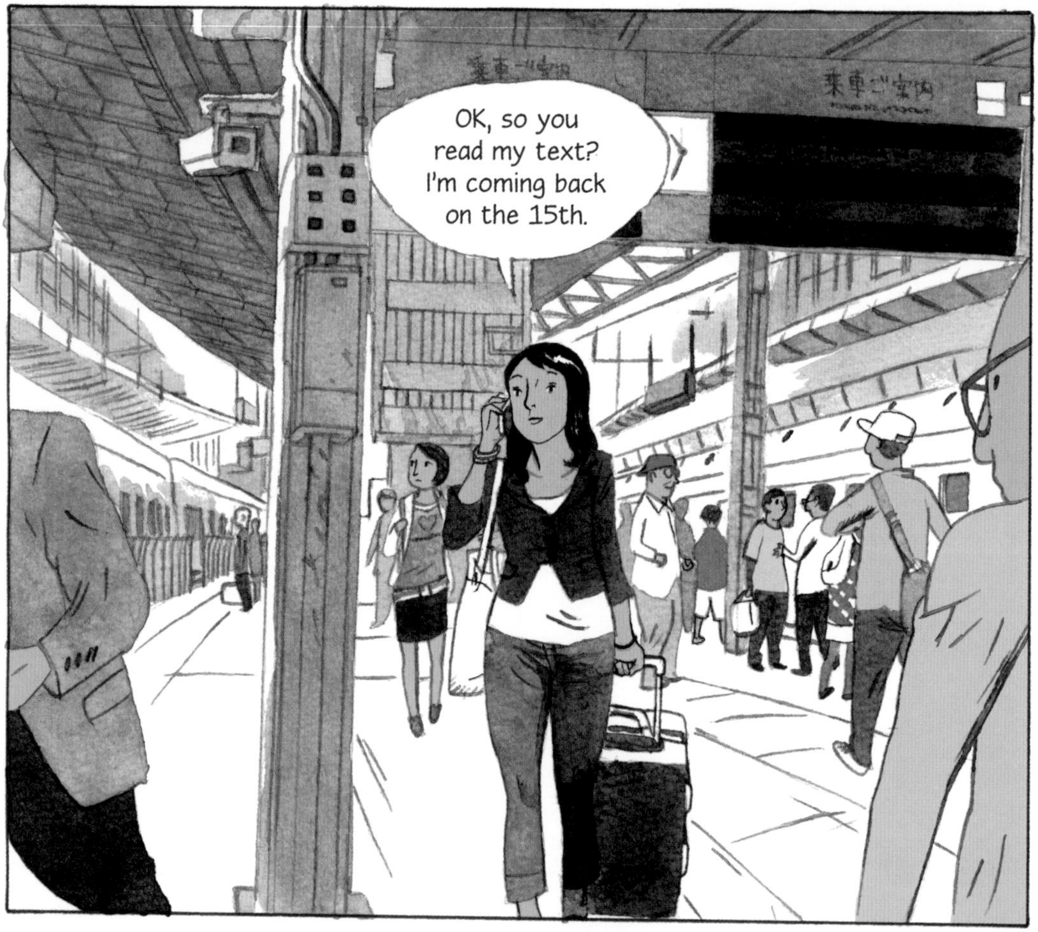
OK, so you read my text? I'm coming back on the 15th.

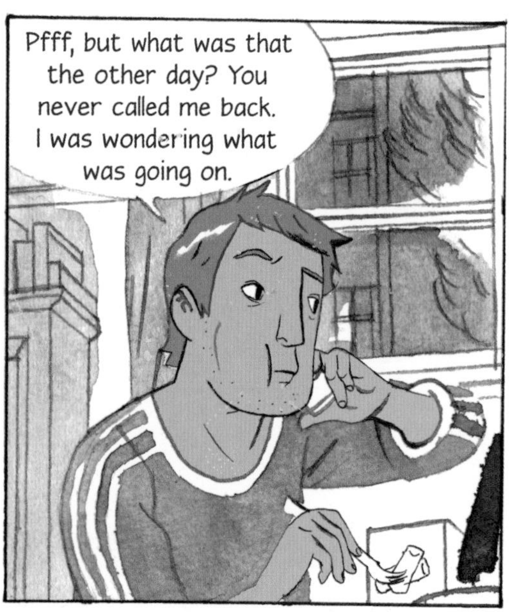
Pfff, but what was that the other day? You never called me back. I was wondering what was going on.

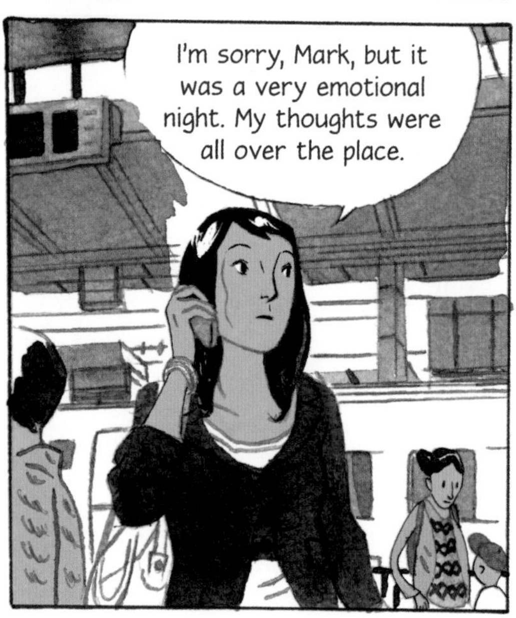
I'm sorry, Mark, but it was a very emotional night. My thoughts were all over the place.

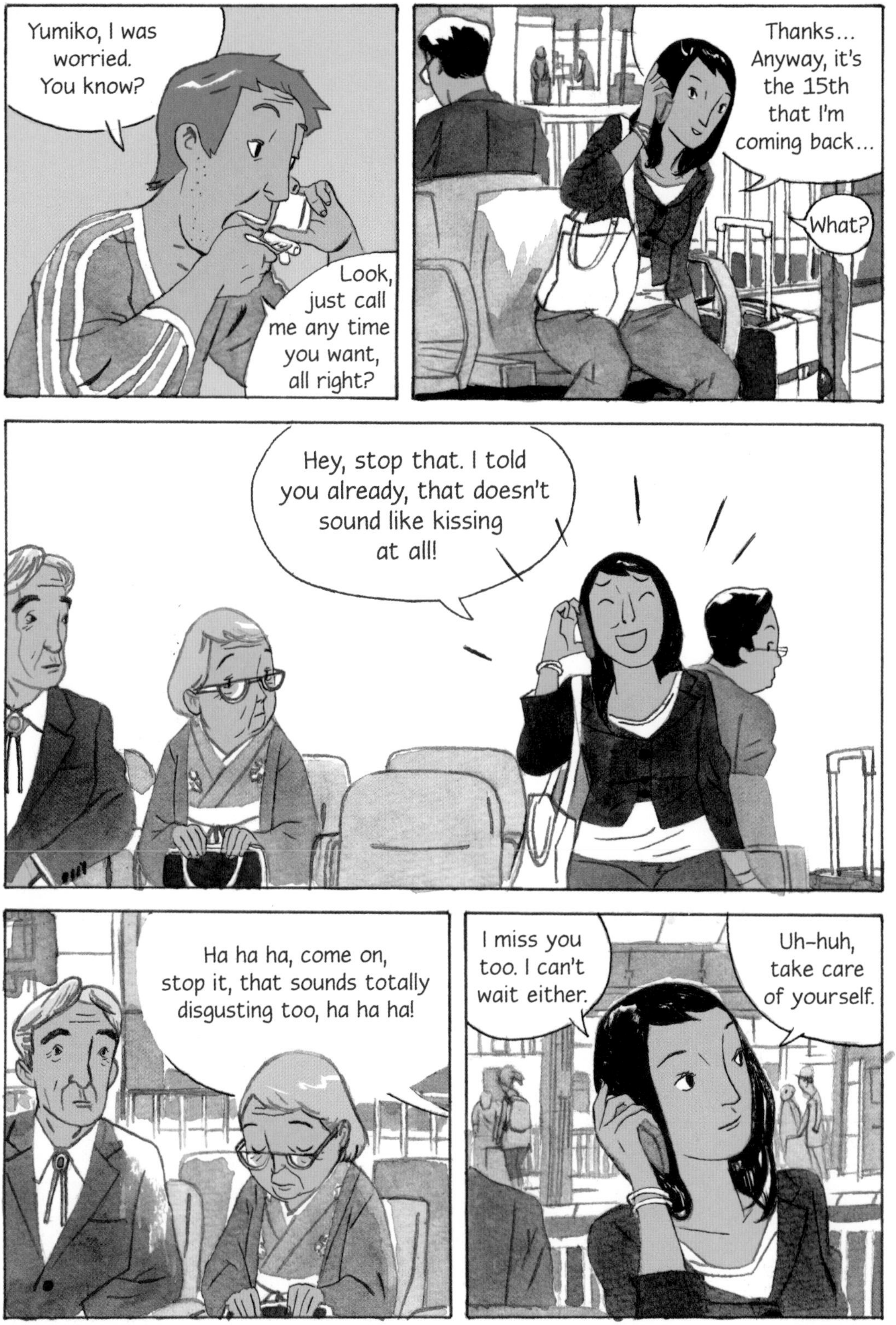
Yumiko, I was worried. You know?
Look, just call me any time you want, all right?
Thanks... Anyway, it's the 15th that I'm coming back...
What?
Hey, stop that. I told you already, that doesn't sound like kissing at all!
Ha ha ha, come on, stop it, that sounds totally disgusting too, ha ha ha!
I miss you too. I can't wait either.
Uh-huh, take care of yourself.

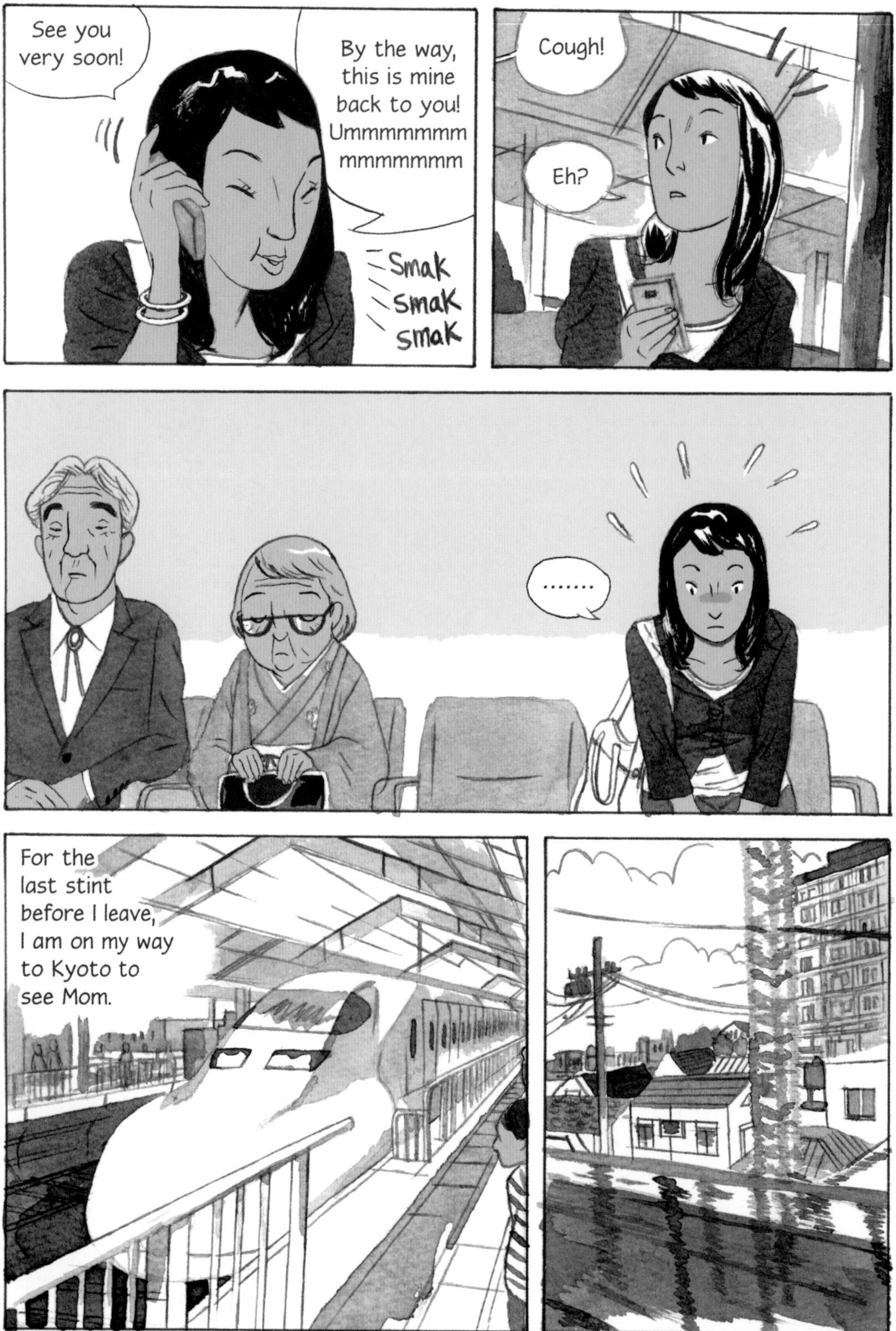
See you very soon!
By the way, this is mine back to you! Ummmmmmm mmmmmmm
Smak
smak
smak
Cough!
Eh?
....
For the last stint before I leave, I am on my way to Kyoto to see Mom.

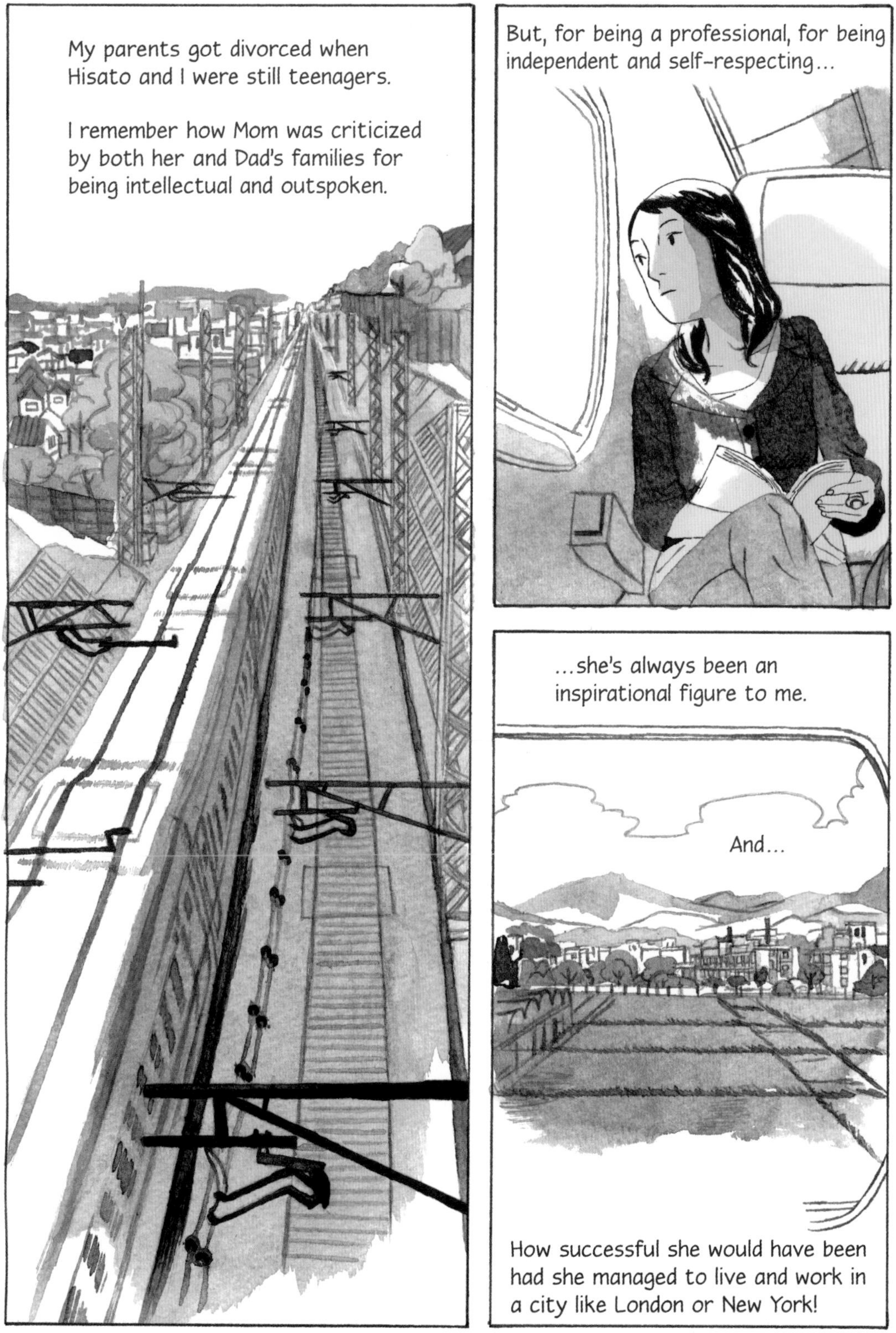
My parents got divorced when Hisato and I were still teenagers.
I remember how Mom was criticized by both her and Dad's families for being intellectual and outspoken.
But, for being a professional, for being independent and self-respecting...
...she's always been an inspirational figure to me.
And...
How successful she would have been had she managed to live and work in a city like London or New York!

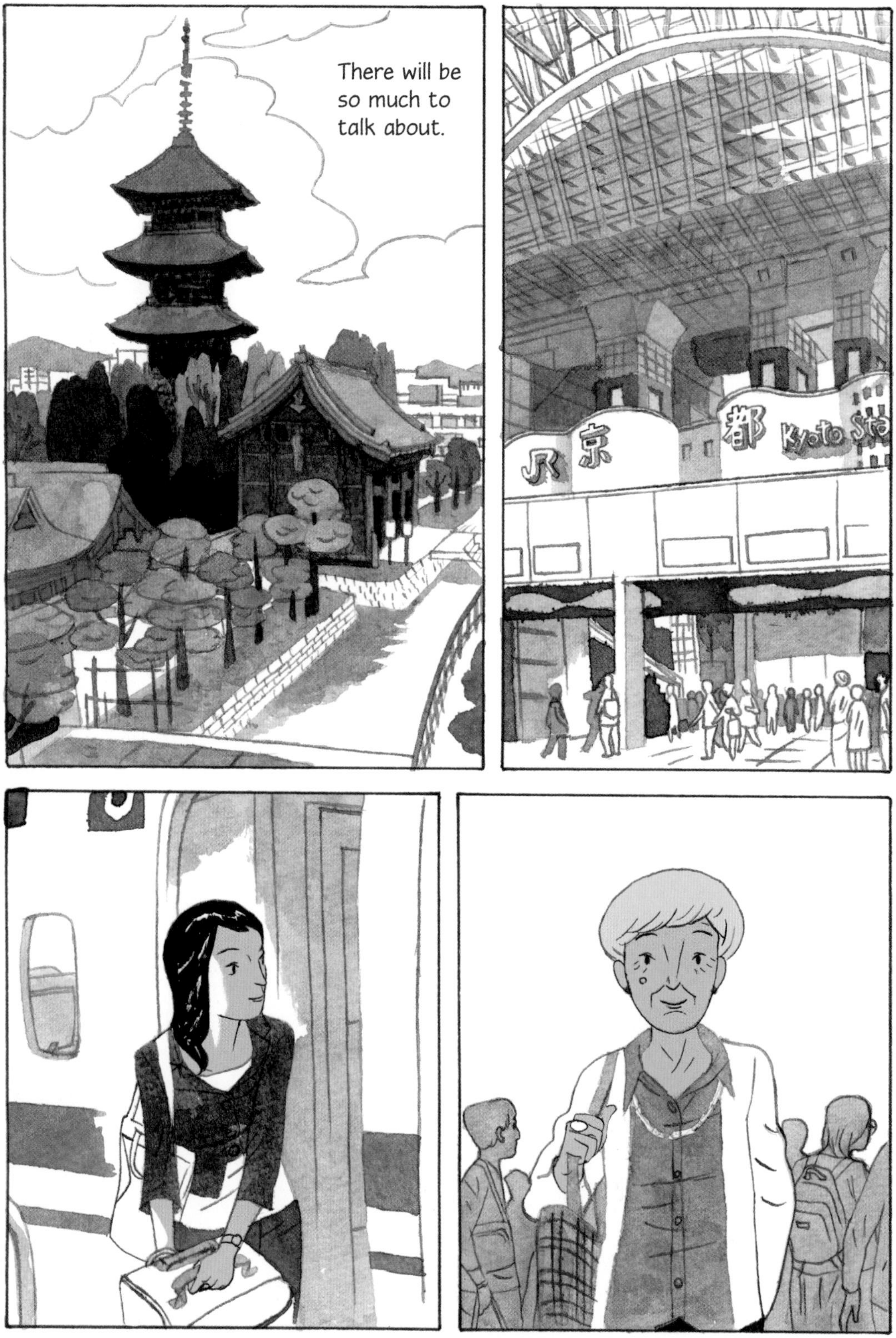
There will be
so much to
talk about.
京
都

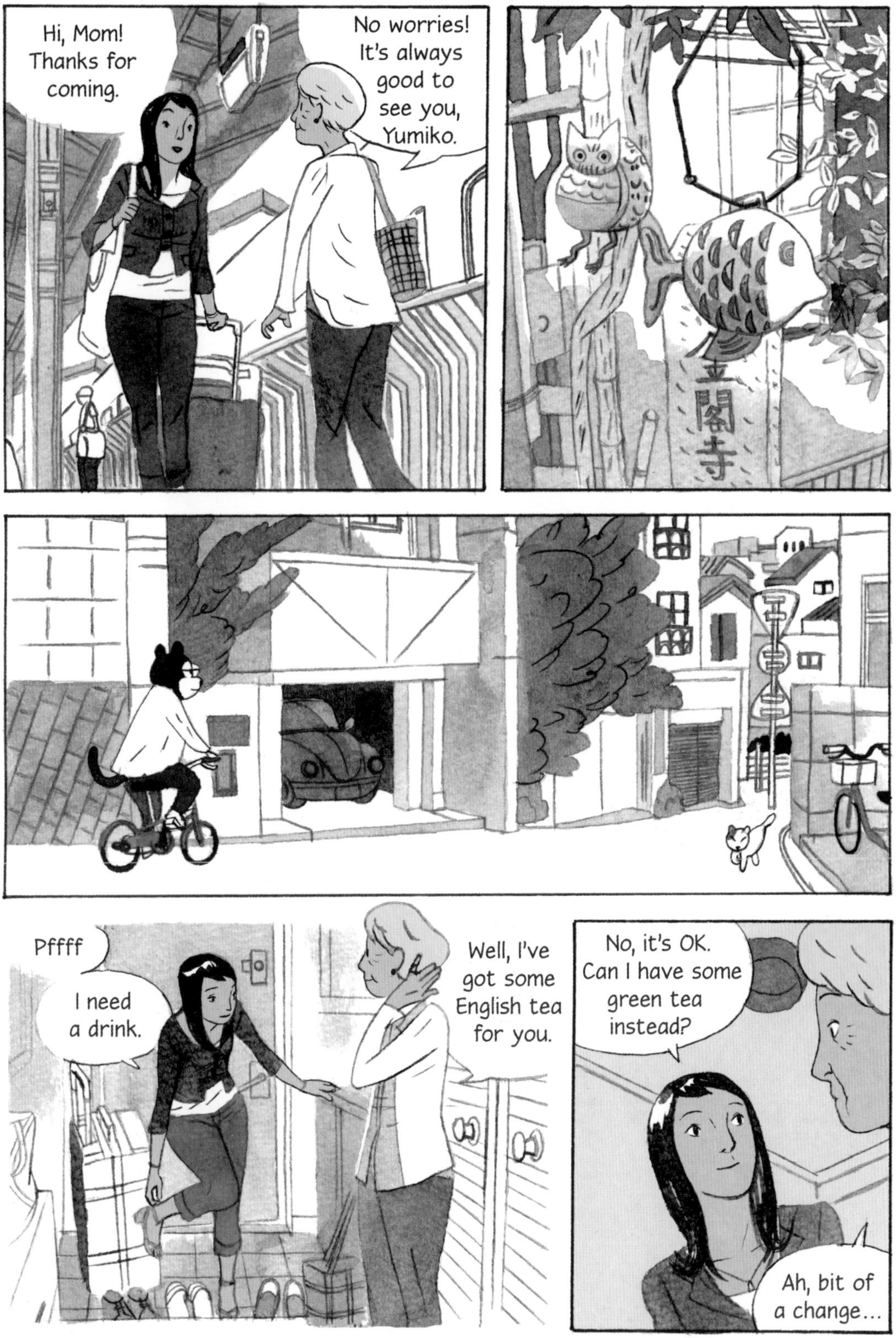
Hi, Mom! Thanks for coming.
No worries! It's always good to see you, Yumiko.
立閣寺
Pffff
I need a drink.
Well, I've got some English tea for you.
No, it's OK. Can I have some green tea instead?
Ah, bit of a change...

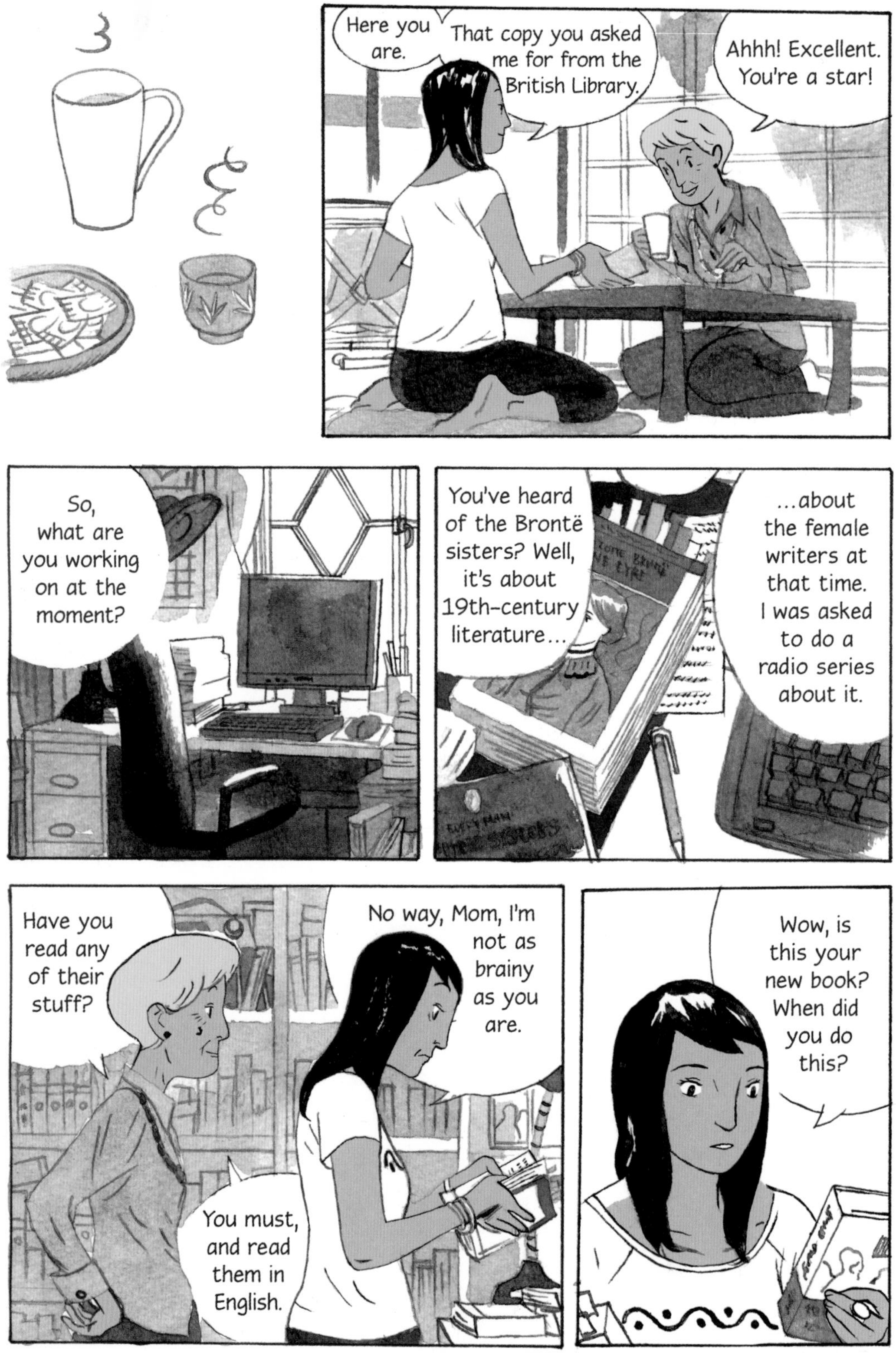
Here you are.
That copy you asked me for from the British Library.
Ahhh! Excellent. You're a star!
So, what are you working on at the moment?
You've heard of the Brontë sisters? Well, it's about 19th-century literature...
...about the female writers at that time. I was asked to do a radio series about it.
Have you read any of their stuff?
No way, Mom, I'm not as brainy as you are.
You must, and read them in English.
Wow, is this your new book? When did you do this?

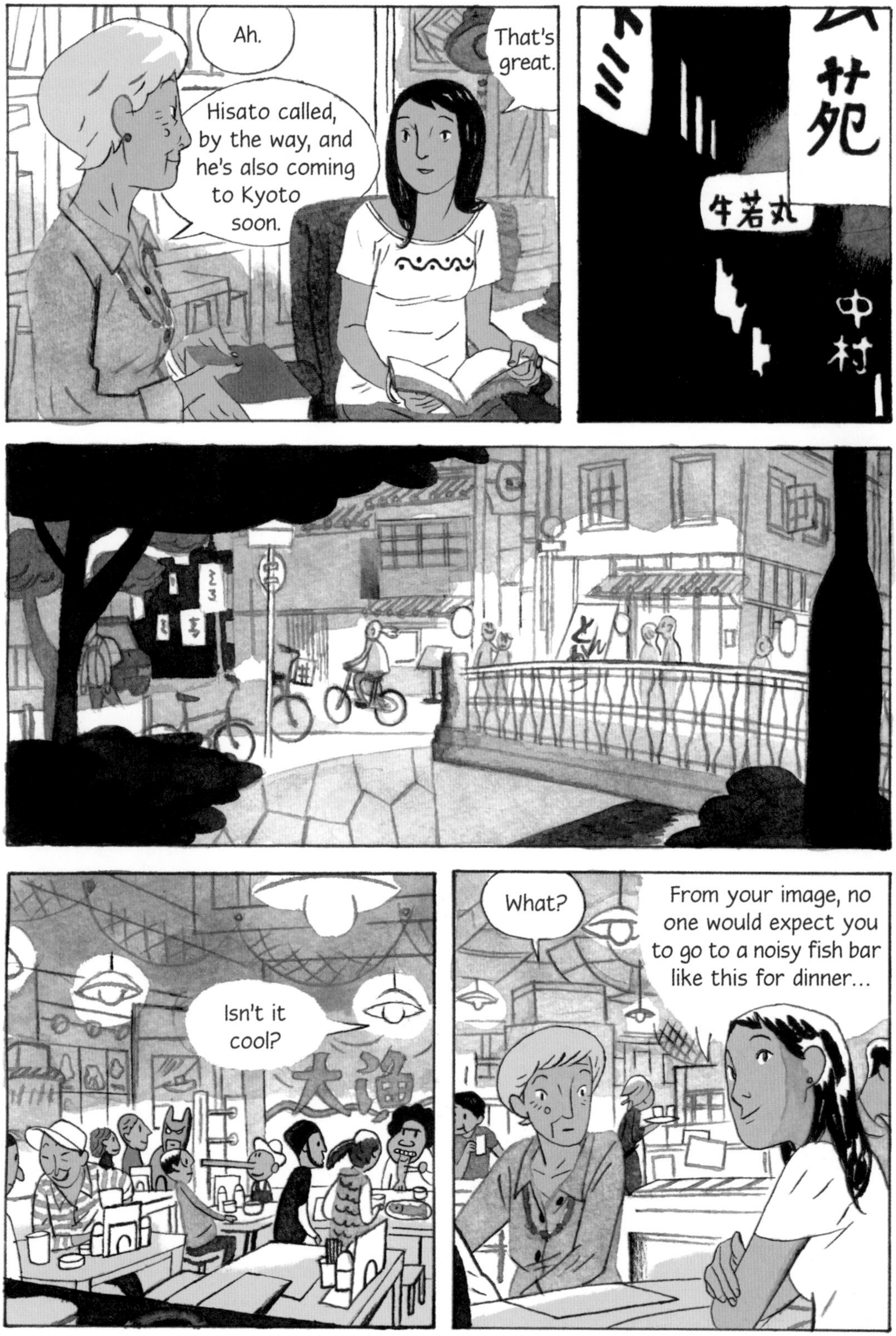
Ah.
Hisato called, by the way, and he's also coming to Kyoto soon.
That's great.
苑
牛若丸
中村
Isn't it cool?
大漁
What?
From your image, no one would expect you to go to a noisy fish bar like this for dinner...

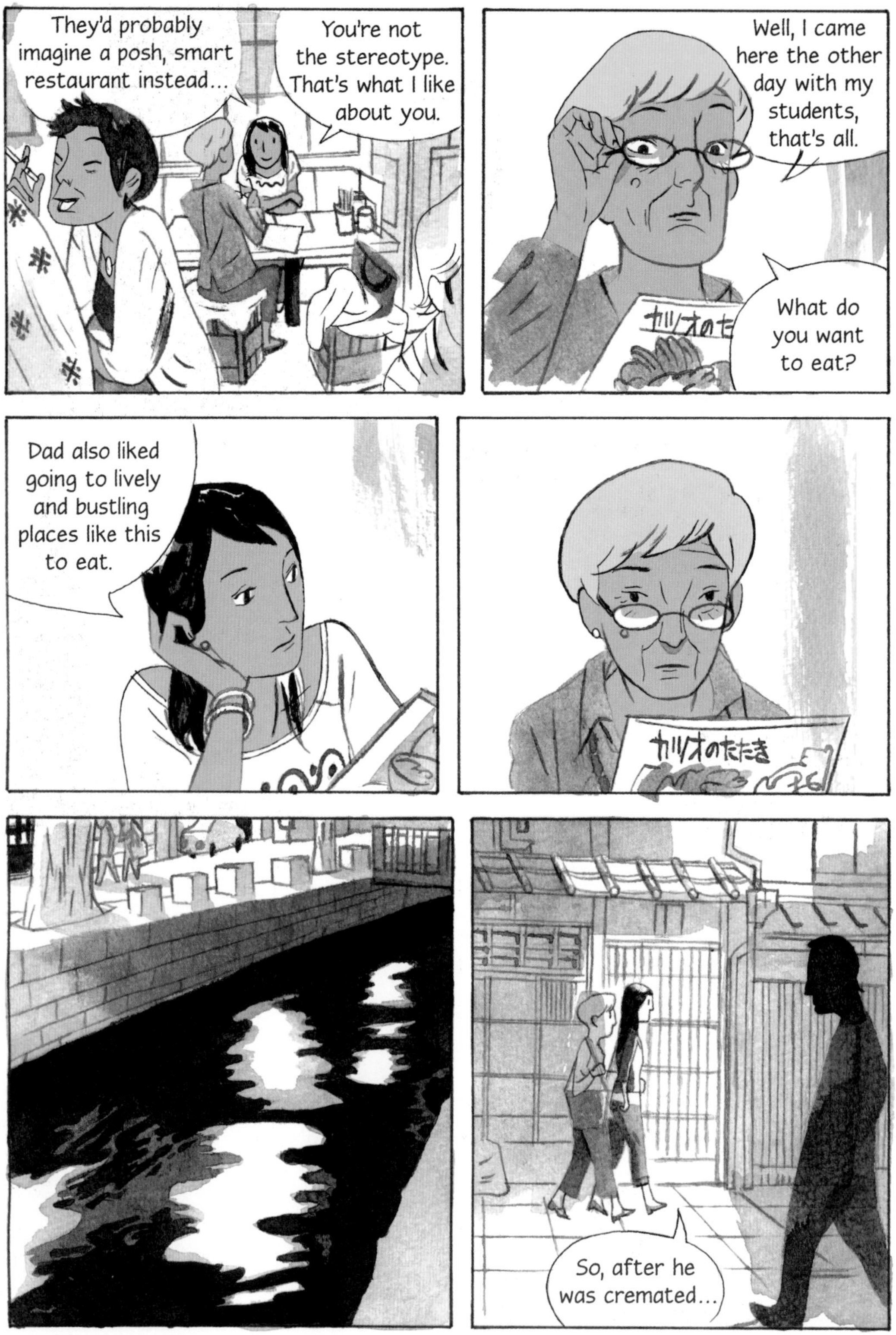
They'd probably imagine a posh, smart restaurant instead...
You're not the stereotype. That's what I like about you.
Well, I came here the other day with my students, that's all.
カツオのた
What do you want to eat?
Dad also liked going to lively and bustling places like this to eat.
カツオのたたき
So, after he was cremated...

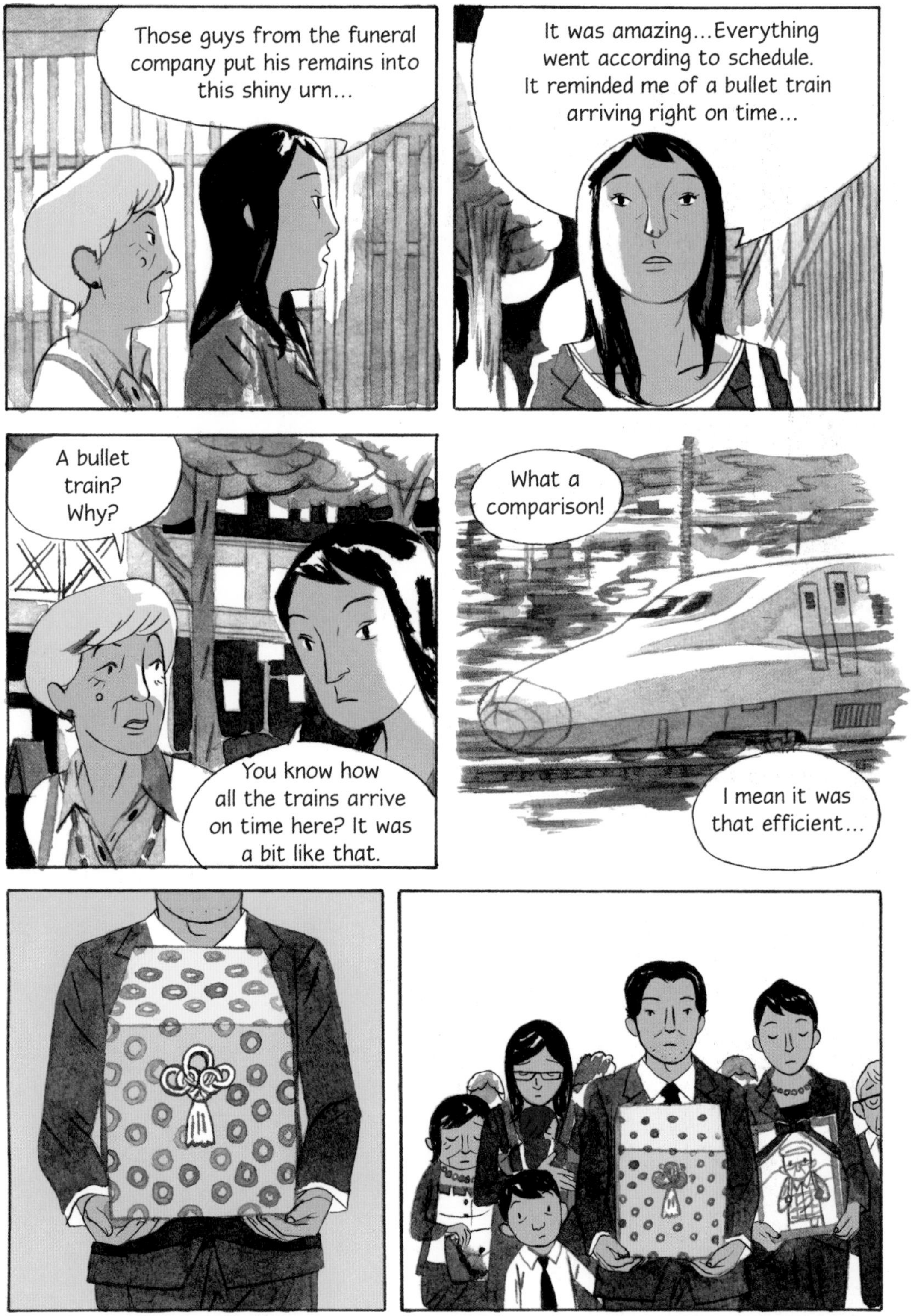

Those guys from the funeral company put his remains into this shiny urn...
It was amazing...Everything went according to schedule. It reminded me of a bullet train arriving right on time...
A bullet train? Why?
You know how all the trains arrive on time here? It was a bit like that.
What a comparison!
I mean it was that efficient...

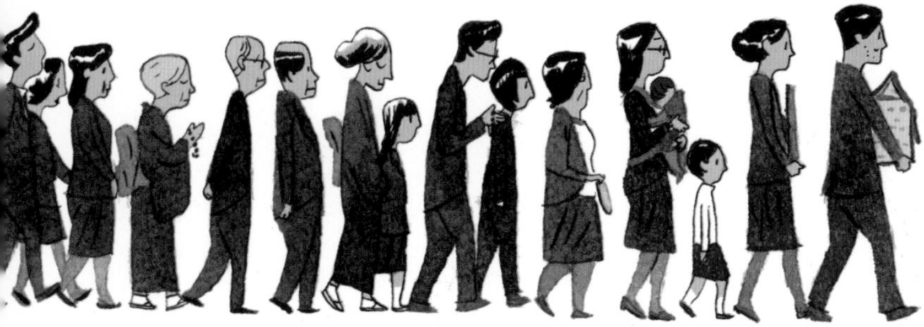

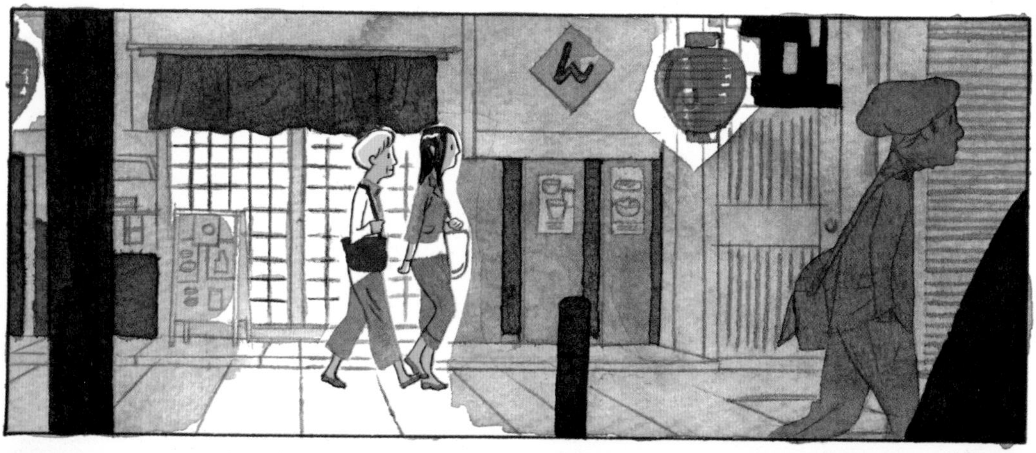

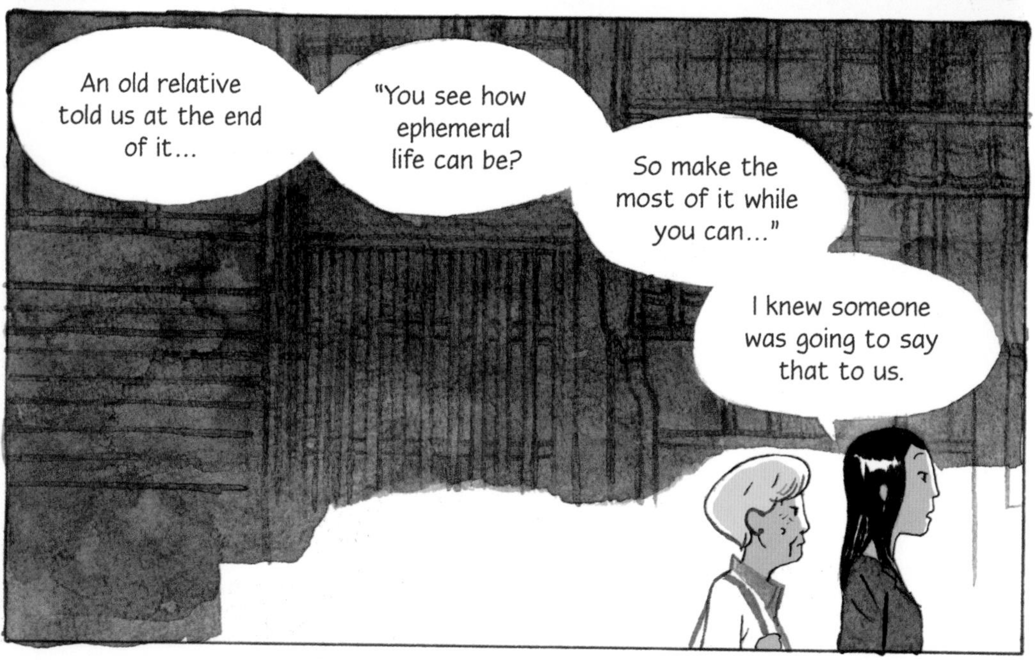
An old relative told us at the end of it...
"You see how ephemeral life can be?
So make the most of it while you can..."
I knew someone was going to say that to us.

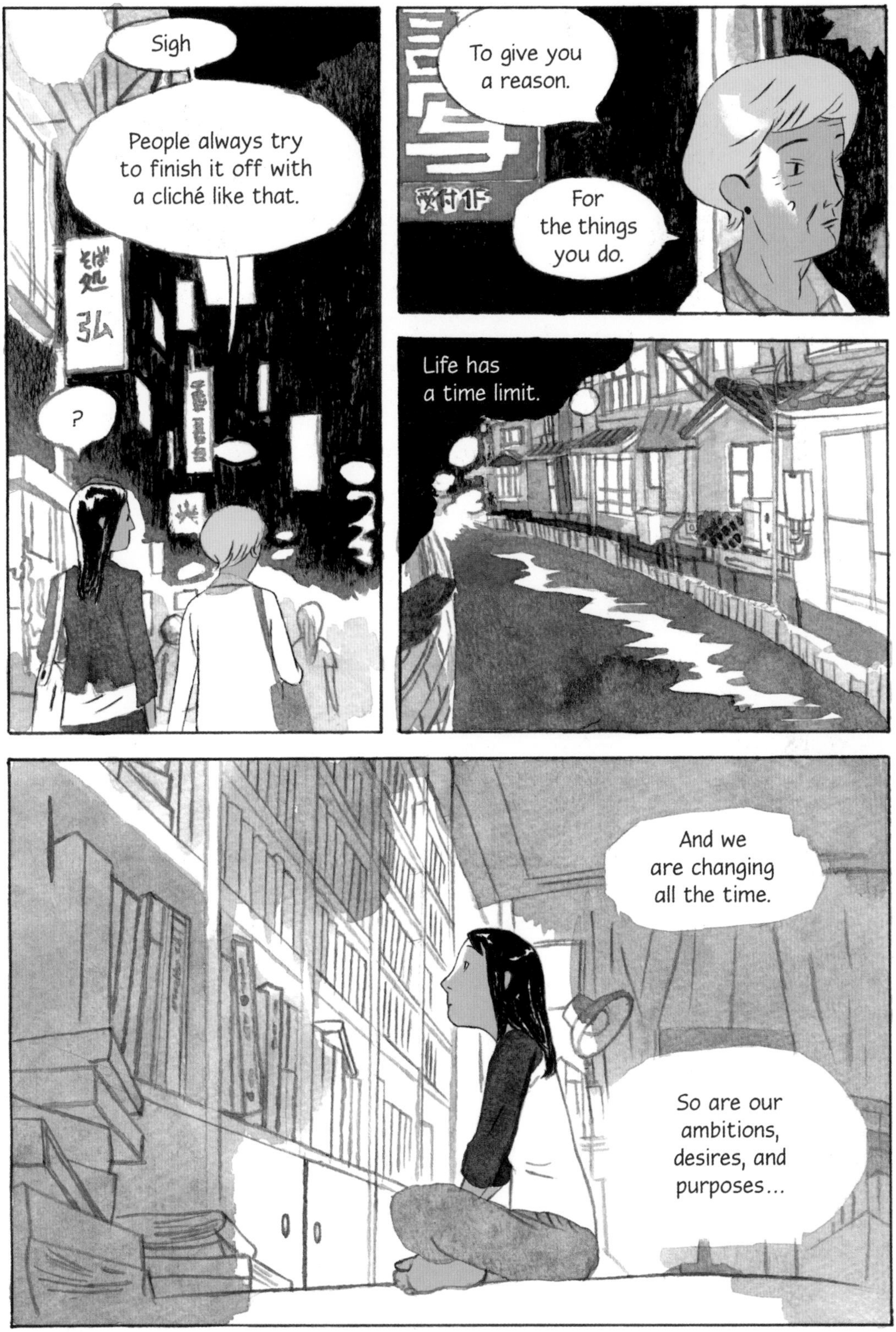

Sigh
People always try to finish it off with a cliché like that.
そば処
弘
?
To give you a reason.
受付1F
For the things you do.
Life has a time limit.
And we are changing all the time.
So are our ambitions, desires, and purposes...

The important thing is...

...to find something that never changes in you.

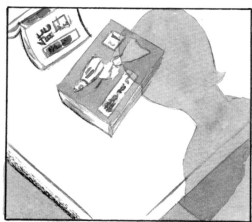

What books are you reading? Are they about Noh theater?

Those are your books, Mom.

I read them ages ago.

I must have been in high school. I suddenly remembered them the other day...

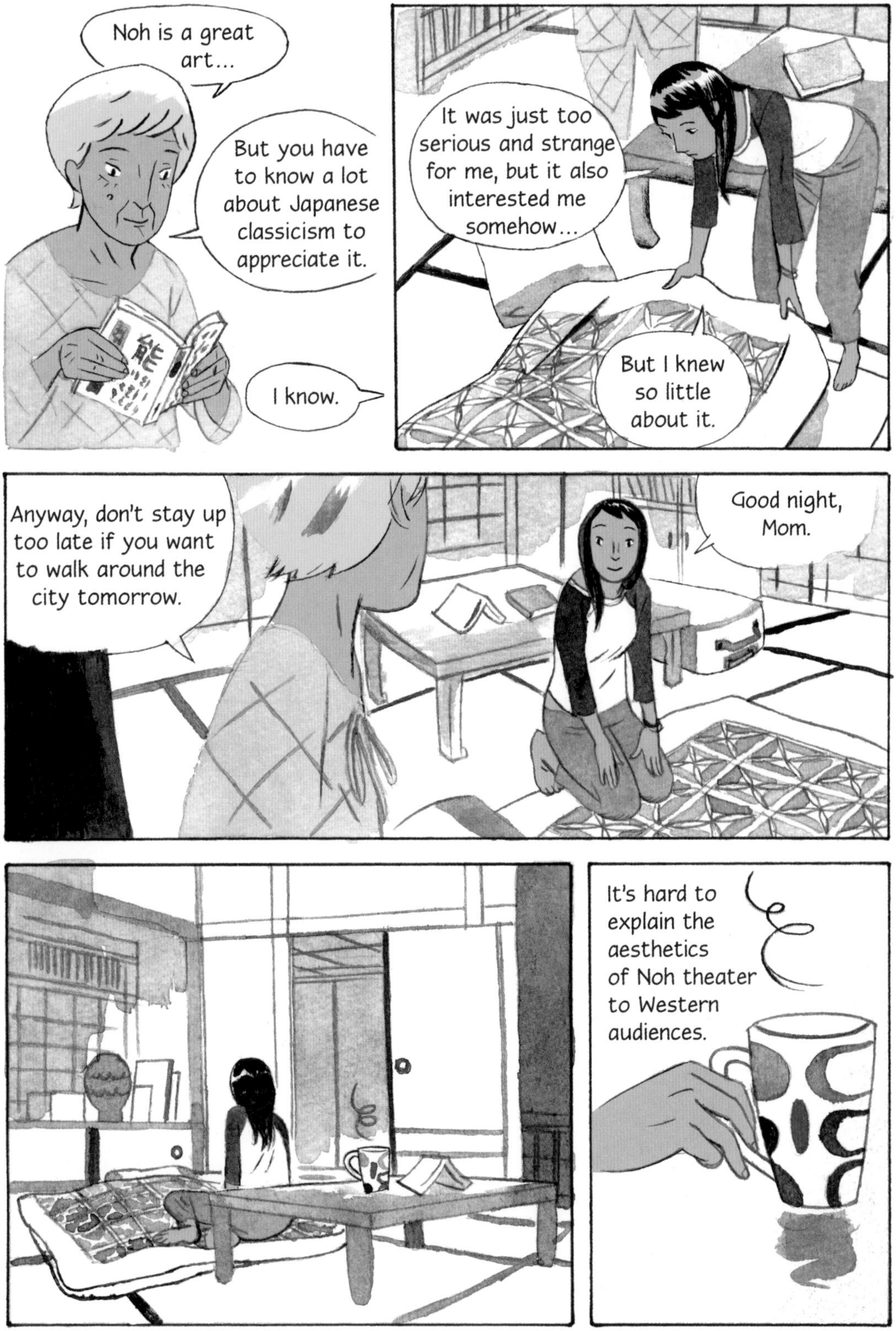
Noh is a great art...
But you have to know a lot about Japanese classicism to appreciate it.
能
I know.
It was just too serious and strange for me, but it also interested me somehow...
But I knew so little about it.
Anyway, don't stay up too late if you want to walk around the city tomorrow.
Good night, Mom.
It's hard to explain the aesthetics of Noh theater to Western audiences.

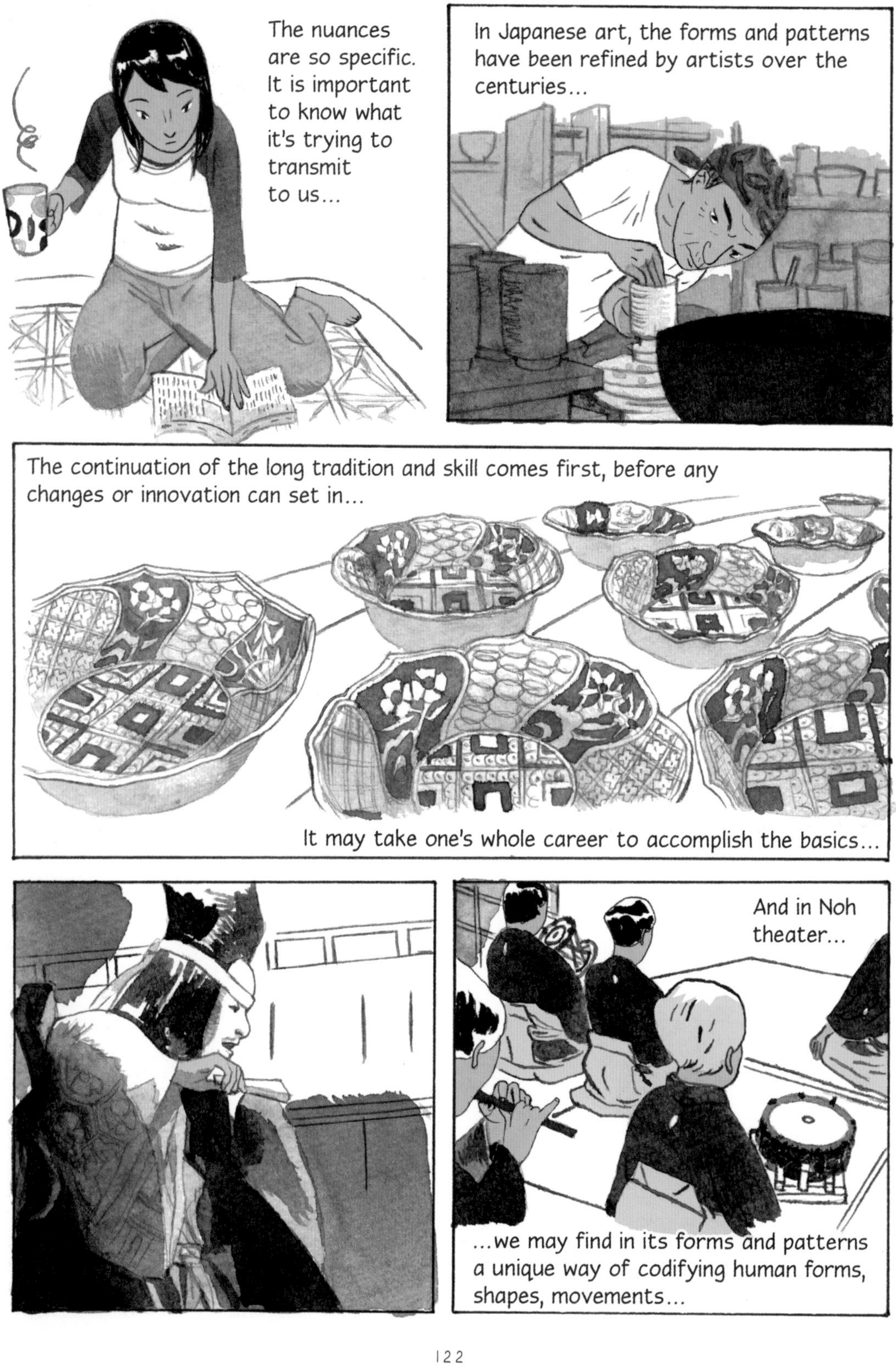
The nuances are so specific. It is important to know what it's trying to transmit to us...
In Japanese art, the forms and patterns have been refined by artists over the centuries...
The continuation of the long tradition and skill comes first, before any changes or innovation can set in...
It may take one's whole career to accomplish the basics...
And in Noh theater...
...we may find in its forms and patterns a unique way of codifying human forms, shapes, movements...

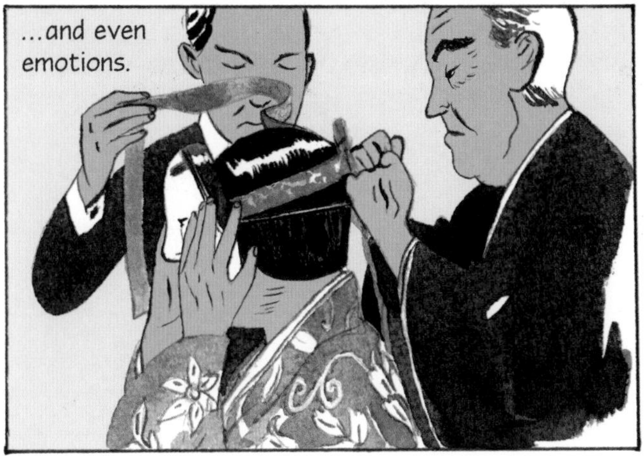
...and even emotions.

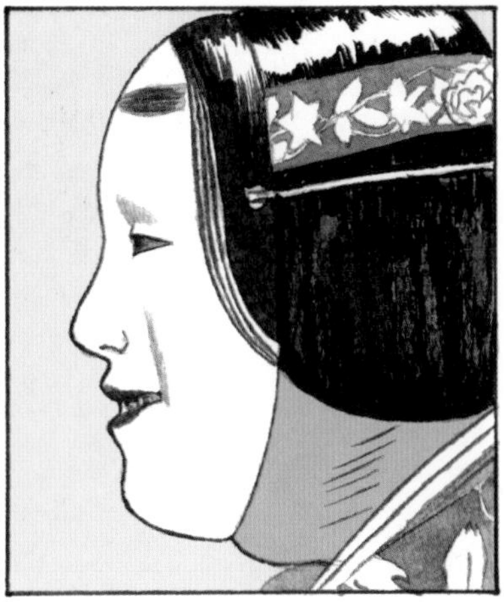

This is a transformation in a ritual sense, to be totally possessed by the theater, or to be subject to it.

In order to express its idea of a transcendental world, one must put one's heart and mind in total resonance with the theatrical role.

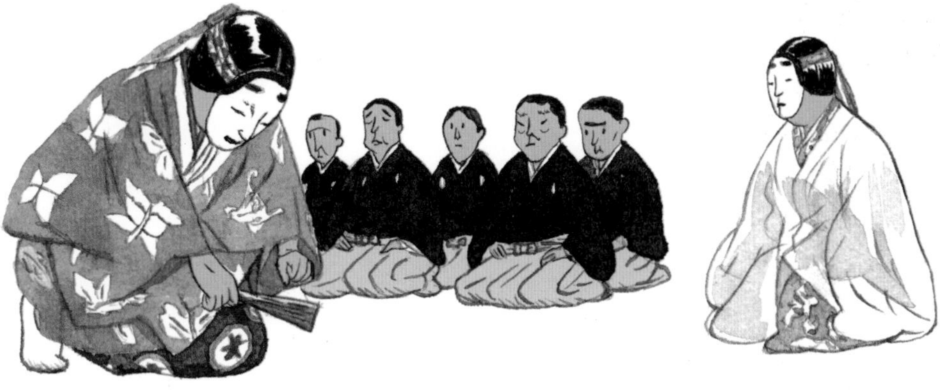

And in the process, all the natural traits are SIMPLIFIED.

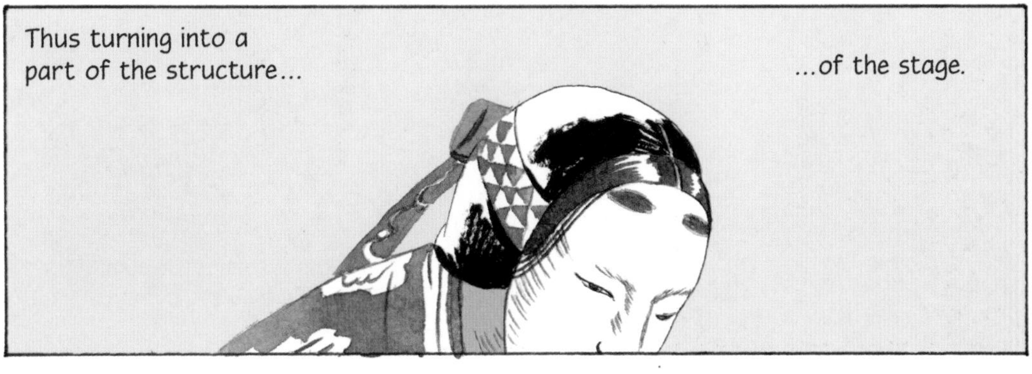
Thus turning into a part of the structure...
...of the stage.

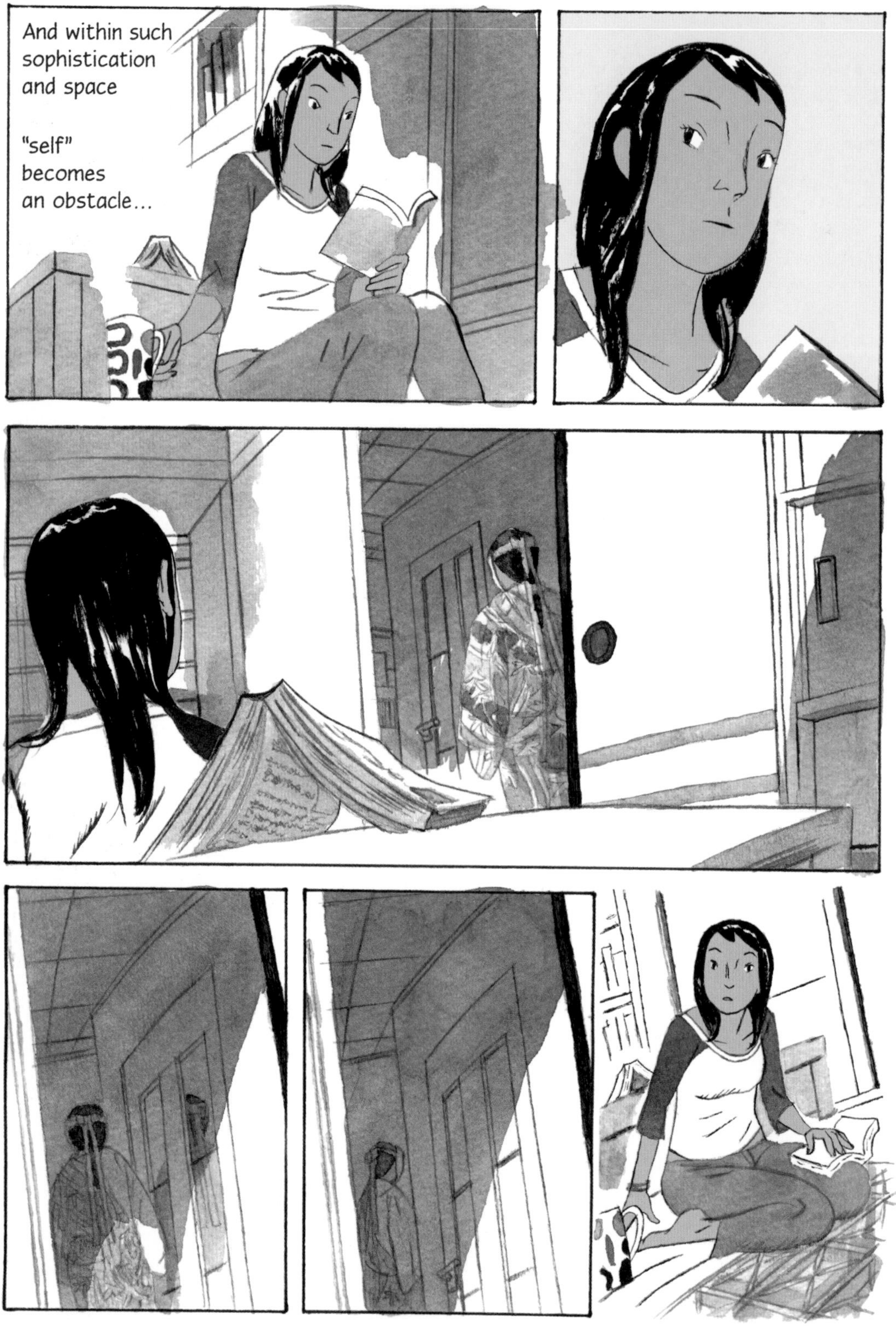
And within such
sophistication
and space

"self"
becomes
an obstacle...

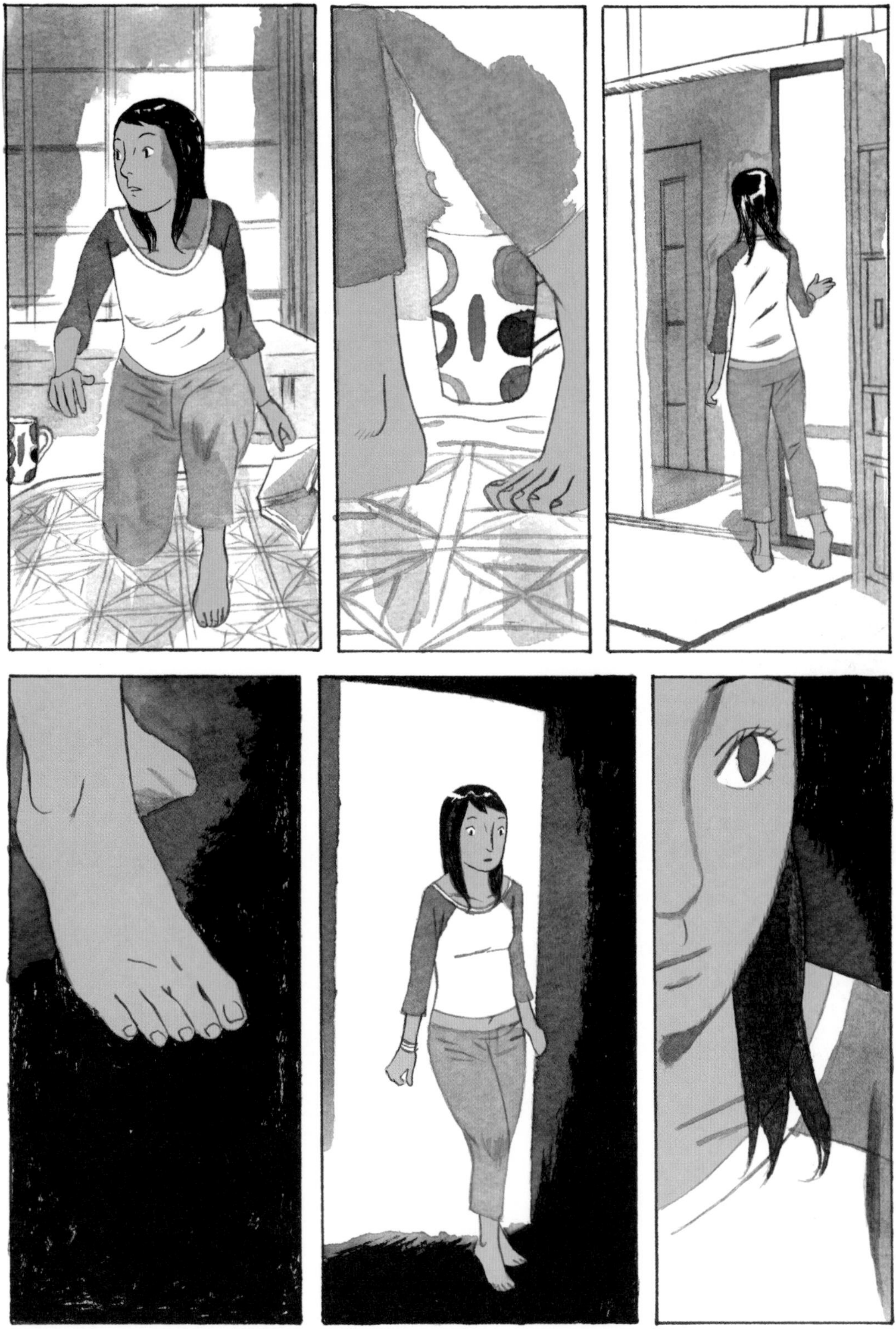

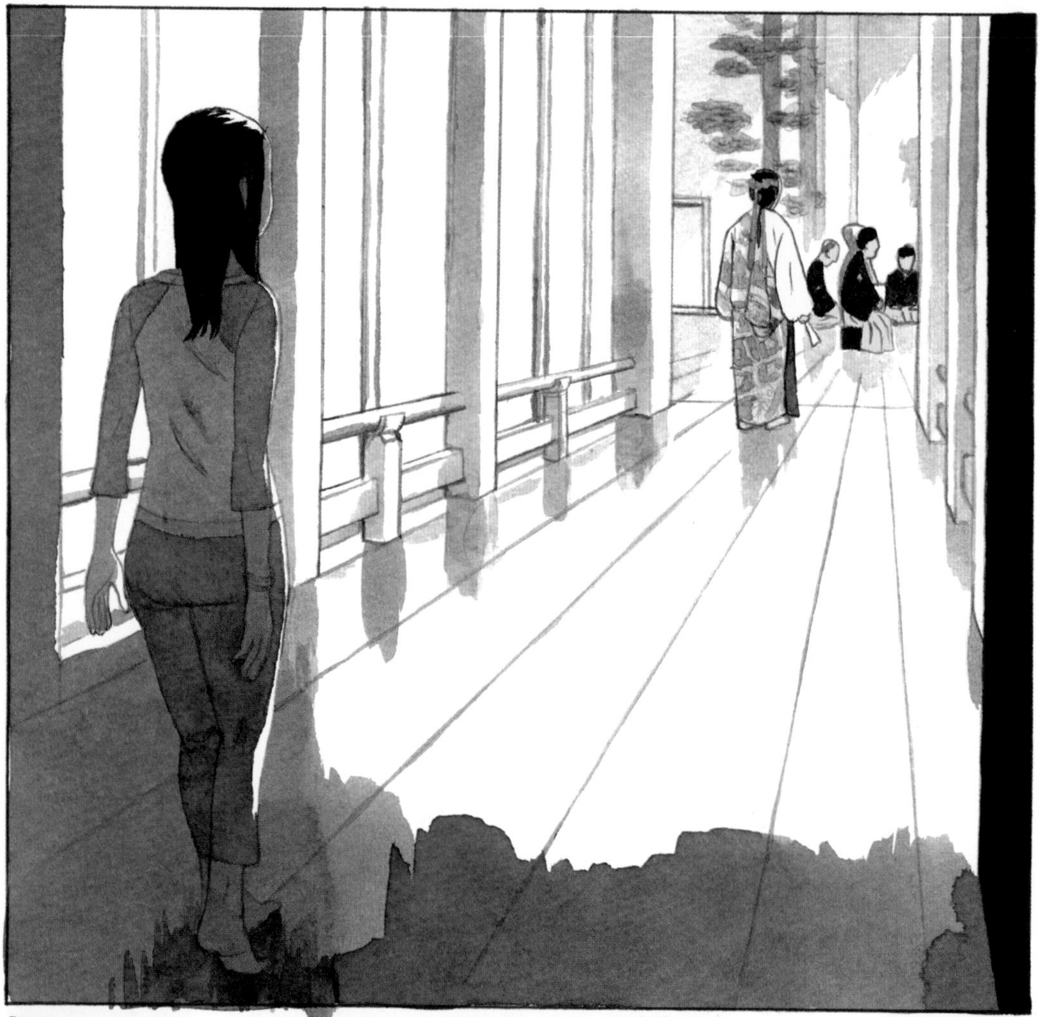

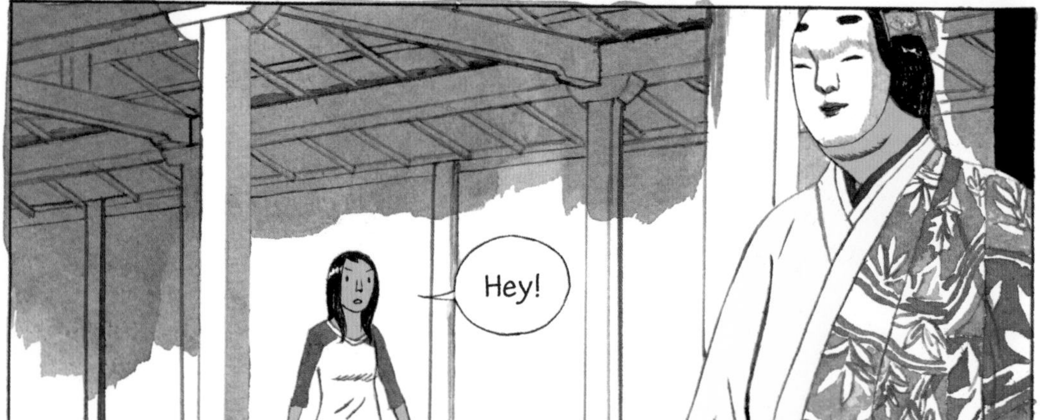
Hey!

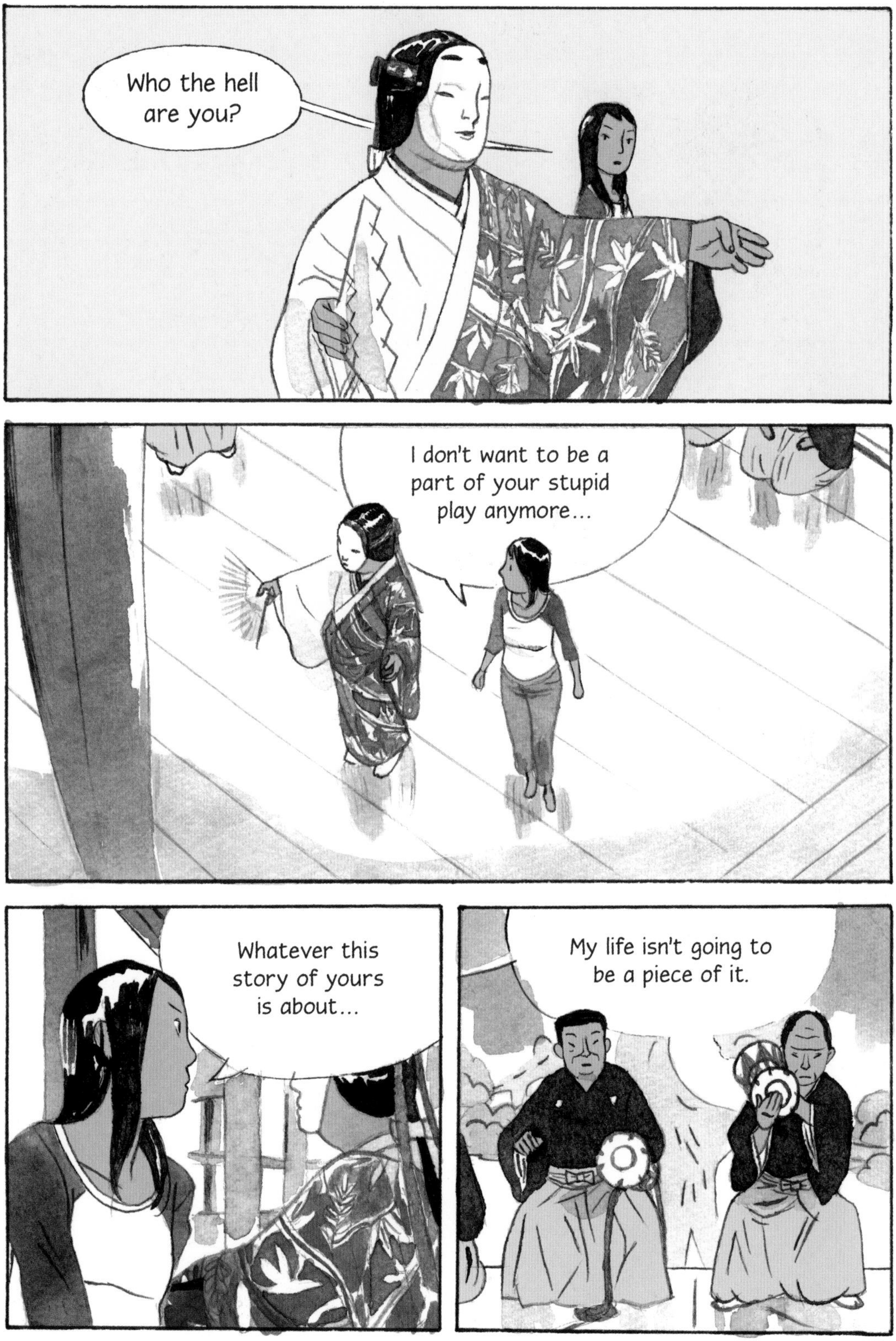
Who the hell are you?
I don't want to be a part of your stupid play anymore...
Whatever this story of yours is about...
My life isn't going to be a piece of it.

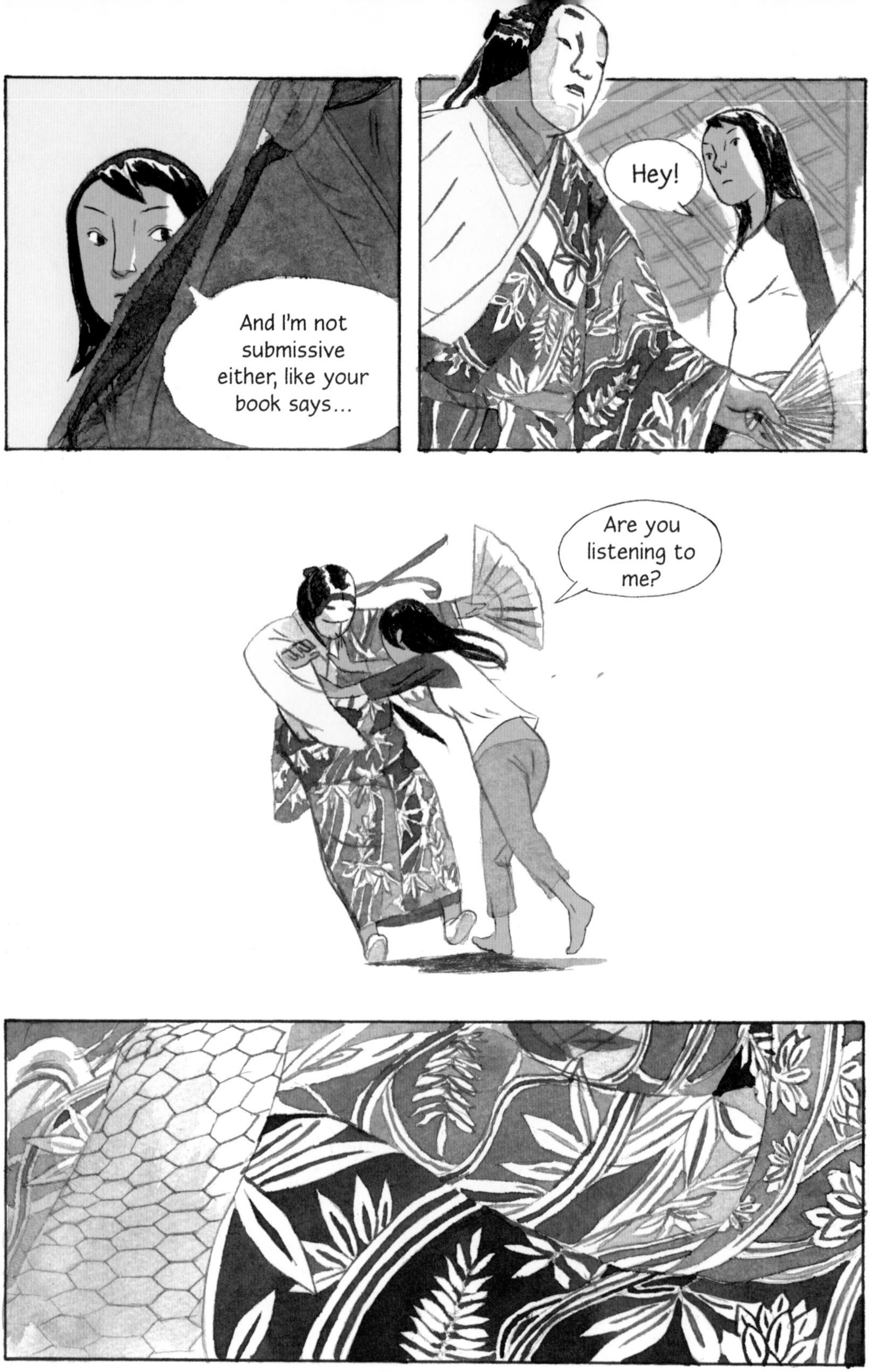
And I'm not submissive either, like your book says...
Hey!
Are you listening to me?

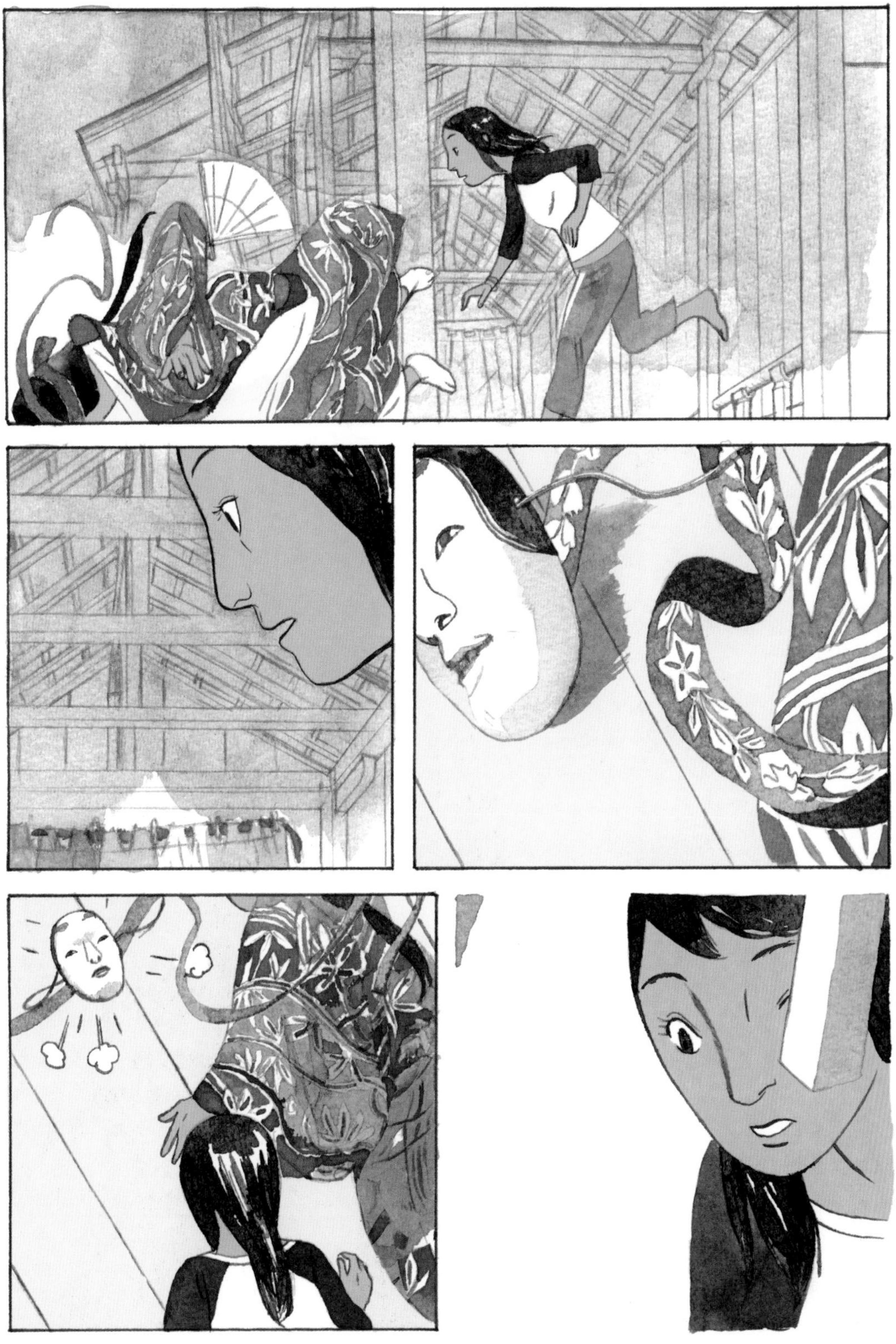

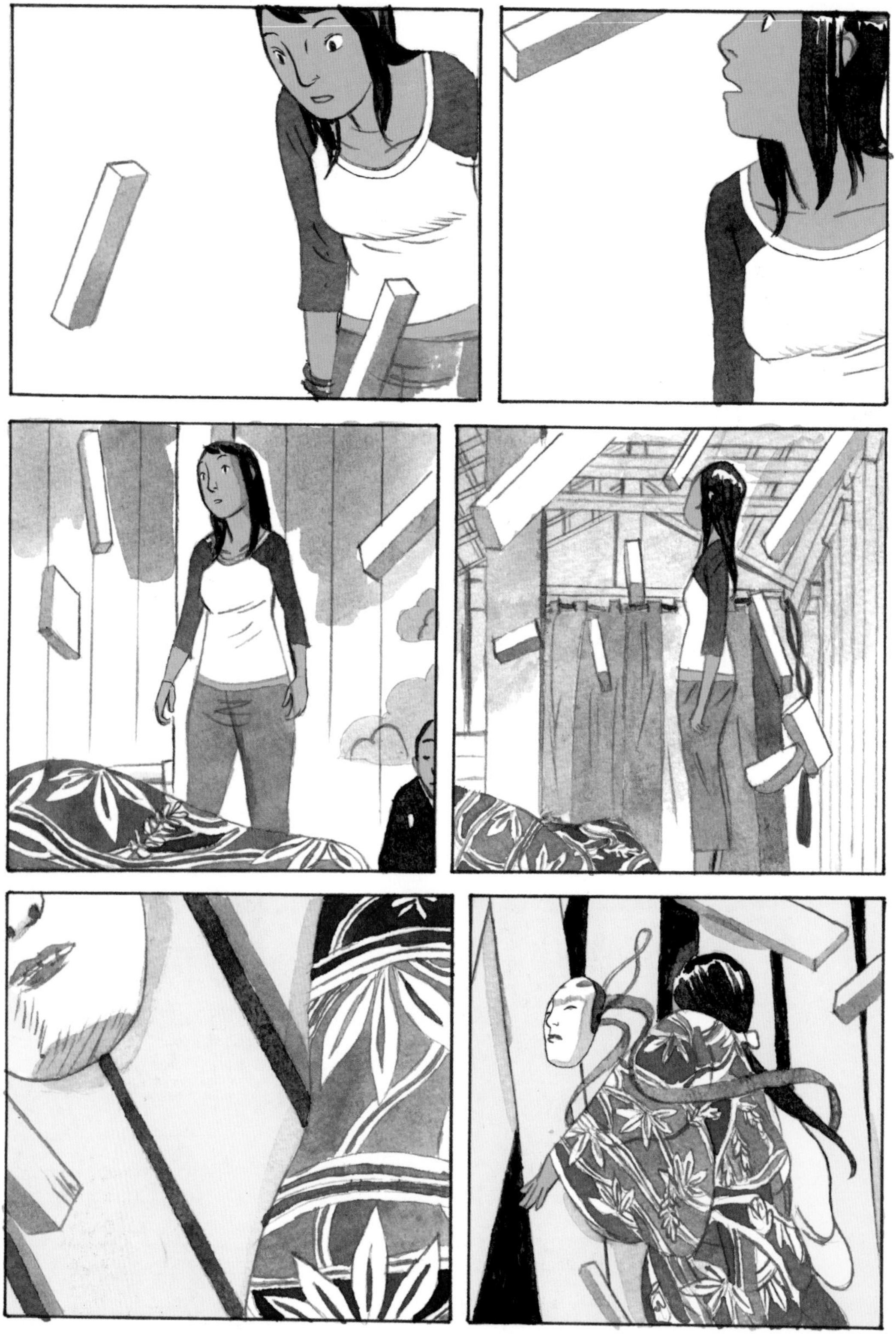

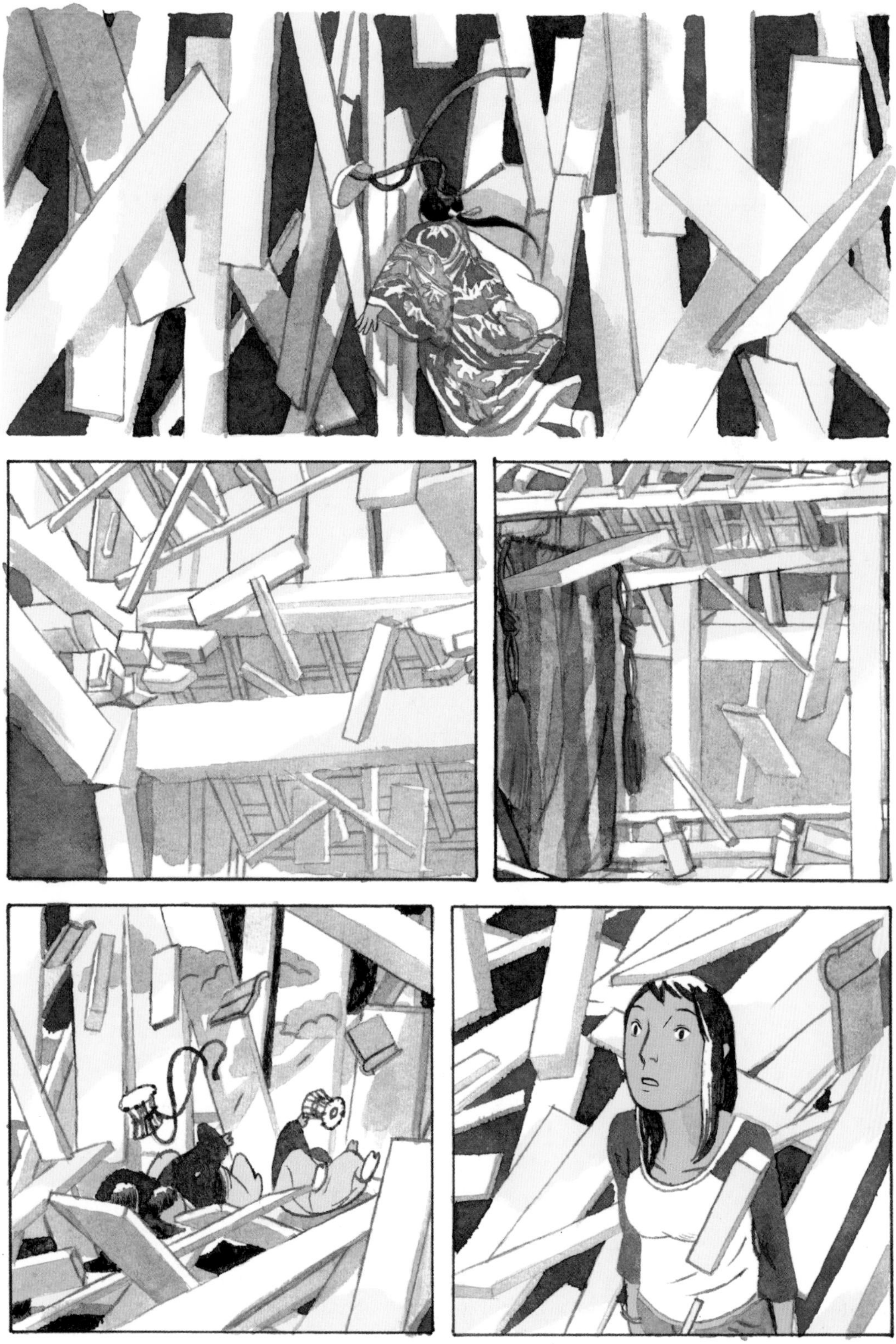

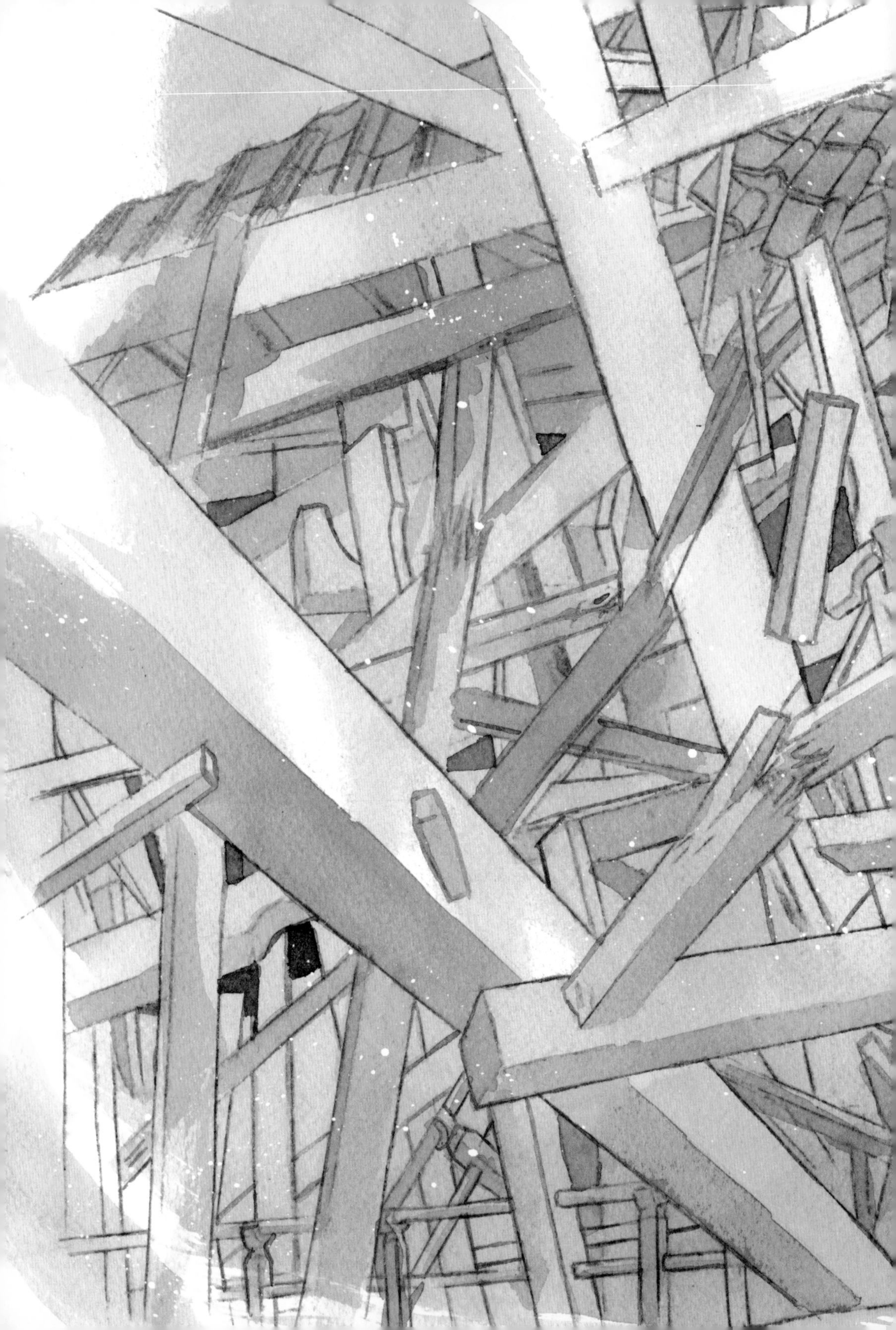

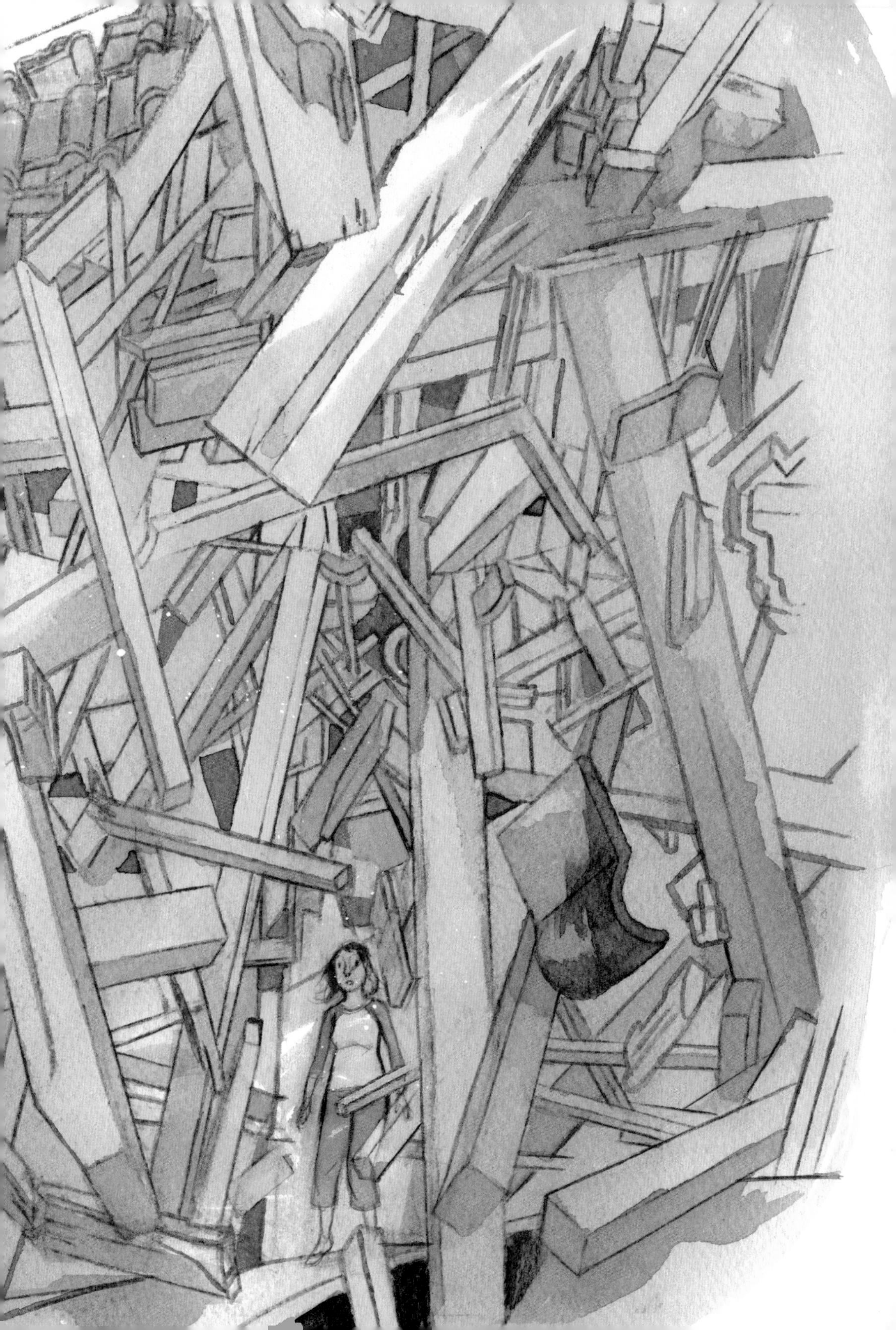

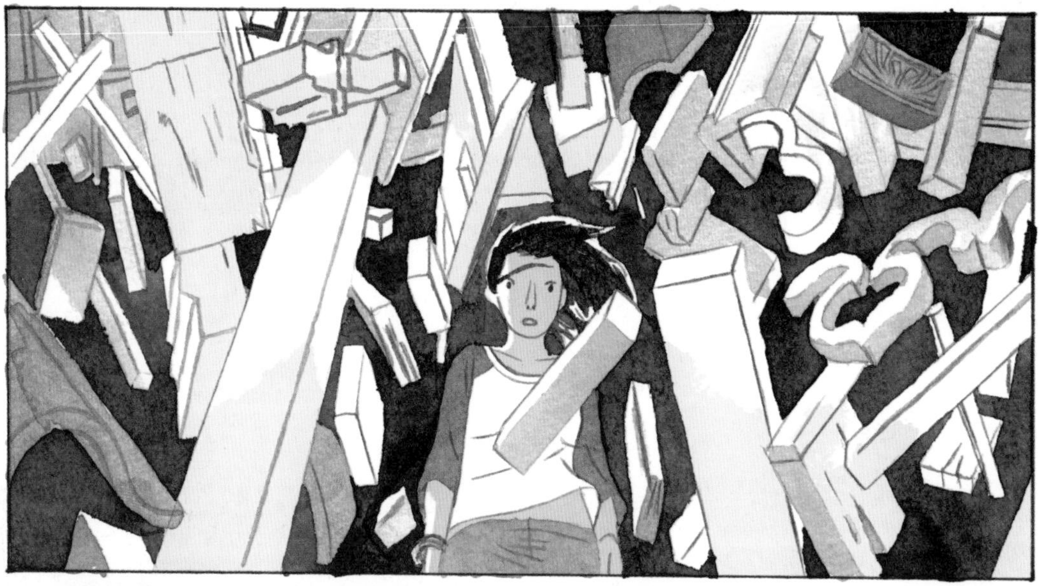
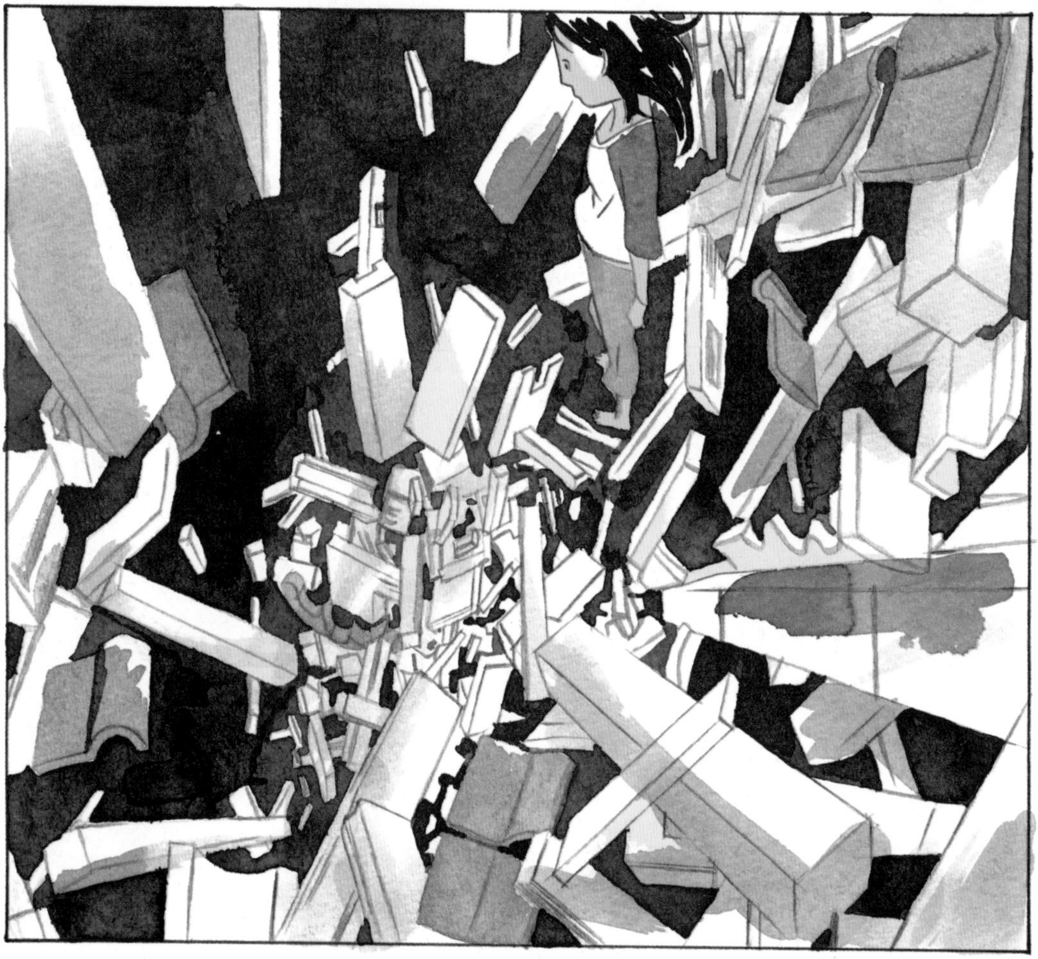

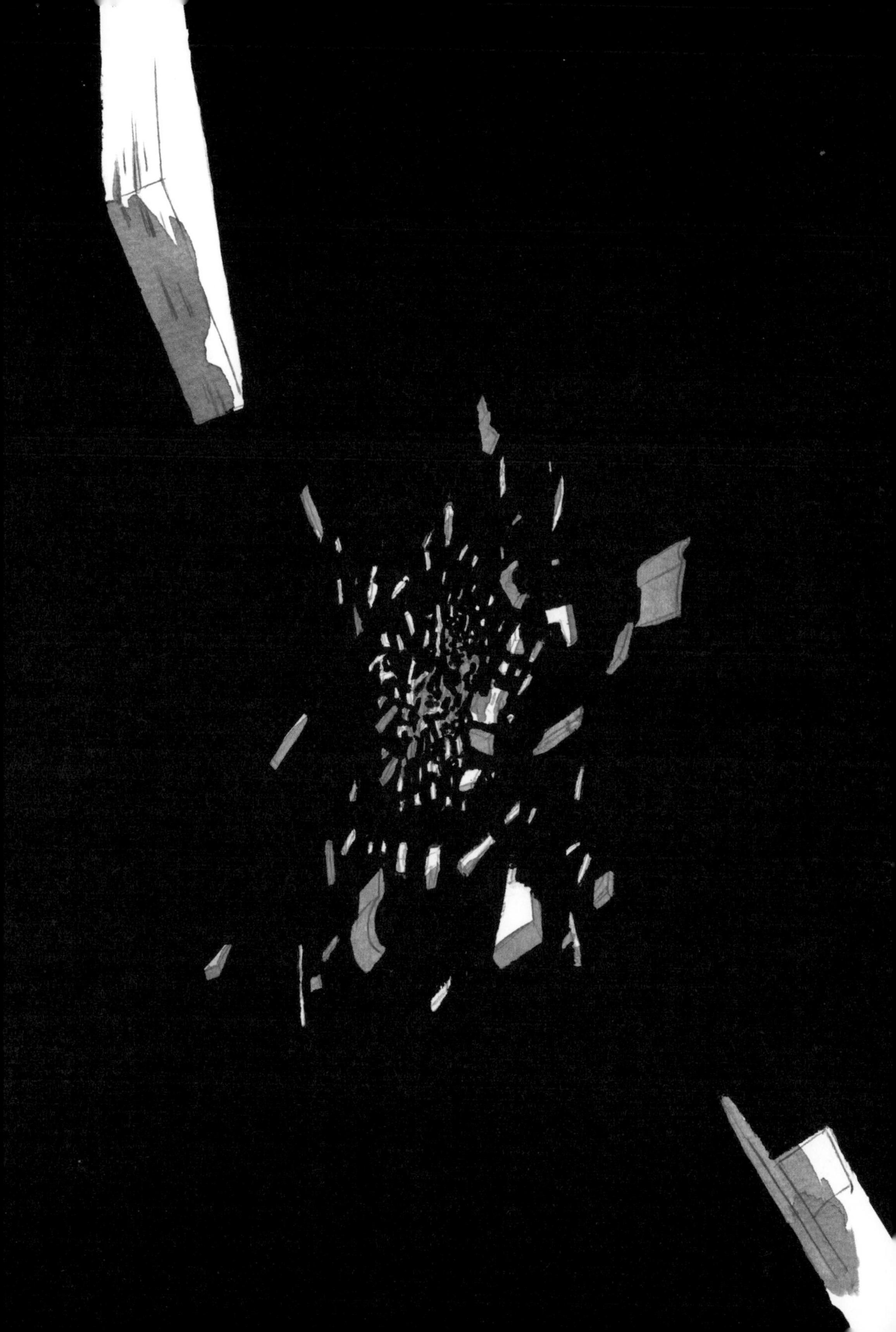

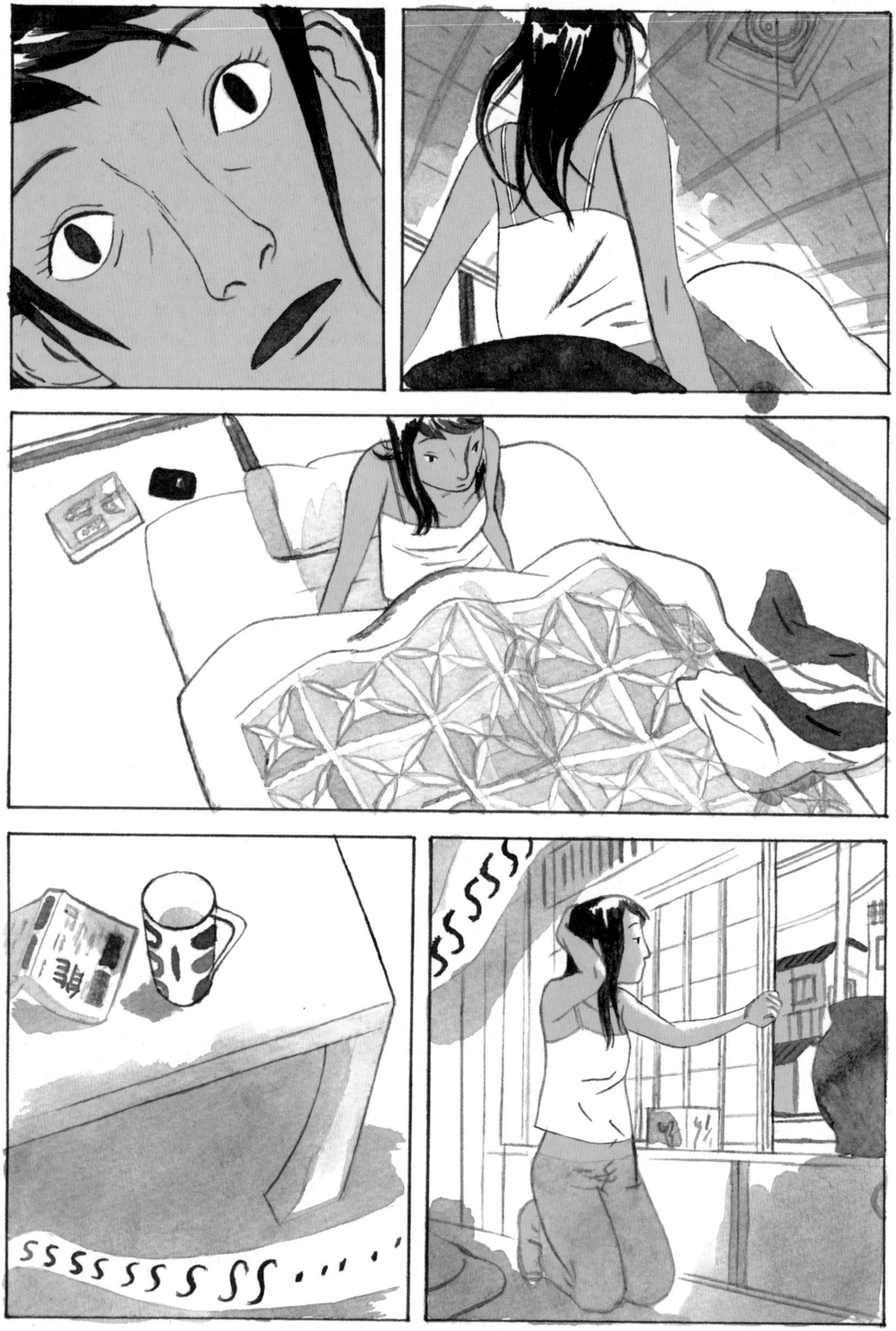
SSSSSSSSSS....
SSSSSS

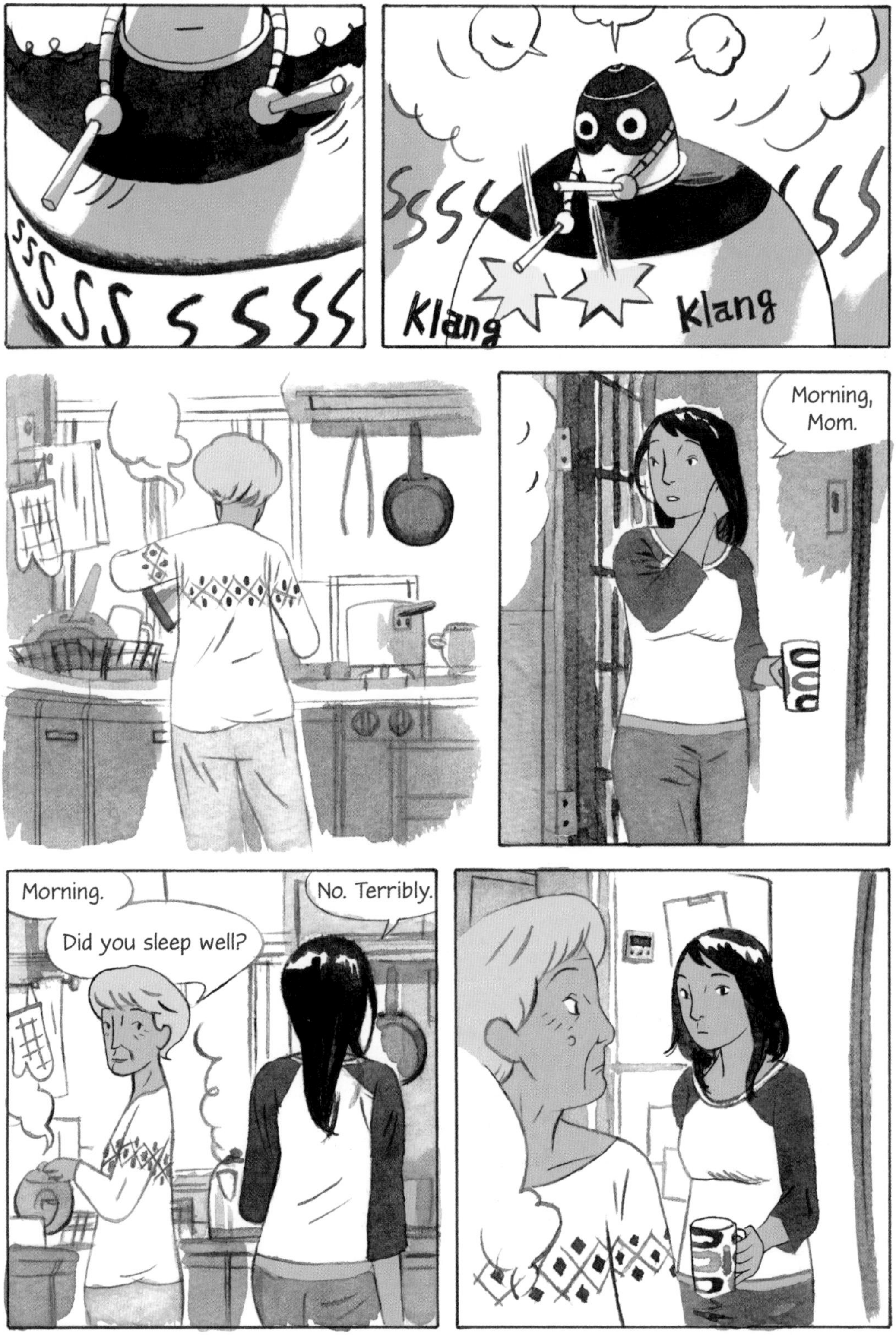
SSSSSSSS SSSS
SSSS
SSS
Klang
Klang
Morning, Mom.
Morning.
Did you sleep well?
No. Terribly.

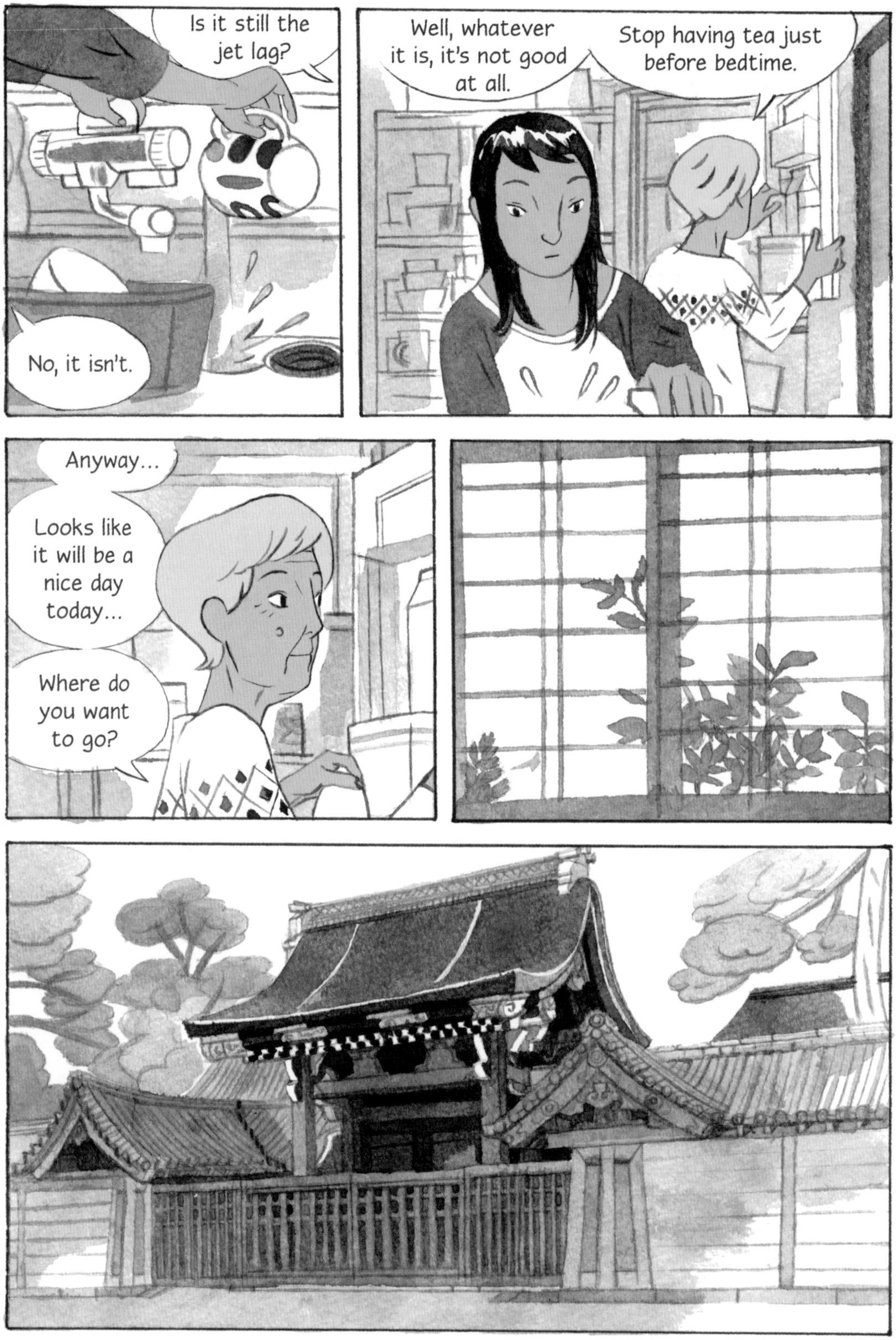
Is it still the jet lag?
No, it isn't.
Well, whatever it is, it's not good at all.
Stop having tea just before bedtime.
Anyway...
Looks like it will be a nice day today...
Where do you want to go?

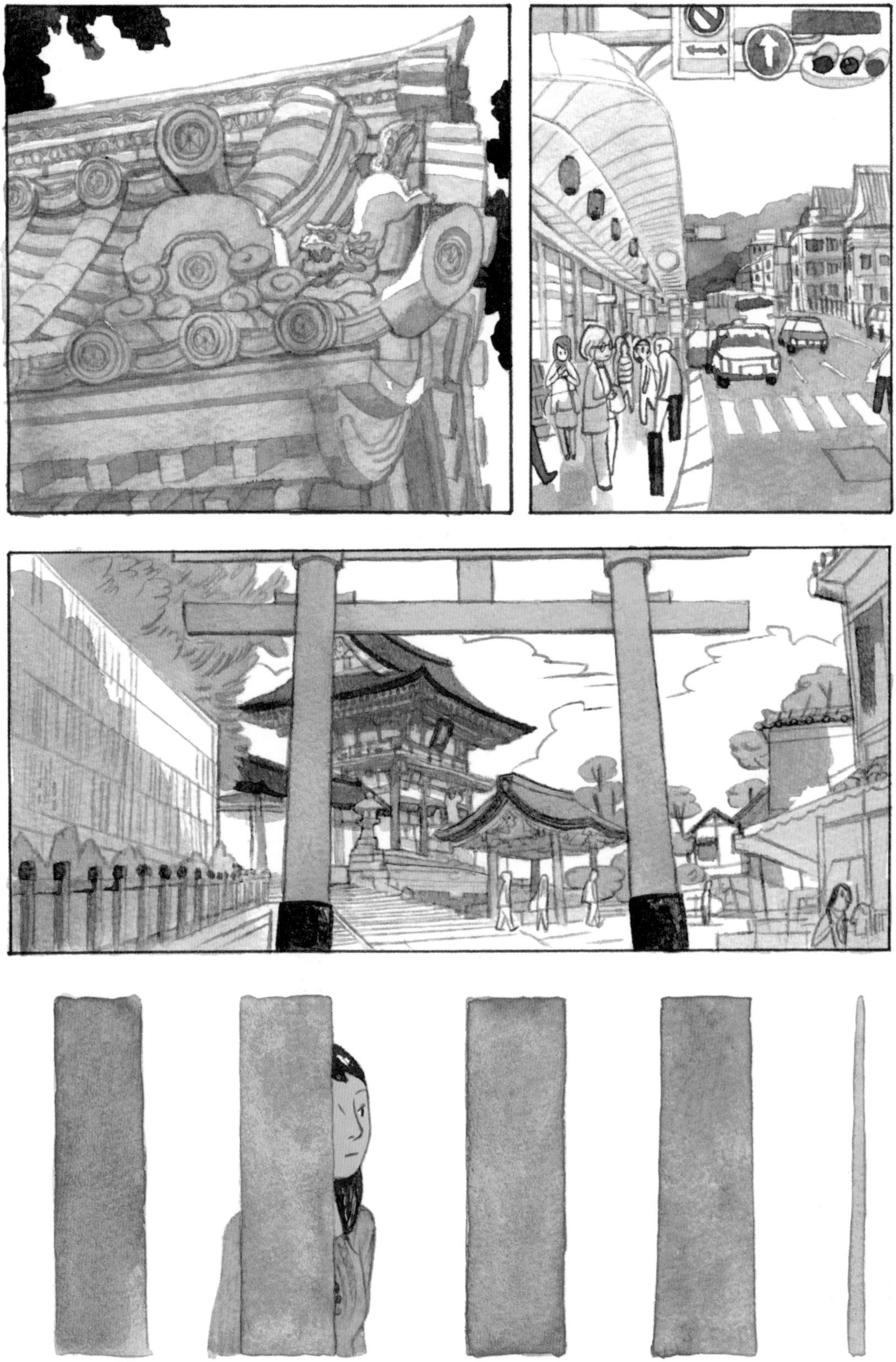

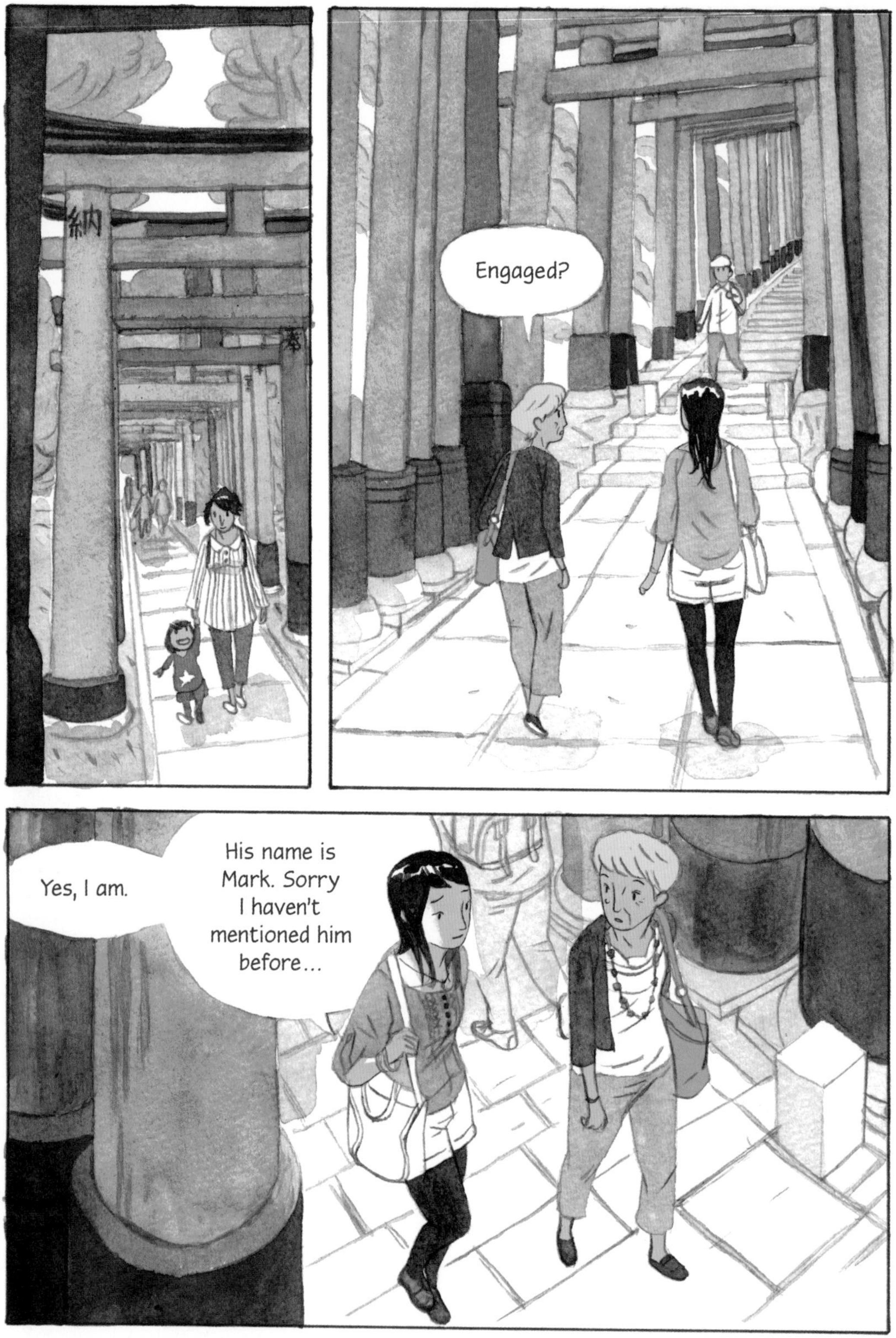
納
Engaged?
Yes, I am.
His name is Mark. Sorry I haven't mentioned him before...

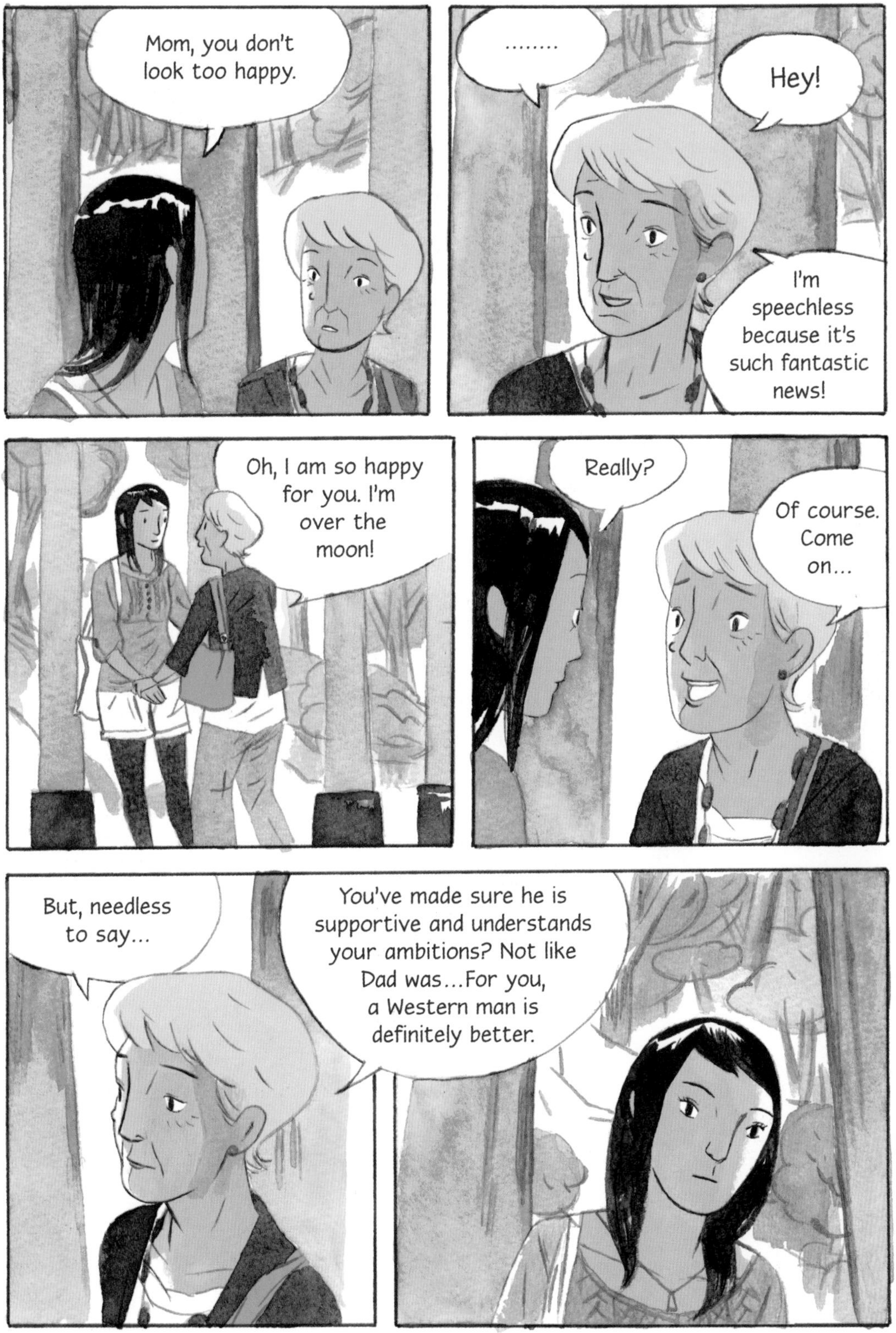

Mom, you don't look too happy.
....
Hey!
I'm speechless because it's such fantastic news!
Oh, I am so happy for you. I'm over the moon!
Really?
Of course. Come on...
But, needless to say...
You've made sure he is supportive and understands your ambitions? Not like Dad was...For you, a Western man is definitely better.

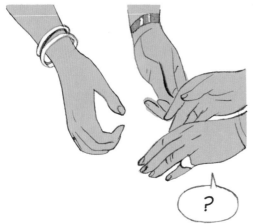

?

Yumiko, are you all right?

I don't think Dad would have liked me marrying over there.

He always wanted me to come back, and now I probably won't.

....

What do you mean, Yumiko? Why do you say that?

I was planning to leave England and come back here...

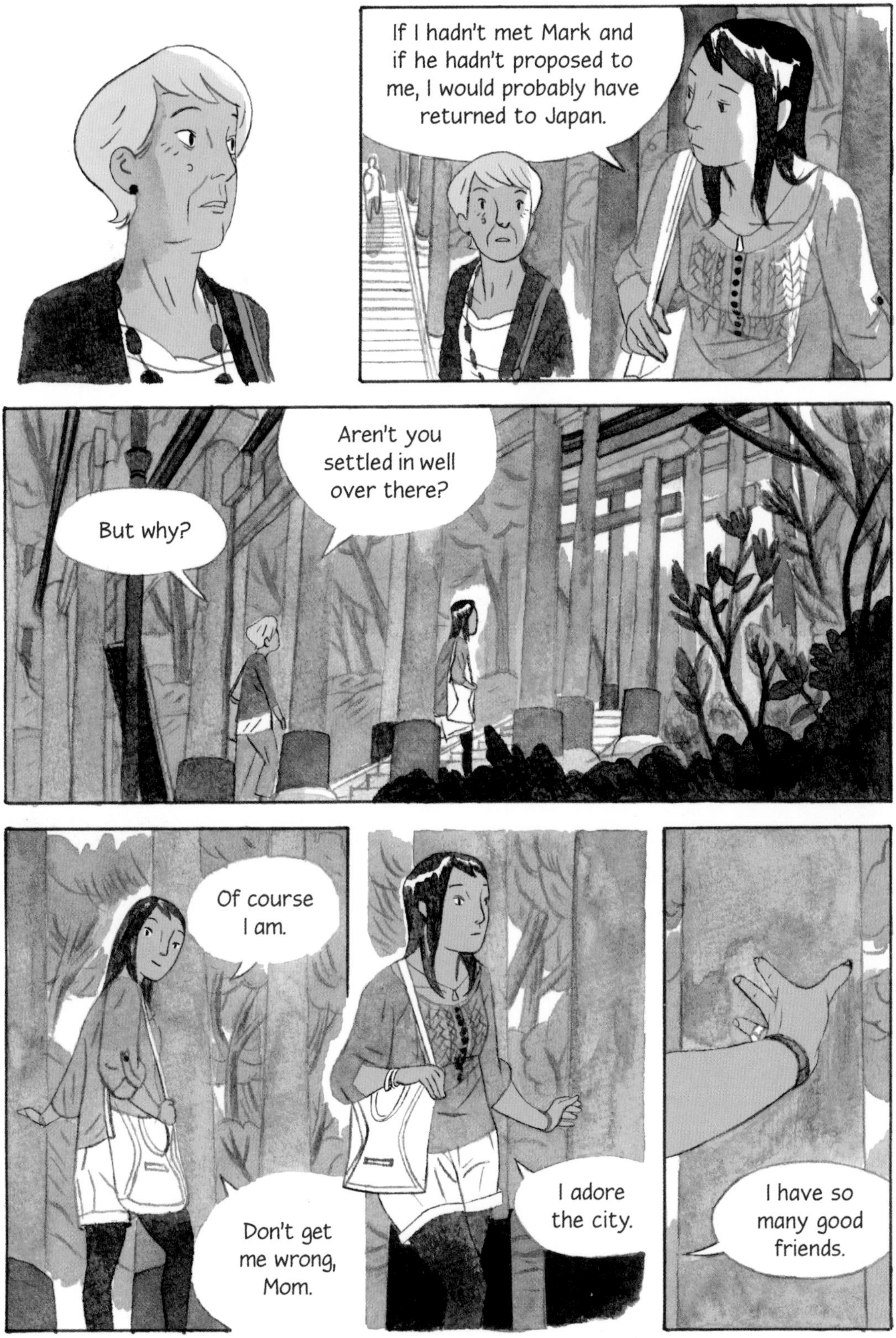
If I hadn't met Mark and if he hadn't proposed to me, I would probably have returned to Japan.
But why?
Aren't you settled in well over there?
Of course I am.
Don't get me wrong, Mom.
I adore the city.
I have so many good friends.

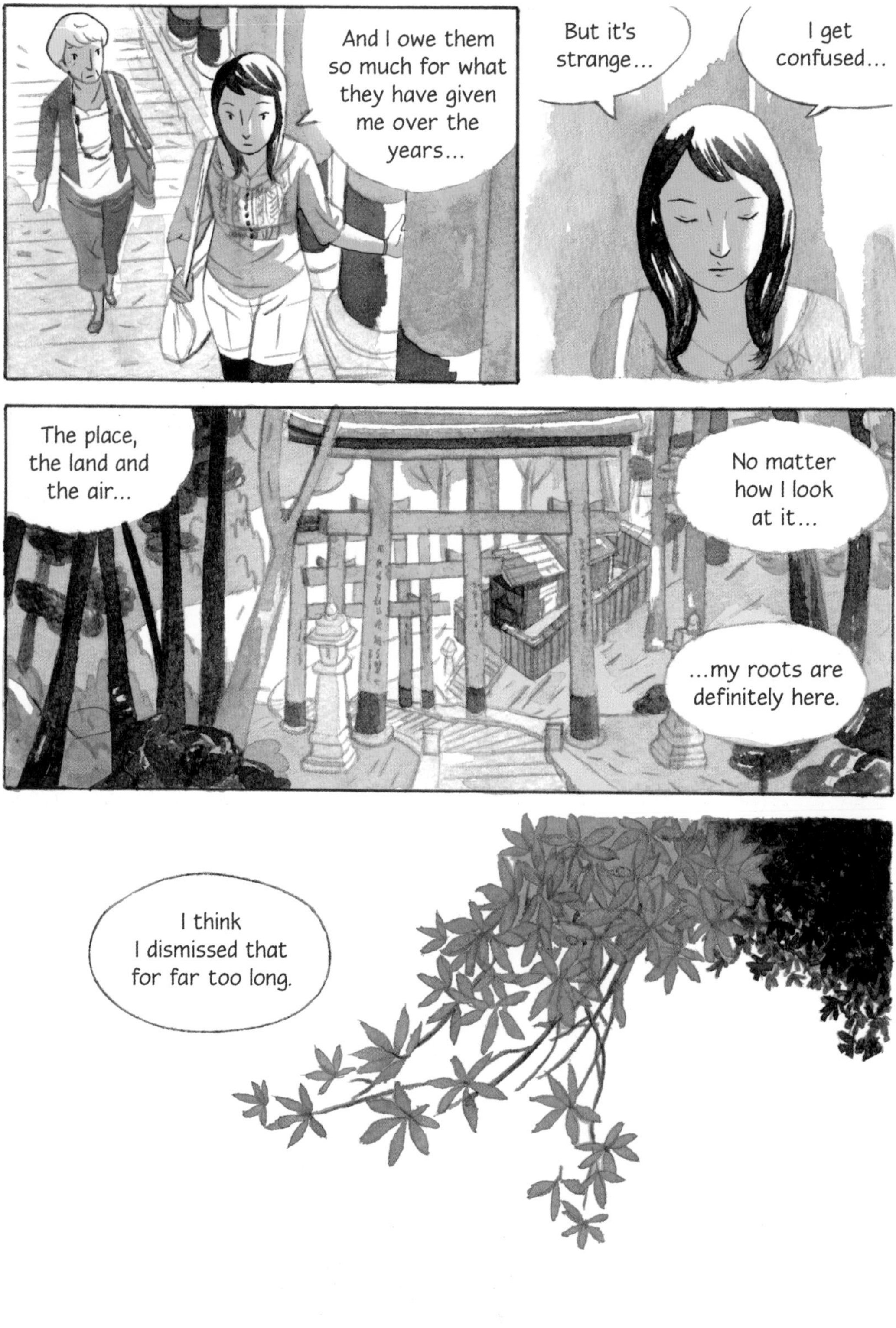
And I owe them so much for what they have given me over the years...
But it's strange...
I get confused...
The place, the land and the air...
No matter how I look at it...
...my roots are definitely here.
I think I dismissed that for far too long.

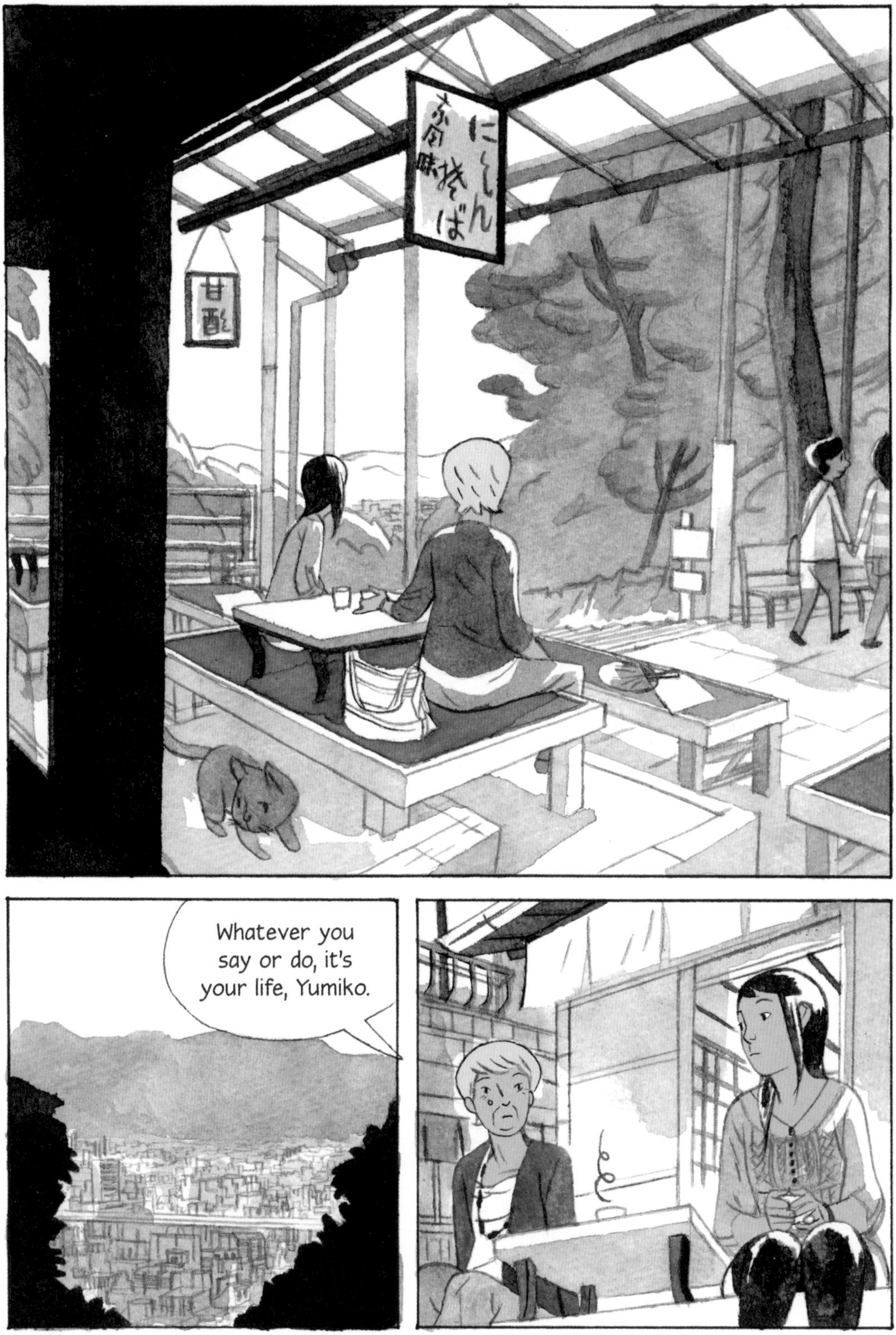
にしんそば
Whatever you say or do, it's your life, Yumiko.

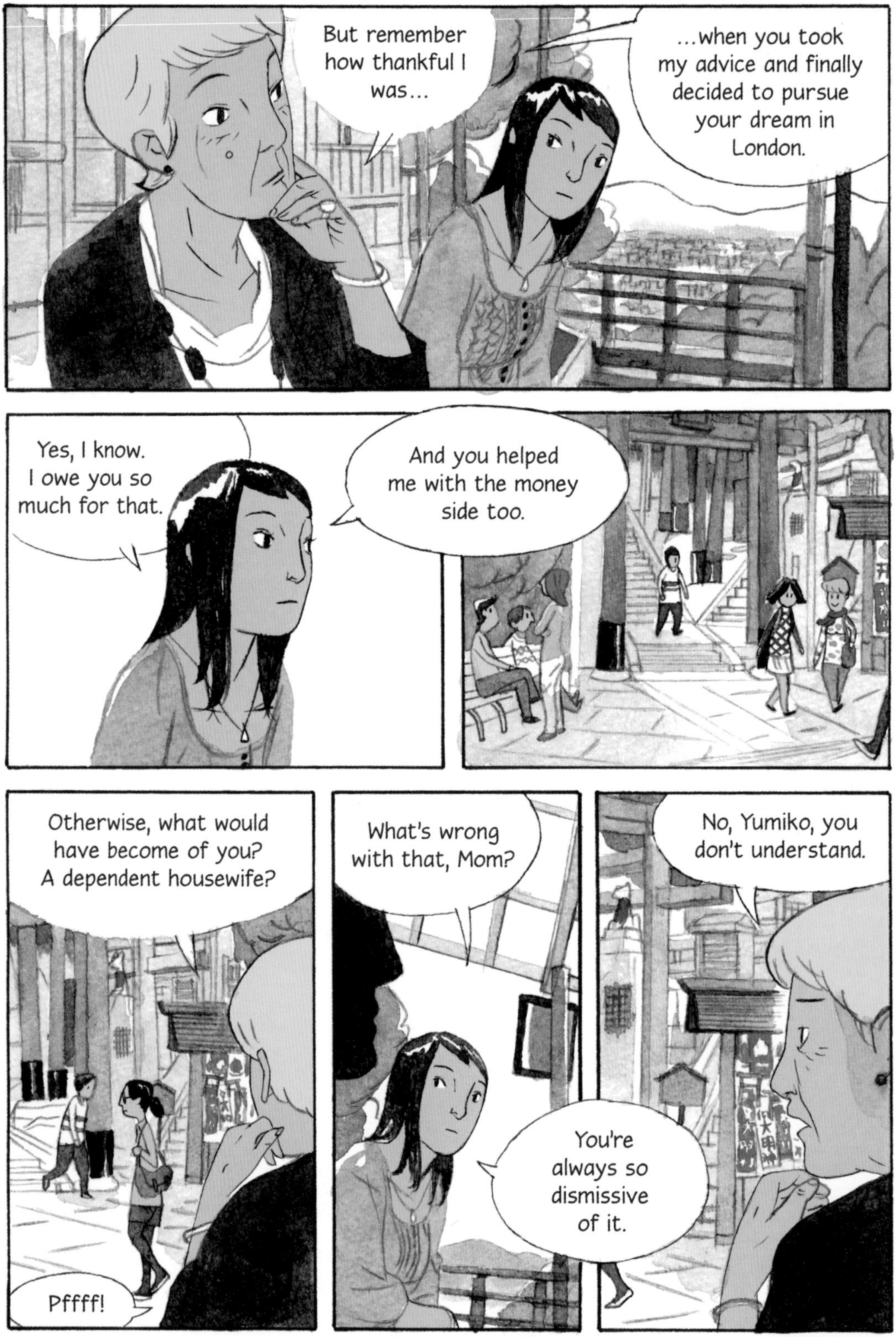
But remember how thankful I was...
...when you took my advice and finally decided to pursue your dream in London.
Yes, I know. I owe you so much for that.
And you helped me with the money side too.
Otherwise, what would have become of you? A dependent housewife?
Pffff!
What's wrong with that, Mom?
You're always so dismissive of it.
No, Yumiko, you don't understand.

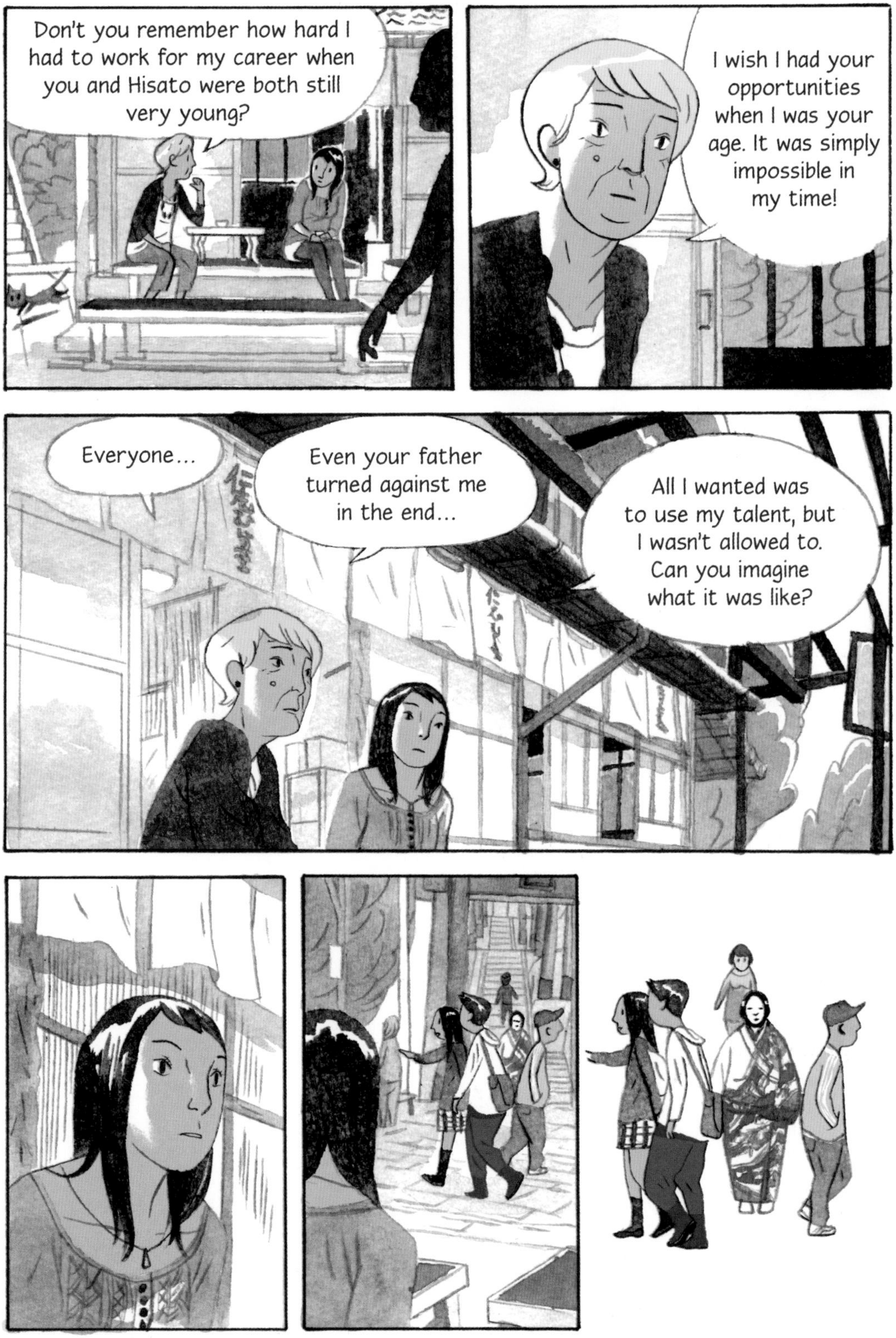
Don't you remember how hard I had to work for my career when you and Hisato were both still very young?
I wish I had your opportunities when I was your age. It was simply impossible in my time!
Everyone...
Even your father turned against me in the end...
All I wanted was to use my talent, but I wasn't allowed to. Can you imagine what it was like?

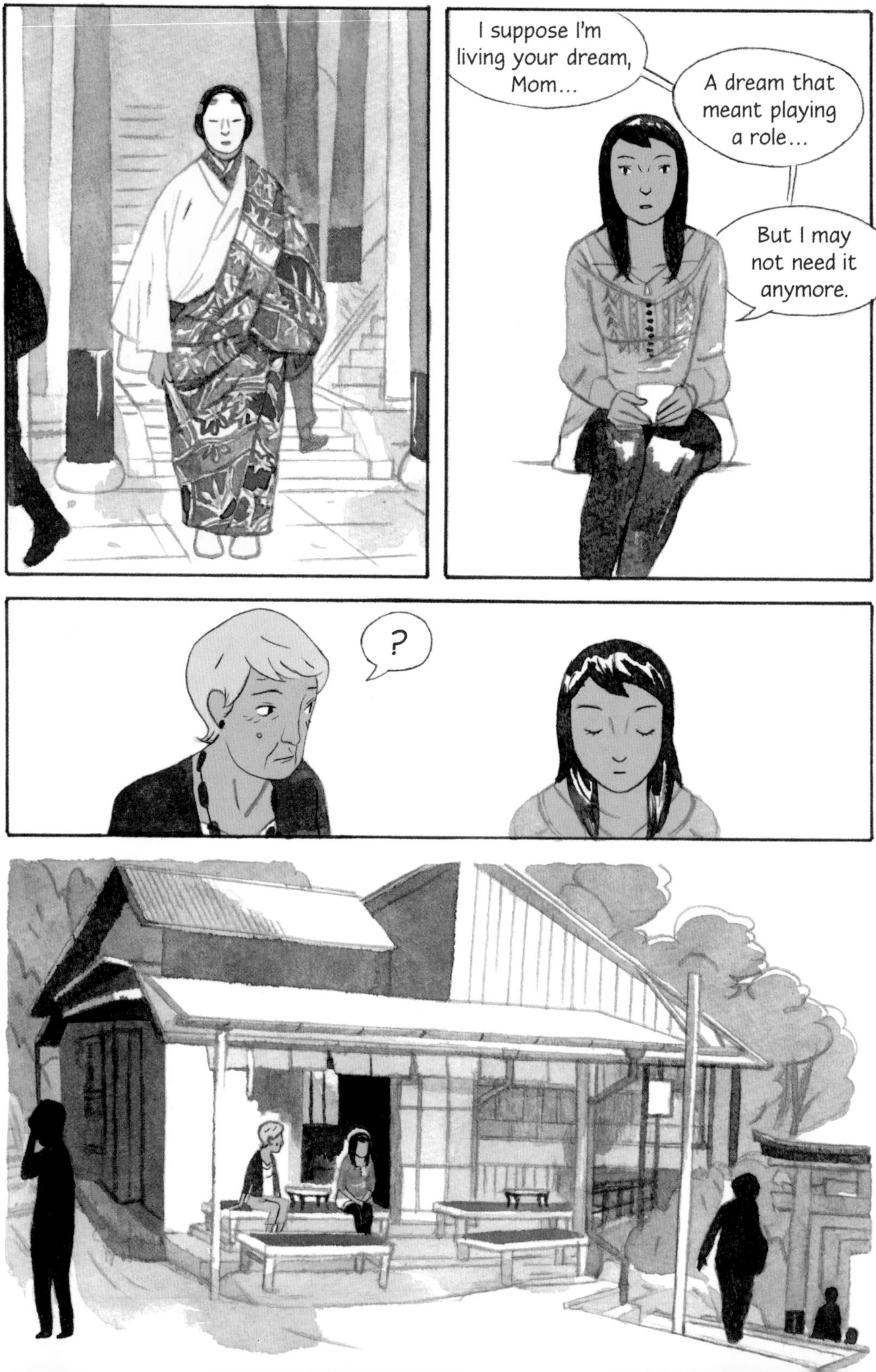
I suppose I'm living your dream, Mom...
A dream that meant playing a role...
But I may not need it anymore.
?

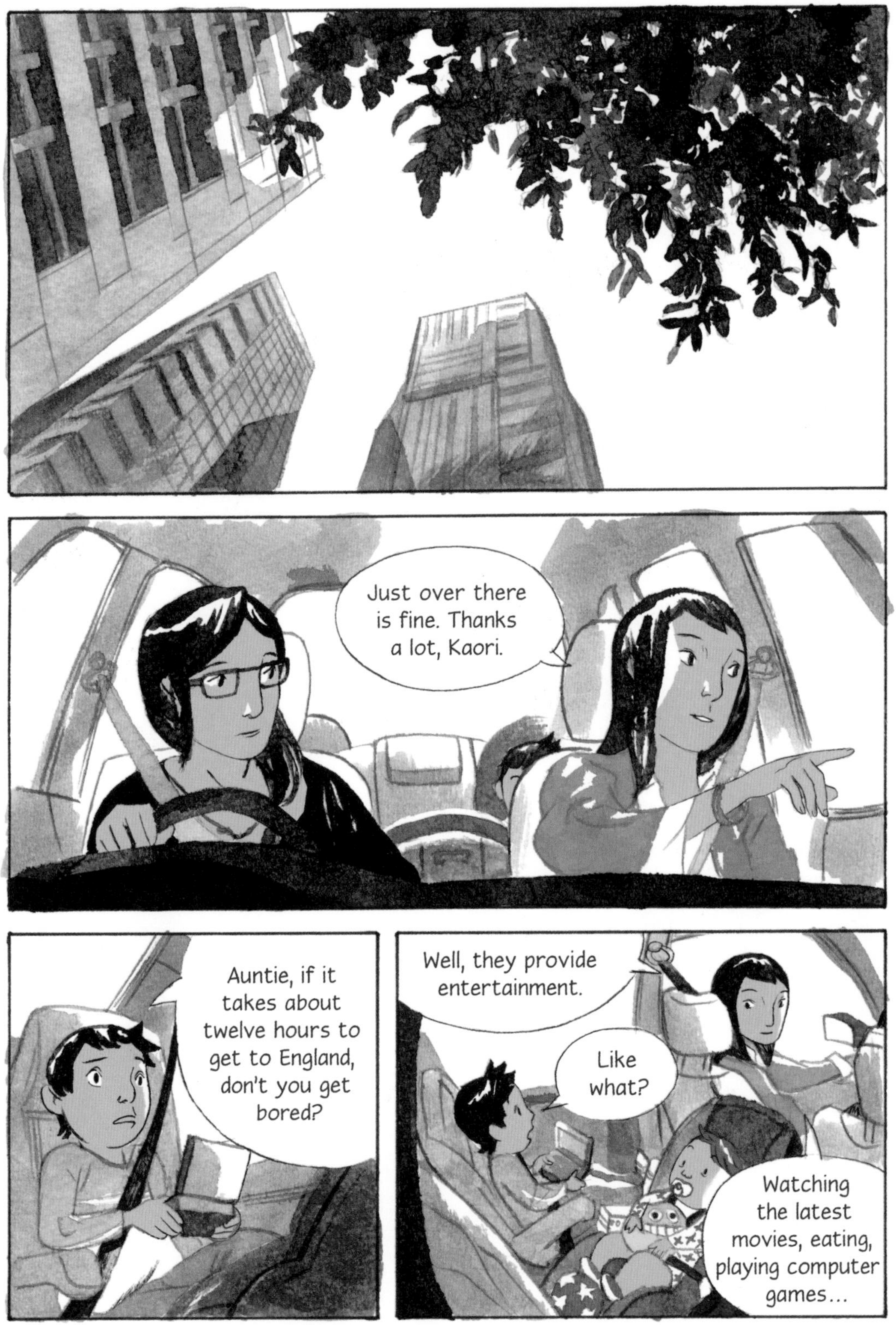

Just over there is fine. Thanks a lot, Kaori.
Auntie, if it takes about twelve hours to get to England, don't you get bored?
Well, they provide entertainment.
Like what?
Watching the latest movies, eating, playing computer games...

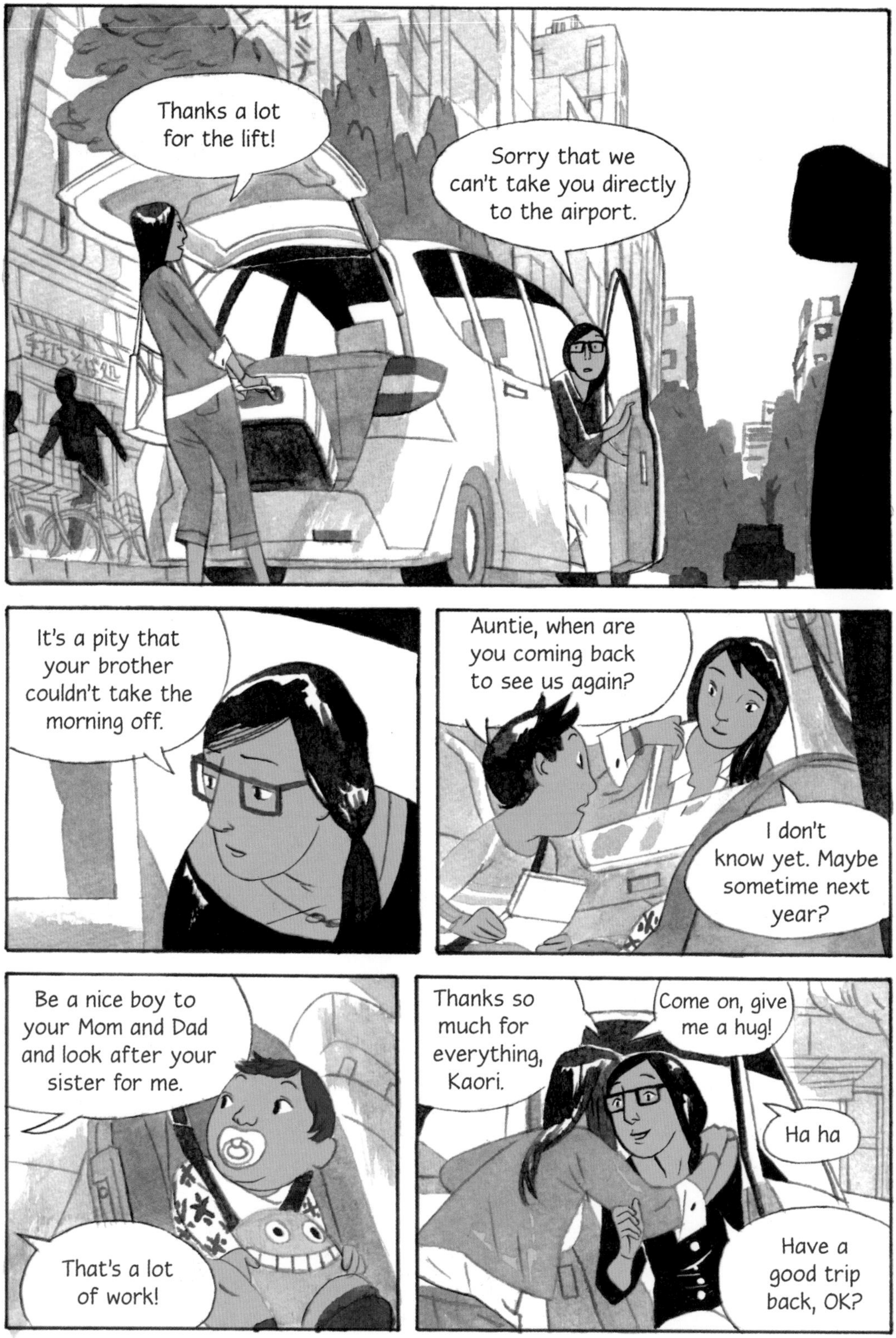
Thanks a lot for the lift!
Sorry that we can't take you directly to the airport.
It's a pity that your brother couldn't take the morning off.
Auntie, when are you coming back to see us again?
I don't know yet. Maybe sometime next year?
Be a nice boy to your Mom and Dad and look after your sister for me.
That's a lot of work!
Thanks so much for everything, Kaori.
Come on, give me a hug!
Ha ha
Have a good trip back, OK?

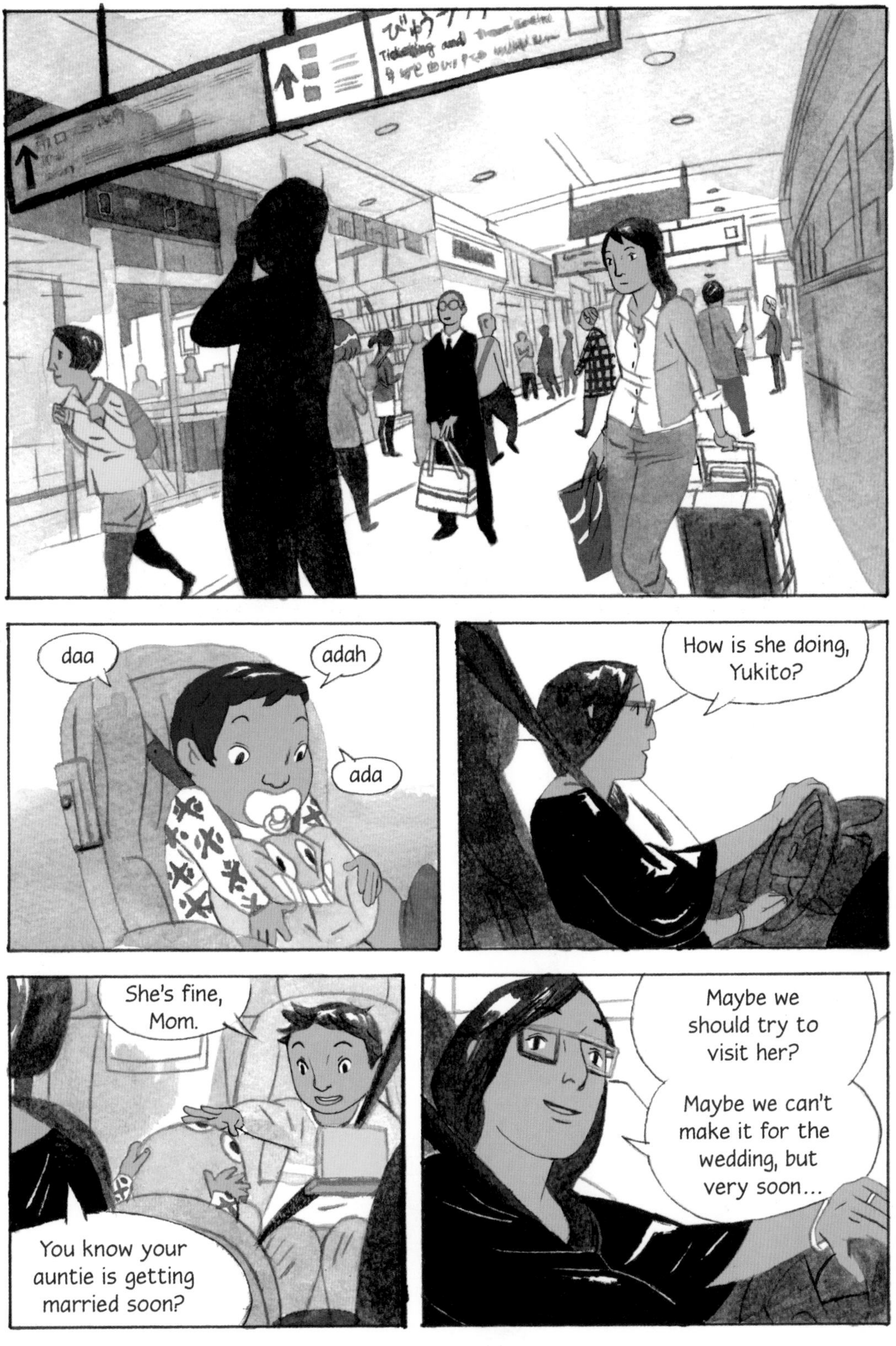
daa
adah
ada
How is she doing, Yukito?
She's fine, Mom.
You know your auntie is getting married soon?
Maybe we should try to visit her?
Maybe we can't make it for the wedding, but very soon...

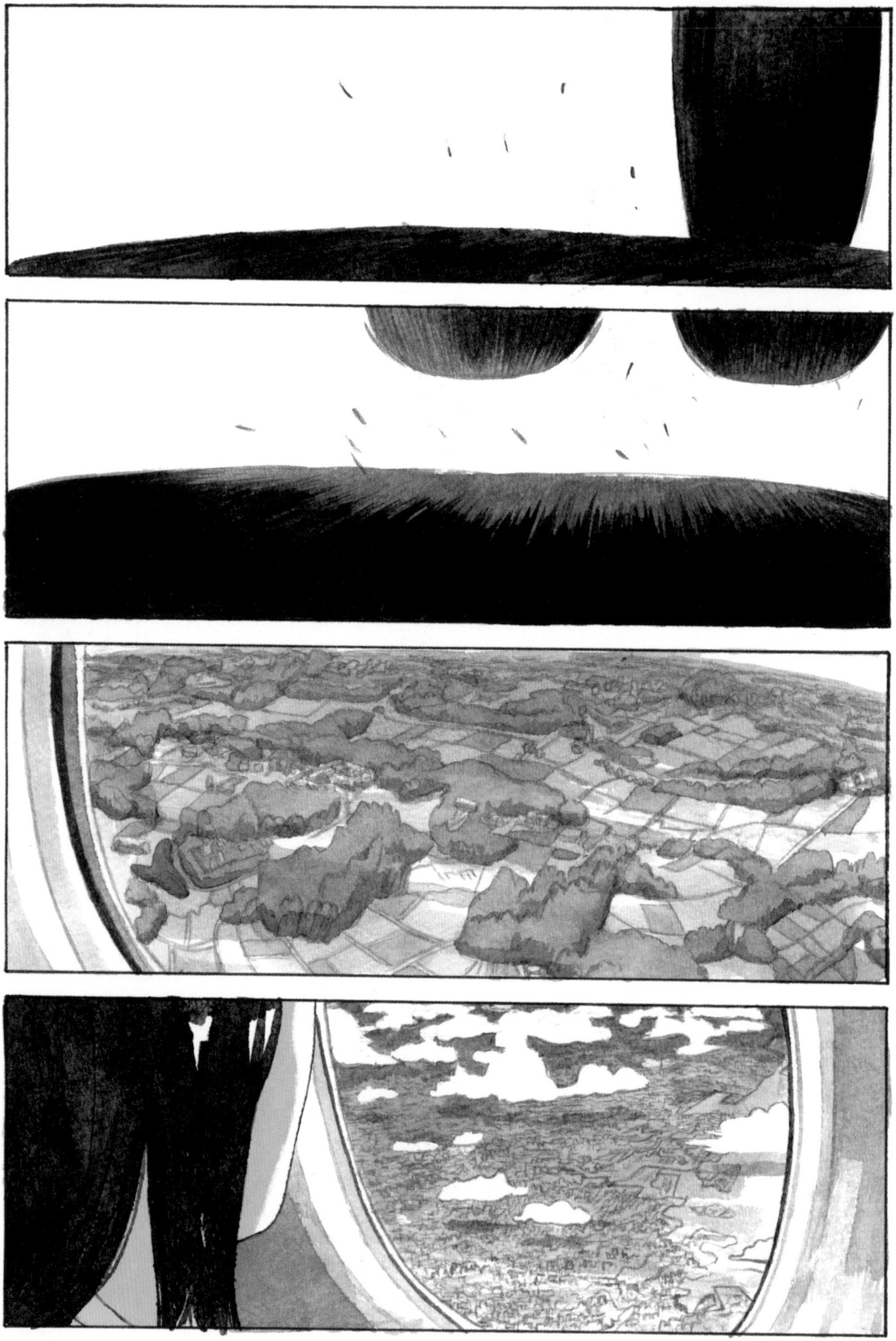

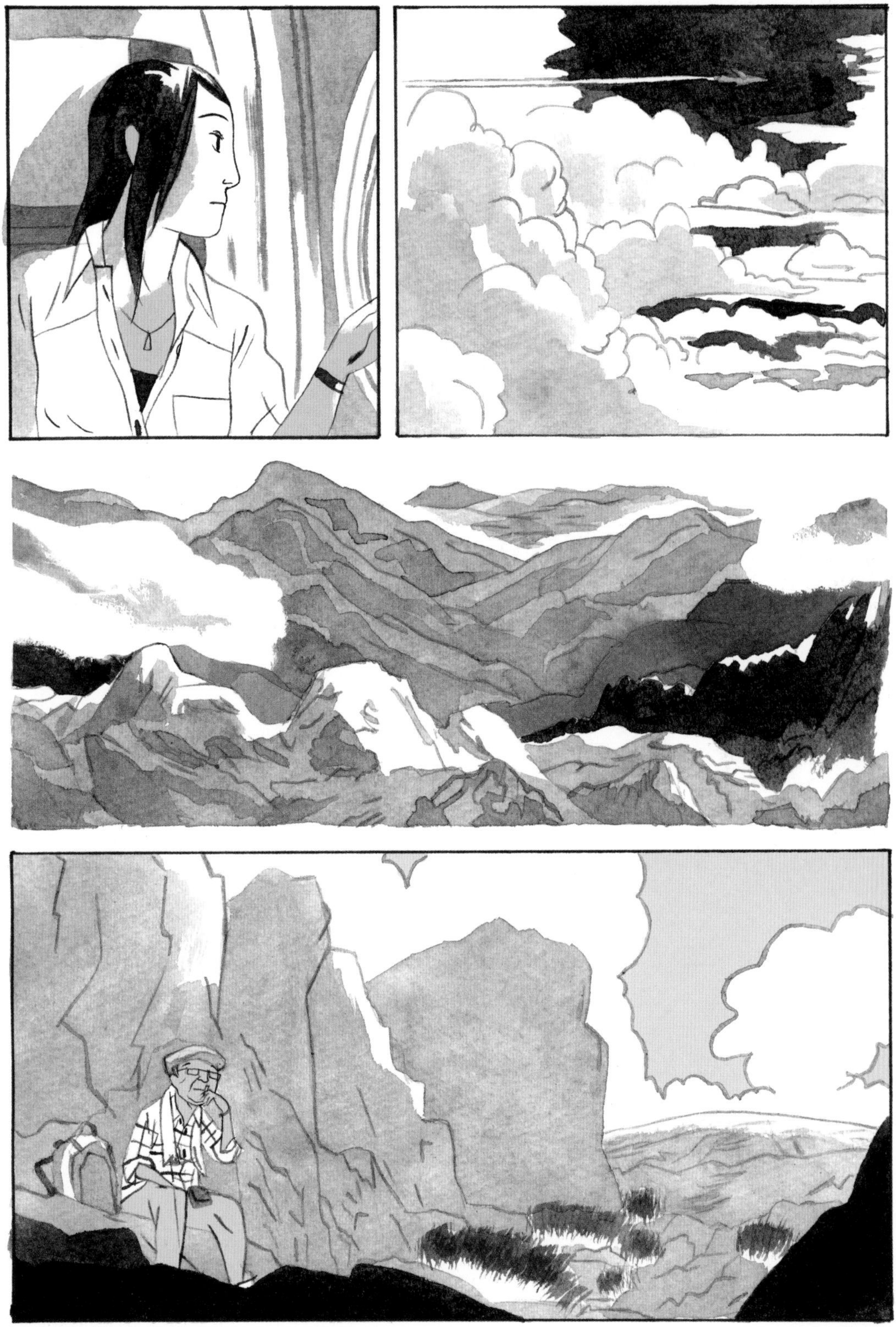

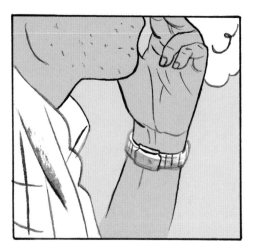

Eh?

Why do you ask?

Huh!

Come on, Yumiko. Don't be silly.

Do whatever you want. You don't need to ask my permission... You know that.

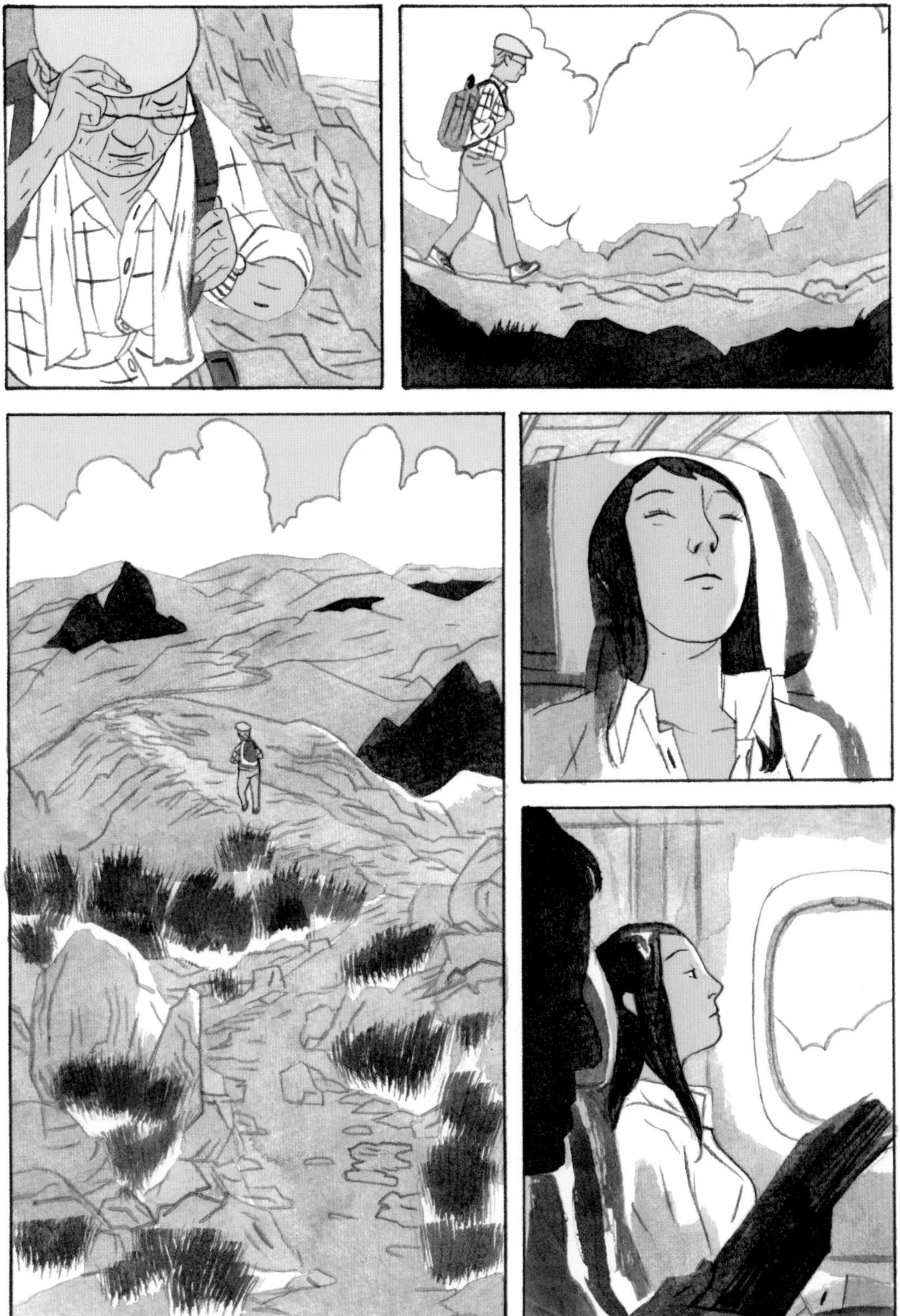

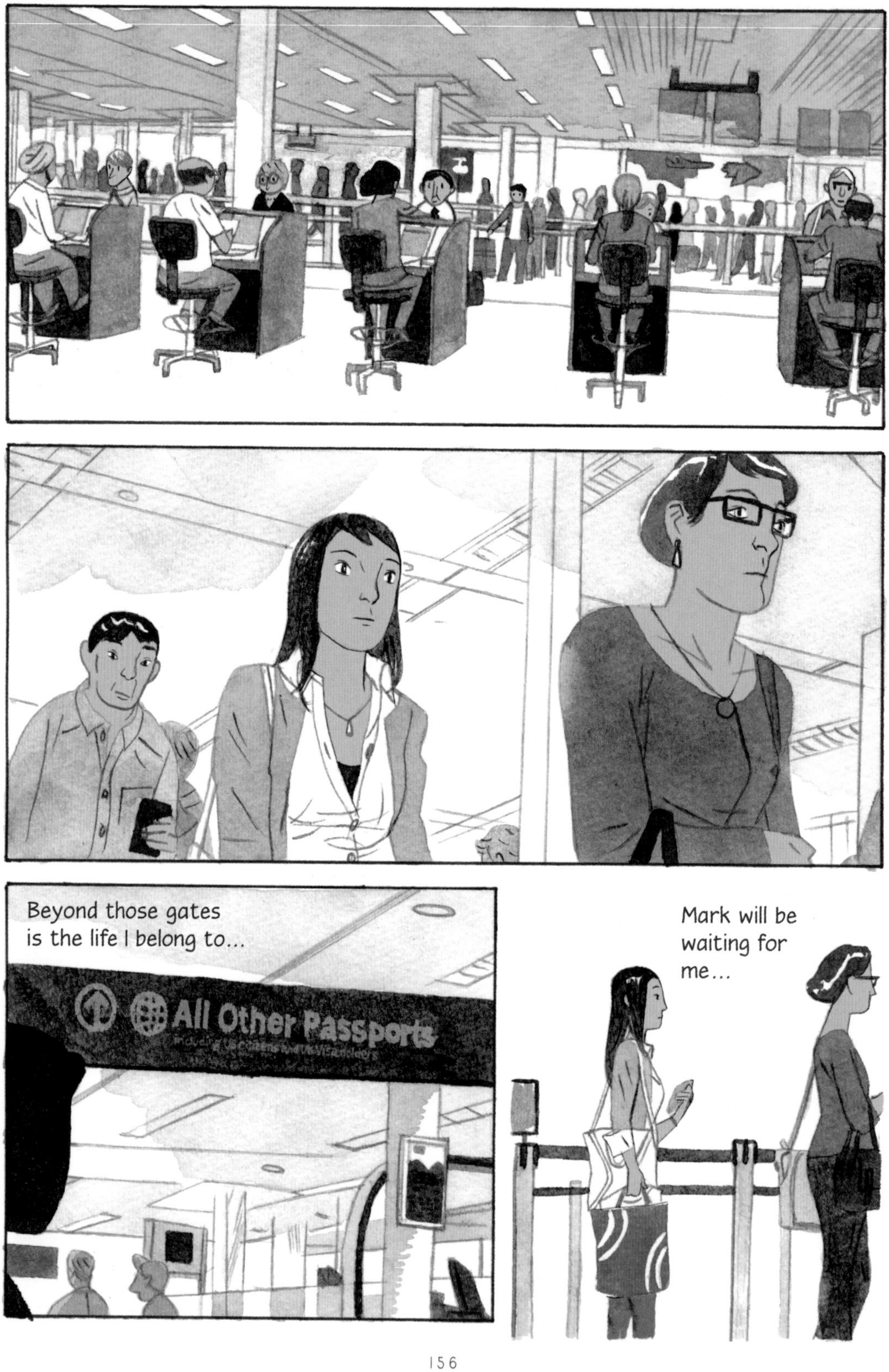

Beyond those gates
is the life I belong to...
All Other Passports
Mark will be
waiting for
me...

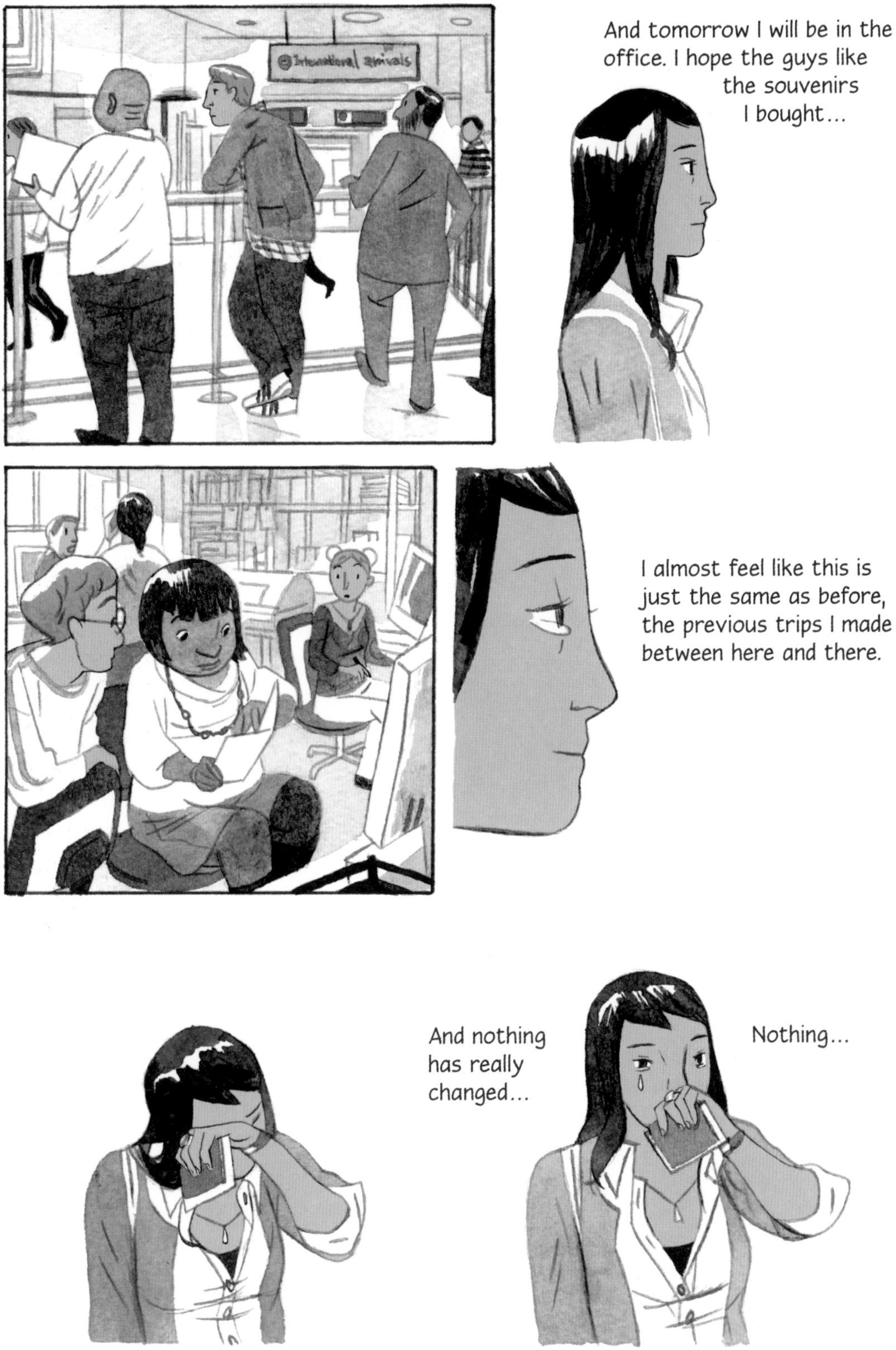
International arrivals
And tomorrow I will be in the office. I hope the guys like the souvenirs I bought...
I almost feel like this is just the same as before, the previous trips I made between here and there.
And nothing has really changed...
Nothing...

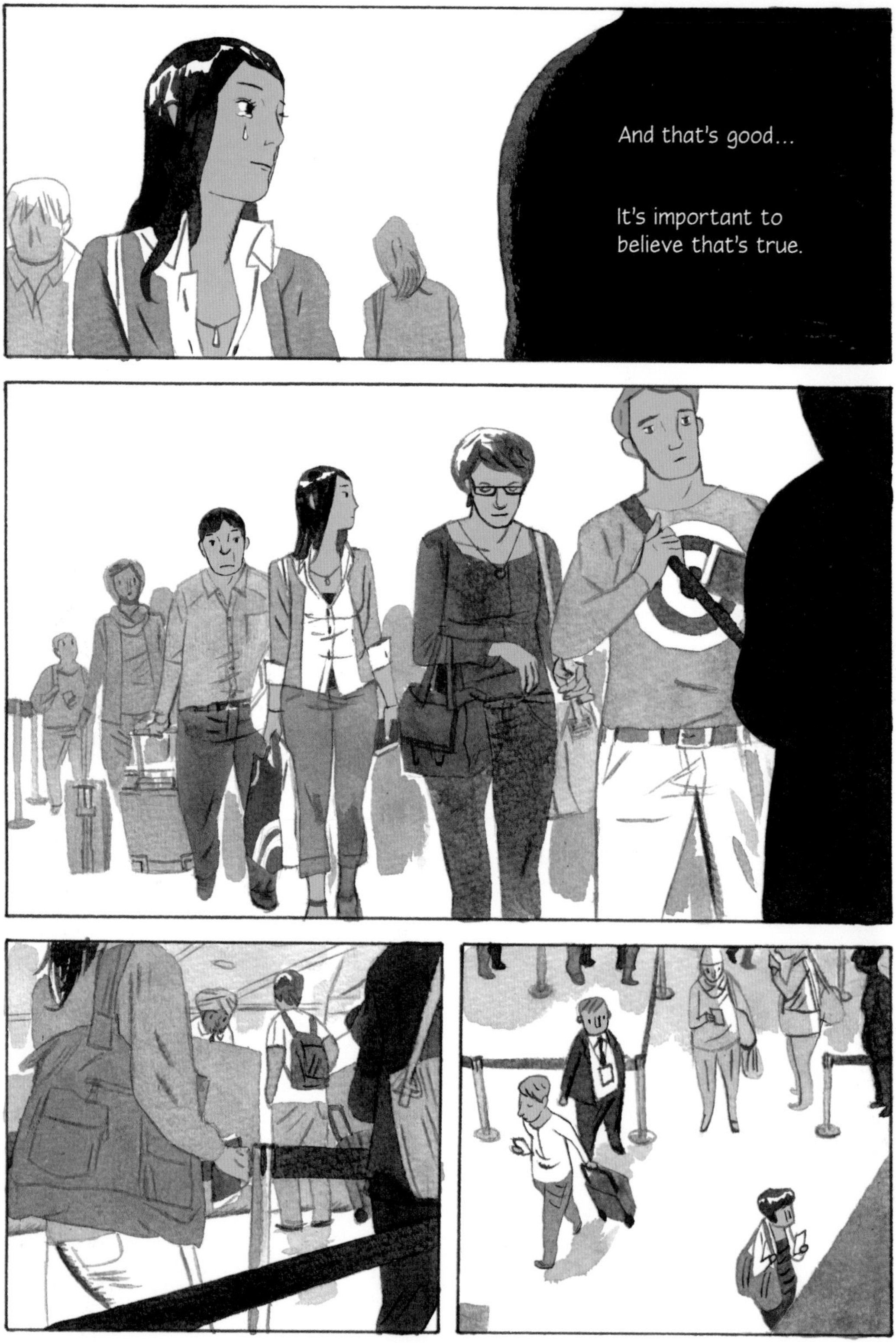
And that's good...
It's important to
believe that's true.

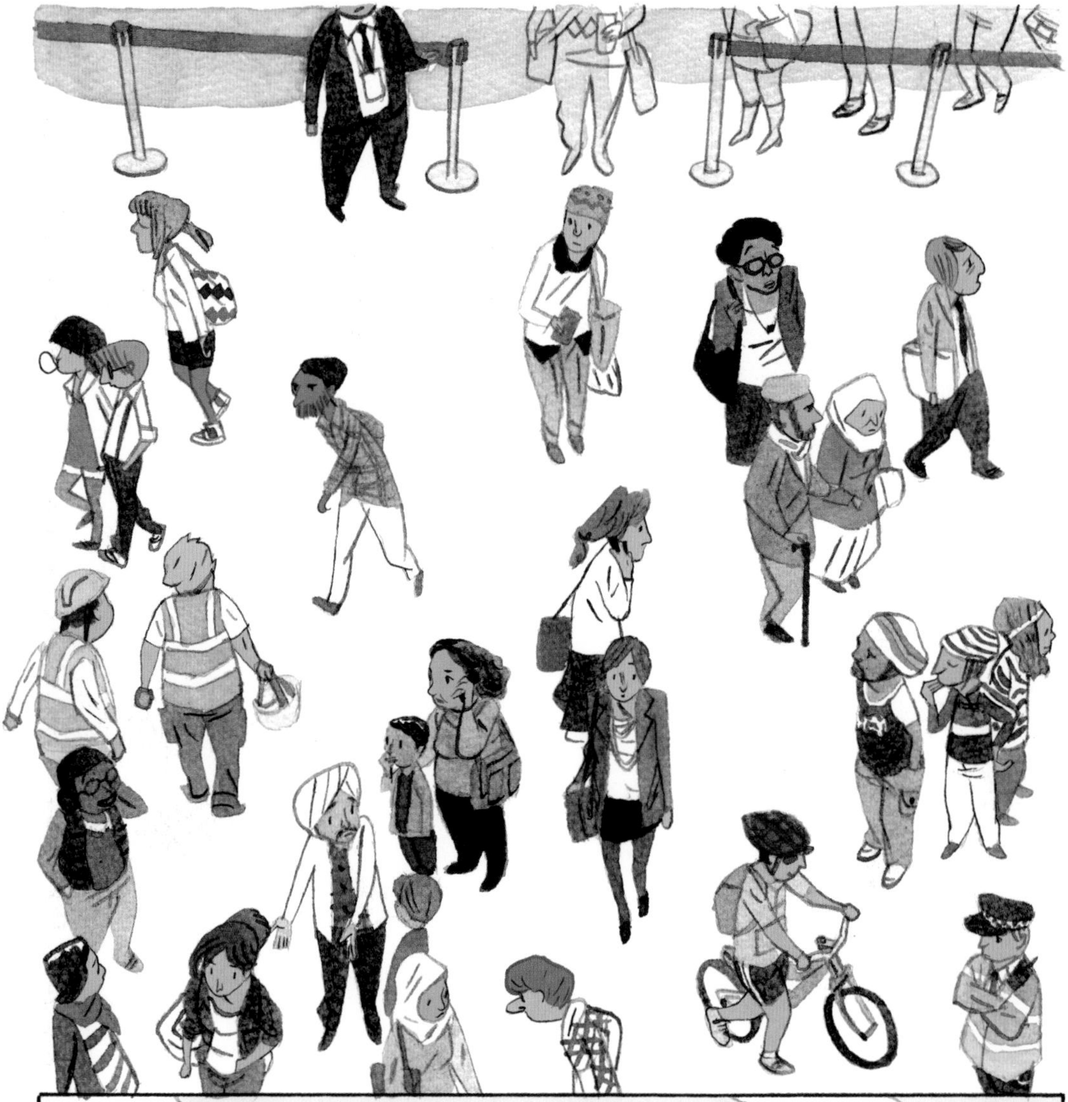

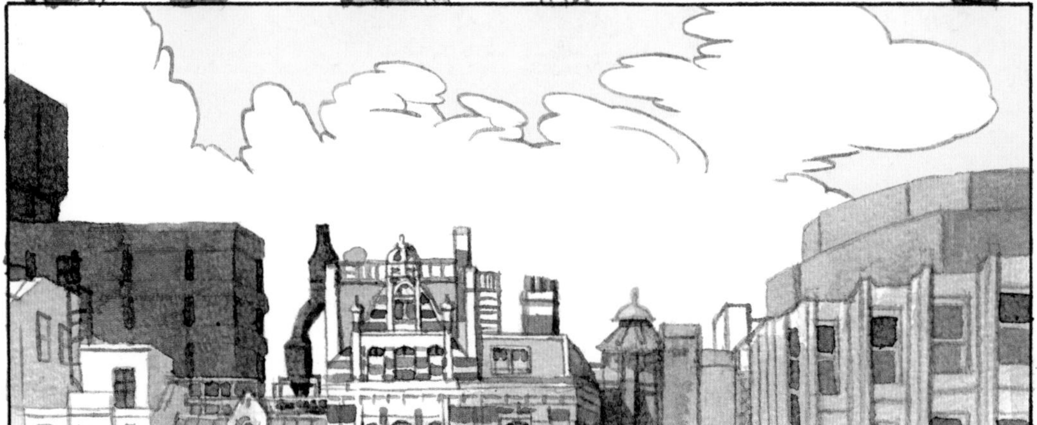

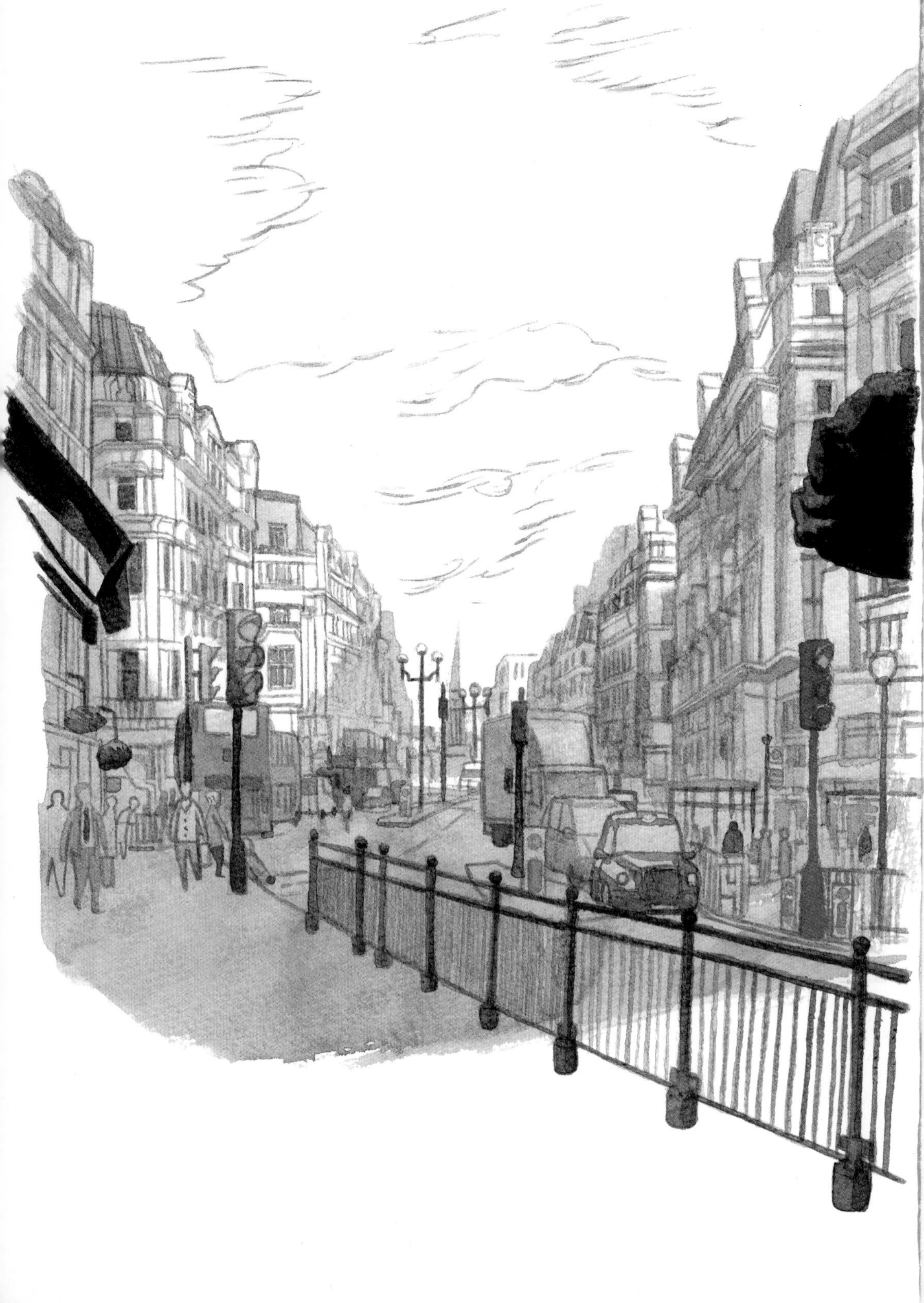